Implementing Public Policy

Implementing Public Policy

An Introduction to the Study of Operational Governance

Second Edition

Michael Hill and Peter Hupe

Los Angeles | London | New Delhi
Singapore | Washington DC

First edition published 2002
Reprinted 2010, 2011, 2012

SAGE Publications Ltd
1 Oliver's Yard
55 City Road
London EC1Y 1SP

SAGE Publications Inc.
2455 Teller Road
Thousand Oaks, California 91320

SAGE Publications India Pvt Ltd
B 1/I 1 Mohan Cooperative Industrial Area
Mathura Road
New Delhi 110 044

SAGE Publications Asia-Pacific Pte Ltd
3 Church Street
#10-04 Samsung Hub
Singapore 049483

Library of Congress Control Number 2008925136

British Library Cataloguing in Publication data

A catalogue record for this book is available from
the British Library

ISBN 978-0-4129-4798-5
ISBN 978-0-4129-4799-2 (pbk)

Typeset by C&M Digitals (P) Ltd., Chennai, India
Printed in Great Britain by the MPG Books Group
Printed on paper from sustainable resources

CONTENTS

PREFACE TO THE FIRST EDITION[1]

This book reviews the literature on public policy implementation, relating it to contemporary developments in thinking about governance. It stresses the continuing importance of a focus upon the implementation part of policy processes. Accordingly it goes on to suggest strategies for future research on implementation and identifies modes of managing implementation.

We are very grateful to Ian Holliday for commissioning the book for Sage Politics Texts, and for the support he has given us during our work. We also wish to thank Lucy Robinson of Sage for her support of the venture, and Lauren McAllister and Justin Dyer for all their help with the preparation of the manuscript.

We are particularly grateful to Marianne Vorthoren for her assistance throughout the whole project. She always reacted with good humour to our relentless demands for articles. While we were teaching, doing consultancy and other jobs, she helped to ensure that our work on the book went on. At the last stages of preparation of the manuscript we benefited enormously from Vicky Balsem's typographical and word-processing expertise. Thanks are also due to Jantiene van Elk for her bibliographical support.

We thank all those who provided comments on a draft of the manuscript. In addition to Ian Holliday, these were (in alphabetical order): Bob Hudson, Walter Kickert, Stephen Mitchell, Larry O'Toole, Christopher Pollitt and Arthur Ringeling.

We are grateful to the board of the research group Waardering in en van het openbaar bestuur (The Evaluation of Government) at the Department of Public Administration at Erasmus University, Rotterdam, particularly the chair and treasurer, Arthur Ringeling and Harry Daemen, for their financial support. Similar thanks go to the School of Social Sciences and the Department of Public Administration of Erasmus University, Rotterdam, particularly Wim Derksen, Jan Hakvoort and Percy Lehning, the (then) Dean, for approving Peter Hupe's arrangement to spend his concentrated research time in the second semester of 2000–1 at Goldsmiths College, University of London. Similar thanks go to Nirmala Rao, at that time Head of the Department of Social Policy and Politics at Goldsmiths College, for hospitality for our work, and to the Warden of Goldsmiths, the late Ben Pimlott, for his approval of our affiliations to the College.

Our wives, Betty and Nynke, have both been wise and patient, very committed to what we are doing, while giving us the space to get on with our work. They have been supportive and tolerant when mealtime conversation turned to the book. We therefore dedicate this book to them.

Note

1   This preface has been amended slightly.

PREFACE TO THE SECOND EDITION

The first edition of this book, published in 2002, was well received by peer reviewers in several journals of political science and public administration. It has appeared on reading lists for curricula in those disciplines across the world. It thus is obvious that we felt pleased when David Mainwaring of Sage asked us to prepare a second edition of the book.

In this second edition both much and little have changed. Concerning the latter, we have maintained our view on what the top-down/bottom-up controversy has brought to the state of implementation theory and research conceived as a sub-discipline between political science and public administration. In the first three chapters, therefore, only minor changes have been made. What also has remained the same is our clinical view of the future of implementation studies; see the final chapter. As long as people engage in collective endeavours, intentions will have to be turned into achievements – as legitimately as possible. That fact justifies the expectation that the study of the ways this happens will endure, despite the changing labels for such a study.

New elements concern the increased importance of the concept of governance and the development of *governance research* when related to that. The essence of both seems a widening of scope, away from vertical means/ends schemes as the only thinkable approach in practice as well as in theory. In fact, in this second edition we particularly elaborate on these themes in more detail, because they were already present in the first edition of the book. More specifically we can give the following overview of changes.

As indicated, the first three chapters have been only lightly adapted. In view of insights gained since 2002, in Chapter 4, we have reformulated the range of issues addressed in implementation theory. In doing so, we do not give a substantively different state of the art, but the way we present the issues has changed. In Chapter 5, we focus on the historical and societal environment within which implementation is being studied, as we did in the first edition. More explicitly, however, we position the policy-implementation paradigm in what we consider as a historical development. In Chapter 6, we present our meta-theoretical framework of analysis as an alternative to the widely used stages approach to the analysis of public policy. This is something we did in the first edition, but now it has been elaborated in a separate chapter. In the first edition we included both a research review and a set of recommendations on doing research. The former has been removed but the latter has been expanded in Chapter 7 (and aligned with the account of the issues in Chapter 4), drawing on experience from the previous research review and our efforts to keep up with more recent articles and monographs. In Chapter 8, we look at the practice of implementation, as we did in the corresponding chapter in the first edition. The difference is that now we explore the dimensions of contextual variety more systematically. As far as the conceptual part of the chapter is concerned (modes of governance), where previously we were rather prescriptive, our stance is now that those who make prescriptions need to take into account the ways in which policy and institutional contexts will differ. In the final chapter, the general argument of the book is summarized, and some promising developments are identified.

Several colleagues were kind enough to give their comments on drafts of the first edition of this book; they are acknowledged in the parts of the earlier preface reproduced above. We remain grateful to them. Since then we have had the chance to develop our ideas further in several publications and in many classes and seminars. From these we wish to highlight the contributions of the editors, and anonymous reviewers, of *Public Management Review, Policy and Politics* and *Public Administration* for comments on articles published in those journals in which we have developed our thinking between the two editions.

Michael Hill would like to express his thanks to Wayne Parsons and Ken Young who invited him to participate in research and teaching at Queen Mary College, University of London, and to Raymond Kuhn who extended his visiting professorship there for three more years from 2008. Students from a lively MA course, with participants from UK central and local government and from many other countries, have taught him a great deal. He is also grateful to Nicola Vick and Perri 6 for involving him in a research study of the implementation of the English direct payments scheme. Susan Balloch and Philip Haynes at the Health and Social Policy Research Centre at the University of Brighton have continued to be invaluable sources of support and have kept him in touch with applied research.

From February till October 2007, Peter Hupe was visiting professor at the Public Management Institute in Leuven. He would like to thank his colleagues there, as well as at the Department of Public Administration, Erasmus University, Rotterdam, his institutional base, for enabling this affiliation. These thanks regard in particular Geert Bouckaert, Marleen Brans and Manu Gerard in Leuven, and Kees van Paridon, Victor Bekkers and Henk Schmidt in Rotterdam. Weekly teaching to both Flemish and Dutch students made it possible to try out a notion like the *trias gubernandi* and other ideas about studying the policy process. At these two universities the students are thanked for their response. In a late stage of the preparation of this book Donald Kettl gave comments on a draft of Chapter 5, which were greatly appreciated.

1

INTRODUCTION

Contents

Introduction

Once upon a time there was a period of intense academic debate about the understanding of the phenomenon of public policy implementation. It lasted from about the moment of the publication of Pressman and Wildavsky's influential book *Implementation* in 1973 until sometime around the end of the 1980s. In 1997, one of us in an article asked whether implementation had become 'yesterday's issue' (Hill, 1997). The answer given to that rhetorical question was: 'No'.

In this book we take a similar stance. In doing so, alongside a discussion of literature explicitly concerned with implementation will be a recognition of four facts. The first is that the phenomenon 'implementation' was a matter of concern and, to some extent, academic study before the word was used. The second fact is that, as we have discovered whenever we have attempted computerized literature reviews, the word 'implementation' is used in many contexts by writers who approach it from very different backgrounds to the public administration and public management specialists who also use it. Third, it is a fact that such writers, without using the word 'implementation', may equally explore it in ways which public administration specialists regard as relevant. Fourth, implementation inevitably takes different shapes and forms in different cultures and institutional settings. This last point is particularly important in an era in which processes of 'government' have been seen as transformed into 'governance'. The latter means that a wider range of actors may be participating and that simplistic hierarchical models are being abandoned. Hence linking the study of implementation with the study of governance is a central element in this book.

This is an exploration of the state of the art of the study of implementation as what we consider to be a sub-discipline of political science and public administration. Our objective in this book is to bring together the major insights presently available from implementation theory and research. We do not present a new theory on implementation here, but rather give an overview and make relevant connections. Because of the latter, the exercise can be called 'synthesizing' or 'third-generation', terms used by Goggin et al. (1990). Specifically, however, when we observe inconsistencies, anomalies or conflicts in or between implementation publications, we see it as our primary task to report on these before, eventually, making suggestions to 'solve' them.

Throughout all this literature, examination of implementation – simply 'what happens between policy expectations and (perceived) policy results' (DeLeon, 1999a: 314–15, paraphrasing Ferman, 1990: 39) – has had a dual character. There has been a concern *to explain* 'what happens' and a concern *to affect* 'what happens', with inevitably many of those interested in the first question being interested in the second too. In this book we will primarily look at efforts to explain what happens, and consider issues concerning studying and researching implementation. We think it important to be aware of these two questions as separate, not in the least because they are related in a specific way. Good research we see being assisted if a measure of detachment can be achieved from the preoccupations of those who want to control events. Effective control we consider as being facilitated by a sensitivity to both the complexity of the task and the nature of the normative issues at stake.

We also recognize that the issues of understanding the process and the issues of controlling it may be of interest to rather different readers. In the last analysis, however, our primary focus on efforts to explain 'what happens' is justified by the fact that if one lacks understanding, one is less likely to be able to control. At the same time we are aware of the possibility that different kinds of audiences may want to use the book in rather different ways. Hence we will introduce what is to follow by describing the contents of the chapters in a way that takes that concern into account.

Structure of the book

In this chapter we will introduce some key conceptual issues, in particular asking what we are talking about when we use the word 'implementation' and terms related to it.

Chapter 2 starts from the proposition that, just as in the real world, 'implementation' existed before this label was invented (otherwise how could the medieval cathedrals have been built?), there was some kind of 'implementation theory' before and beyond the kind of studies we usually refer to with this term. In Chapter 2, this type of theory, some of it in early political science, some of it in sociological and socio-legal work, is discussed.

Chapter 3 goes on to examine the theoretical work that blossomed around and after the publication of Pressman and Wildavsky's *Implementation* (1973), work that can be seen as a kind of dialogue between 'top-down' and 'bottom-up' approaches to theory. Chapter 4 looks at the way theory has developed since efforts were made to synthesize these alternative categories of approaches. Together these chapters reflect the body of theoretical knowledge incorporated in implementation studies. Readers who are familiar with the theory, or particularly impatient to see what new things we have to say, may want to skip over these chapters. They will find many references back to specific parts of them in the later chapters.

Chapter 5 positions the development of our topic in its societal context, exploring the relevance of policy implementation in the practice of public administration. That chapter particularly considers the implications of the changing nature of governance for the study of implementation.

Against the background of these implications, in Chapter 6, studying implementation is positioned in an analytical framework that, on a meta-theoretical level, may serve as an alternative to the so-called 'stages model' of the policy process.

Chapter 7 explores research on implementation, drawing upon much empirical work done in recent years. Methodological and programmatic issues are discussed. Suggestions are offered on how to do implementation research, pitfalls are identified and ways to avoid them are suggested. This chapter is particularly pertinent for those whose concern is with questions about how implementation can be studied.

Chapter 8 elaborates on that topic in terms of the framing of recommendations from implementation studies, suggesting that such activities have to be located in an understanding of institutional contexts and policy objectives.

Chapter 9, the final chapter, is about the future of implementation studies. Given the rise of a scholarly field like public management and new research topics like 'public service performance' (Boyne et al., 2006) the status of studying policy implementation is assessed.

Some matters of definition

Public policy

Implementation, to us, means just what Webster and Roger say it does: to carry out, accomplish, fulfill, produce, complete. But what is it being implemented? A policy, naturally. There must be something out there prior to implementation; otherwise there would be nothing to move toward in the process of implementation. A verb like 'implement' must have an object like 'policy'. But policies normally contain both goals and the means for achieving them. How, then, do we distinguish between a policy and its implementation?

With these sentences Pressman and Wildavsky (1984: xxi) highlight a question that is of more than linguistic relevance. They continue:

> We can work neither with a definition of policy that excludes any implementation nor one that includes all implementation. There must be a starting point. If no action is begun, implementation cannot take place. There must be also an end point. Implementation cannot succeed or fail without a goal against which to judge it. (1984: xxii)

The question at stake here is one of logic. In its most general form, the act of 'implementation' presupposes a prior act, particularly the 'cognitive act' of formulating what needs to be done and making a decision on that. In everyday terms, while we may vary what we do when we take action, we very often make a decision to take action – go on a journey, for example – and think about how to do it, before carrying out that action. But two further groups of questions follow from that basic one. The first is, who is the formulator, who is the decision-maker and who is the implementer? If they are not integrated as a single actor, there is a need to identify the variety of actors involved. The second group of questions is about whether the formulator or decision-maker has more power, or a role that is more legitimized, than the implementer. The former group of questions concerns empirical ones, while within the latter group the one about legitimacy addresses a normative issue. The act of formulation and decision-making may take place 'at the bottom'. But even then, it is to be followed by implementation; otherwise the former act remains without consequences. The logical connotation of the original question may be called the '*implementation follows formulation and decision theorem*'.

If implementation in the context of public administration presupposes policy, what is then meant by policy, and particularly by public policy? In academic writings on the latter subject, many definitions are provided. Partly, the variety has to do with semantics, partly with diversity in the stress on a specific aspect of the phenomenon as observed in the real world. From the available variety of definitions, we will use Hogwood and Gunn's. They identify the following elements in the use of the term 'public policy'. Although policy is to be distinguished from 'decision', it is less readily distinguishable from 'administration'. Policy involves behaviour as well as intentions, and inaction as well as action. Policies have outcomes that may or may not have been foreseen. While policy refers to a purposive course of actions, this does not exclude the possibility that purposes may be defined retrospectively. Policy arises from a process over time, which may involve both intra- and inter-organizational relationships. There is a difficult issue here about what is exactly meant by public, since private actors may participate in all aspects of public policy-making. Thus, Hogwood and Gunn say, 'Public policy involves a key, but not exclusive, role for public agencies' (1984: 23). The implication of 'key' may be seen in the extent to which the involvement of government legitimizes the action. We could invoke here the notion of 'state' action, but that too takes us into a complex issue in the modern world (explored further in Chapter 5).

Policy is subjectively defined. Hogwood and Gunn summarize this characterization in the following definition: 'Any public policy is subjectively defined by an observer as being such and is usually perceived as comprising a series of patterns of related decisions to which many circumstances and personal, group, and organizational influences have contributed' (ibid.: 23–4). Other authors also underline the subjective aspect in the definition of public policy. Heclo (1972: 83), for instance, states that what is 'policy' and certainly what is *'the* policy' depend on the observer.

For obvious reasons, this subjectivity has not prevented authors from offering *ex cathedra* a specific definition that can serve as a way of talking about public policy in similar terms. In his textbook, Anderson, for instance, gives the following definition of policy: 'A purposive course of action followed by an actor or set of actors in dealing with a problem or matter of concern ... Public policies are those policies developed by governmental bodies and officials' (1975: 3). Similar definitions can be found in various public policy textbooks (see, for instance, Kuypers, 1973; Hoogerwerf, 1978; for a variant, see Van de Graaf and Hoppe, 1989). In this kind of definition, public policy is about means and ends, which have to have a relationship to each other. Where the political functionaries provide the objectives, it is the task of administrators to develop the appropriate instruments. That they are expected to do so in as systematic a way as possible, stems from the fact that these administrators are doing their work in public service, dealing with collective problems. Public policy focuses on what Dewey (1927) once described as 'the public and its problems'. Similarly what Lasswell called the 'policy orientation' (Lerner and Lasswell, 1951; Lasswell, 1970) is problem-focused, multi-disciplinary, uses multiple methods and is contextual. In his textbook on public policy, Parsons refers to what can be called a 'clinical' attitude as characteristic of 'the policy sciences': 'Knowledge of society could provide a way of making it better' (1995: 20). Parsons describes the title of Wildavsky's book *Speaking Truth to Power* (1979) as a typical expression of the belief in social science as a form of engineering or medicine. Parsons sees the policy focus as most closely associated with the contributions of four scholars: Harold Lasswell, Herbert Simon, Charles Lindblom and David Easton. Lindblom's position is special, in the sense that he stresses 'non-rational' aspects of policy that have to do with power, social interaction and the connections between various phases and stages.[1]

What, in general, is striking about the definitions of public policy indicated here is the purposive character public policies are expected to have, and the way in which they are expected to be related to (societal) problems. For implementation theory and research, this means that contextualization is important; 'implementation' is always connected to specific policies as particular responses to specific problems in society.

The policy cycle

Since Lasswell's seminal publications on public policy it has become quite usual to speak of a 'phase' or 'stage' model of the policy process. When we broaden our scope and look beyond this process in a narrow sense, in fact, we can observe a variety of analytical ways of distinguishing between different 'stages' in the process from thinking to action.

Many writers have set out models of the 'stages' of the policy process (see, for example, Simon, 1945; Lasswell, 1956; Mack, 1971; Rose, 1973; Jenkins, 1978; Hogwood and Gunn, 1984; Dror, 1989). Typically these models embrace processes regarding how issues get on the agenda, followed by initiation (Jenkins) or 'deciding to decide' (Hogwood and Gunn), then information assembly, followed by more precise formulation. After this, the models include application and implementation. Finally, there may be feedback and evaluation, and at the end decisions about 'policy maintenance, succession or termination' (Hogwood and Gunn, 1984: 4). Perhaps the most differentiated model is presented by Dror (1989: 163–4). He distinguishes between the major stages of meta-policy-making, policy-making and post-policy-making. Because each of these has sub-stages, there is a total of 18 (sub-) stages. 'Executing the policy' is the sixteenth stage in the cycle; so a very 'late' one.

Like the means/end definition of public policy, the stages framework is widely used in textbooks on the subject. Criticizing it, Nakamura (1987) speaks of the 'textbook approach', portraying it as unrealistic. It is said to neglect the sometimes blurred distinctions between the 'phases'. In general, it is judged as rationalistic (Nakamura, 1987; D.A. Stone, 1989, 2002; Lindblom and Woodhouse, 1993; see Jenkins-Smith, 1991, for perhaps the most elaborate criticism; and Van Gunsteren, 1976, for a general critique of rationalist thinking in public affairs). Although we understand the nature of these comments, we see a continuing role for the stages framework. It is useful analytically and heuristically for both the study and practice of the policy process. Like Parsons (1995: xvii), we do have an additional requirement, however:

> [T]he idea of 'stages' must be expanded to include a wider contextualization of different frameworks and methods or approaches. There can be no one definition of policy analysis (Wildavsky, 1979: 15), and no one theory or model can capture or explain the complexity involved in what Easton once termed the 'web of decisions' (Easton, 1953: 130) which comprise public policy.

The strength of the stages framework, as stressed by Parsons (1995: 80–1), is that it provides a systematic approach to capture the multiplicity of reality. Each 'stage' relates to a specific part of the context in which public policy is being made, while within that partial context various variables and approaches can be seen as appropriate. It is from this perspective that in Chapter 6 we will develop a framework adapted from the stagist one.

Implementation

What can be called 'public policy', and thus has to be implemented, is the product of what has happened in the earlier stages of the policy process. Nevertheless, the content of that policy, and its impact on those affected, may be substantially modified, elaborated or even negated during the implementation stage, as Anderson points out. '[P]olicy is made as it is being administered and administered as it is being made' (1975: 79). Yet implementation is something separate from policy formation. Only very seldom are decisions self-executing, implying that there is no separate implementation stage. If generally there is such a stage, then there is also a good case for the separate analysis of that part of the policy process. 'Much that occurs at this stage may seem at first glance to be tedious or mundane, yet its consequences for the substance of policy may be quite profound' (Anderson, 1975: 78–9).

One of the most influential definitions of implementation is that formulated by Mazmanian and Sabatier (1983: 20–1):

> Implementation is the carrying out of a basic policy decision, usually incorporated in a statute but which can also take the form of important executive orders or court decisions. Ideally, that decision identifies the problem(s) to be addressed, stipulates the objective(s) to be pursued, and in a variety of ways, 'structures' the implementation process.

Similarly Pressman and Wildavsky say in their preface to their first edition (1973): 'Let us agree to talk about policy as a hypothesis containing initial conditions and predicted consequences. If X is done at time t1, then Y will result at time t2' (1984: xxii). Thus defined, implementation is a complicated process, or rather sub-process. Therefore much can go wrong. 'The longer the chain of causality, the more numerous the reciprocal relationships among the links and the more complex implementation becomes' (ibid.: xxiv). Nevertheless, it is inevitable that this chain is usually long.

Seen 'from the bottom', the perspective on implementation is fundamentally different. For those at the end of Pressman and Wildavsky's implementation 'chain' there is not so much concern about 'the transmission of policy into a series of consequential actions', but a policy–action relationship. The latter rather 'needs to be regarded as a process of interaction and negotiation, taking place over time, between those seeking to put policy into effect and those upon whom action depends' (Barrett and Fudge, 1981a: 4). Many implementation scholars in one way or another refer to what Barrett and Fudge call the 'policy–action continuum'. For Dunsire, policy implementation is seen as pragmatization (1978a: 178). John speaks of 'the post-legislative stages of decision making' (1998: 27), while he elsewhere calls implementation 'the stage in the policy process concerned with turning policy intentions into action' (ibid.: 204). O'Toole identifies the central question in implementation research as: 'What happens between the establishment of policy and its impact in the world of action?' (2000a: 273). Elsewhere he defines policy implementation as 'what develops between the establishment of an apparent intention on the part of government to do something, or stop doing something, and the ultimate impact in the world of action' (ibid.: 266). Earlier, and even more concisely, O'Toole remarked that policy implementation 'refers to the connection between the expression of governmental intention and actual results' (1995: 43). Boiling down all kinds of elaborate definitions, DeLeon calls the study of implementation 'little more than a comparison of the expected versus the achieved' (1999a: 330). We noted in the introduction to this chapter Ferman's particularly concise definition. It is one we will keep very much in mind in this book.

Implementation and policy formation

The process emphasis, ultimately expressed in the continuum between policy and action, implies that in the implementation stage policy-*making* continues. This empirical observation is contrary to the emphasis in the theory of bureaucracy developed from the classic theoretical contributions of Max Weber and Woodrow Wilson. In that theory, discussed further in Chapter 2, administration starts where politics – read here: 'policy' – ends. This characterization of the relation between the two, both as a hierarchy and a strict dichotomy, has been normatively embedded in the institutions of the rule of law and democracy. In the study of politics and government the possibility that, instead, there could be *interaction* between the different phases, as well as between functionaries playing different roles like the ones of decision-maker and implementer, has been ignored for a long while. The fact that the 'black box' of implementation was not opened in much political science influenced by this view was what made Hargrove (1975) speak of the 'missing link'.

What is needed is a way of combining the analytical benefits offered by the 'stages' model with a recognition of the interaction between the stages. We consider that this is best achieved by talking of policy *formation* (rather than making). This is then distinguishable, in most cases, from an implementation process within which policy will continue to be shaped. If the term 'policy-making' stands for the policy process as a whole, then both implementation and policy formation refer to respectively 'late' and 'early' sub-processes in that process. While some authors focus on policy design (Ingraham, 1987; Weimer, 1993) and others on the societal and 'bureau-political' struggle around it (Lindblom, 1965; Allison, 1971), this combined character of thought and action is crucial. Although Allison (1971), in his analysis of the Cuban missile crisis, was one of the first to point out the synchronic relevance of these different views on policy formation, he did not synthesize them. Nevertheless, the interplay between 'intellectual cogitation' and 'social interaction' particularly in the sub-process of policy formation, and expressed in the combination of, respectively, formulation and decision-making, can to a certain degree explain the often ambiguous character of policy that has to be implemented. Therefore this interplay is crucial for the study of implementation (for a systematic elaboration of this mixed character of policy formation – although in Dutch – see Kuypers, 1980; see also Van de Graaf and Hoppe, 1989).

Outputs and outcomes

One of the most influential models of the relationship between politics and administration is Easton's 'political system' (1953). 'Inputs' go into that system and the things that come out are called 'outputs' and 'outcomes'. Implementation can be seen as a part of the 'throughput' taking place within the 'system'. Sometimes, in both the practice and the study of implementation, the distinction between inputs, outputs and outcomes is overlooked. Given, for instance, concern about lack of crime prevention, the political opposition in a legislature may call for more 'police on the street'. The idea is then that a larger number of personnel – in operational service – will automatically lead to a decline in crime. All kinds of intervening, but perhaps less manipulable, variables are often forgotten. In fact, policy inputs ('more police') here are taken automatically to produce policy impacts or outcomes (less crime) (Mazmanian and Sabatier, 1983: 22). Also in 'output' analysis the issues of defining and operationalizing the various categories at stake are sometimes muddled. This is the case, for instance, when the researcher merely looks at indices like expenditures. It is argued here that these should be regarded as 'input' rather than 'output' variables (for an advance of this argument, see Hill and Bramley, 1986; for the use of this argument in the analysis of welfare state performance, see also Mitchell, 1991).

Besides, it can be observed that outputs and outcomes are sometimes confused.[2] A great deal of implementation literature is about the extent to which policy-makers have successfully grappled with the question whether their policies have been properly designed to address the problems they were alleged to address. Not surprisingly it does this in terms of whether wars on poverty, crime, and so on, have actually dealt with those problems. Lane and Ersson argue: 'Thus, outcome analysis in evaluation research came to include all kinds of results that were relevant to the understanding of policies, including outcomes that had no link whatsoever with a policy but affected the evaluation of whether a policy had succeeded or not' (2000: 62). They emphasize the need for a clear distinction between outputs and outcomes, saying of the latter: 'Outcomes are the things that are actually achieved, whatever the objectives of policy may have been. Outcomes are real results, whether intended or unintended, at the same time as outcomes are not government action' (ibid.: 63).

For implementation research, dependent variables may be outputs or outcomes, after the implementation process, but where they are the latter it is particularly important to identify influences that are quite independent of that process. This distinction is explored further in terms of its specific relevance for research in Chapter 7.

Making judgements about implementation

Speaking of outputs and outcomes implicitly or explicitly means making judgements. Comparing what is achieved with what was expected (DeLeon, 1999a) can often lead to the observation of an 'implementation gap' (Dunsire, 1978a). An alternative term is 'implementation failure'. In daily practice such qualifications are easily used. Similarly, in the study of implementation a qualification in terms of 'success' or, more often, 'failure' is commonly given. And indeed, sometimes, as in the case of a specific serious accident or disaster, the use of the label 'policy fiasco' seems justifiable (Bovens and 't Hart, 1996; Bovens et al., 2001). What has to be kept in mind, then, is that the judgement given in such a case, however analytically supported it may be, is in the end – and should be – a normative one. The question here is: Does the researcher or analyst consider this normative judgement as separate from or as integrated into the empirical analysis? Parsons applies Morgan's metaphorical models of organization (1986, 1993) to explore the value of adopting alternative perspectives on implementation failure. He shows that using a different metaphor means looking at and labelling the causes and consequences of implementation failure in a different way. Implementation failure can be seen, for instance, as a result of a poor chain of command and of problems with structures and roles (machine metaphor); as a result of difficult 'human relations' or 'the environment' (organism metaphor); as a result of poor information flows or 'learning' problems (brain metaphor); as a result of labour/management conflict (domination metaphor); as a result of the 'culture' of an organization (culture metaphor); as a result of subconscious forces, group-think, ego defences or repressed sexual instincts (psychic metaphor); as a result of a 'self-referencing' system (autopoietic metaphor); or as a result of power in and around the implementation process (power metaphor) (Parsons, 1995: 489). Important here is that no one metaphor *a priori* provides a better picture. Actually, what one portrays as empirical reality depends upon what kind of metaphor is used.

This interpretative view involves integrating values, although in sets varying according to the metaphor, into the way of looking at the world. When doing so, the researcher is always right, or in any case as long as he or she chooses the metaphor best fitted to the context at hand. A systematic and controlled confrontation between 'theory' and 'empirical reality' is thus avoided. There is no check on the provisional character of knowledge. Because values are completely integrated into the way of looking at reality, any attempt to interpret the findings is irrelevant. There is no sense in discussing from a normative standpoint what the conclusions of an analysis could be, because these form an integral part of such an analysis. From the beginning until the end, the analysts then have positioned themselves between the reader and the empirical object, making an interpretation of the latter independent from theirs difficult.

In fact, at stake here is a classic epistemological issue that divides the 'positivists' in their various variants from the 'interpretivists'. We see the value of metaphorical 'explanations', of the kind presented by Morgan and Parsons, as contributions to public discourse. But as criteria for the development of a field like implementation studies, we think a broader academic engagement is required, aiming at the accumulation of knowledge. Our stance is that, both on different occasions and in several parts of the empirical cycle, we see functions for interpretative contributions, mainly of a heuristic and evaluative ('making sense of') kind. As far as the development of empirical studies is concerned, we consider that such contributions have uses. However, these are particularly functional in the 'early' parts of the empirical cycle, concerning problem definition and the formulation of working hypotheses; as well as in the 'later' parts of that cycle, focusing on the interpretation of findings, the drawing of conclusions and the formulation of advice. Of course, values are always involved. Nevertheless, concepts need to be defined and operationalized in a neutral fashion, so that then there can be an orientation towards testing in one way or another.[3] In the 'middle part' of the empirical cycle we therefore plead for a systematic, theory-driven, and if possible comparative, approach to empirical reality; for conceptual parsimony; and for aiming at the testing of propositions, in a quantitative, qualitative or combined way. In a fully fledged research design the goal will be to explain variance. In any case, our perspective implies a need to make research decisions explicit and to justify epistemological stances when doing implementation research.

Implementation and evaluation

Talking of an 'implementation failure' or 'implementation deficit' means giving a normative qualification as a result of a comparison between what is observed and what is expected, where the latter is defined in terms of the values either of the observer or of one or more of the actors involved in the process. In that sense, an evaluation is then provided. Nevertheless, the distinction between implementation and evaluation as two successive 'stages' in the policy process is analytically relevant enough to maintain. The definitions of evaluation given in the literature vary in broadness. In a monograph on the subject, Fischer defines policy evaluation as 'the activity of applied social science typically referred to as "policy analysis" or "policy science"' (1995: 2). He refers to Dunn, who speaks of policy analysis as an applied endeavour 'which uses multiple methods of inquiry and argument to produce and transform policy-relevant information that may be utilized in political settings to resolve policy problems' (1981: 35). Classic texts are Patton (1978), Rossi and Freeman (1979) and Palumbo (1987), or, for a 'naturalistic' approach, Guba and Lincoln (1987).

Lane asks, as quoted by Browne and Wildavsky in an additional chapter to Pressman and Wildavsky (1984: 204–05):

> Is implementation analysis the same as evaluation analysis? The concept of implementation as evolution amounts to a strong denial of any identity between the two, because if objectives and outcomes continuously interact, how could the outcomes be evaluated in terms of a fixed set of objectives?

Browne and Wildavsky conclude that the conceptual distinction between evaluation and implementation is important to maintain, however much the two overlap in practice. They state: 'Evaluators are able to tell us a lot about what happened – which objectives, whose objectives, were achieved – and a little about why – the causal connections' (ibid.: 203).

Table 1.1   Implementation and evaluation research

	Implementation	Evaluation
Object	Process/Behaviour Outputs Outcomes Causal connections	Outcomes/Values links
Research act	Description Explanation Theory building and testing Analytical judgements	Value judgements

Parsons makes the implementation/evaluation distinction by indicating that evaluation examines 'how public policy and the people who deliver it may be appraised, audited, valued and controlled', while the study of implementation is about 'how policy is put into action and practice' (1995: 461). The conceptualization used in this book can be summarized as shown in Table 1.1.

Implementation research

Theory and research on public policy implementation concern 'the development of systematic knowledge regarding what emerges, or is induced, as actors deal with a policy problem' (O'Toole, 2000a: 266). In 1973, Pressman and Wildavksy were amazed that there was so little that deserved the heading 'implementation research'. Some years later they described the situation quite differently (1984: 163):

> The study of implementation is becoming a growth industry: tens, perhaps hundreds, of studies are underway now. Yet researchers are visibly uneasy. It is not so much that they expect to discover all the right answers; they are not even sure they are asking the right questions ... But this uneasiness is not surprising, for the attempt to study implementation raises the most basic question about the relation between thought and action: How can ideas manifest themselves in a world of behavior?

Implementation research has grown to what can be seen as a sub-discipline, developed particularly within the disciplines of political science and public administration. In the past 30 years, the field has flourished (see Saetren, 2005), but disappointment has been expressed about the low degree of theoretical coherence and the lack of cumulative effect from the research undertaken (O'Toole, 1986). Some authors are very dismissive: 'While the concept of implementation remains useful as a conceptual tool to understand the failure and success of policy, the project of creating implementation analysis as a separate field of study has largely failed' (John, 1998: 30). In Chapter 5, we look at the development of the field in its societal context, exploring reasons for such a negative judgement – a judgement that we can understand, but do not agree with. Why we are more positive on both the state and the future of the field has to do with the recent emergence of the phenomenon and the concept of 'governance'.

Governance

Somewhere in the 1990s, 'governance' or 'new governance' was seen as having arrived (Pierre and Peters, 2000). This term refers to the way in which collective impacts are produced in a social system. Several authors have provided definitions of the concept of governance already, others focus on a specific sort of governance, while some authors distinguish different models of governance.[4]

Lynn et al. define governance as 'regimes of laws, administrative rules, judicial rulings, and practices that constrain, prescribe, and enable governmental activity' (1999: 2–3). In Rhodes' view, governance 'refers to self-organizing, interorganizational networks' (1997: 15), while for Wamsley, governance 'connotes the use of authority in providing systemic steering and direction' (1990a: 25), and stands for 'choosing, prioritizing, directing and steering' (1990b: 114). In McGregor's definition, the term 'governance' refers to 'the application of power and authority in a way that commits relevant political actors to managerial decisions' (1993: 182). Stoker (1991) speaks of an 'authority, exchange and governance paradigm'. Referring to Clarence Stone (1989), he calls governance 'creating the capacity to act', bringing together the resources required to accomplish the collective ends of society' (Stoker, 1991: 51).

Kooiman (1999) gives a classification of the various ways in which the term 'governance' has been used in the literature thus far. He adds some categories to the list Rhodes (1997) made earlier. Kooiman distinguishes ten different meanings of the term: (1) governance as the minimal state; (2) corporate governance; (3) governance as new public management; (4) 'good governance'; (5) governance as socio-cybernetic governance; (6) governance as self-organizing networks; (7) governance as '*Steuerung*' (German) or '*sturing*' (Dutch); (8) governance as international order; (9) 'governing the economy' or economic sectors; and, finally, (10) governance and governmentability. In the anthology of six definitions Kooiman next selects, he gives as his own: 'solving problems and creating opportunities, and the structural and processual conditions aimed at doing so' (1999: 69).

By adding an adjective, several authors particularly focus on a specific *sort* of governance. Kooiman, for instance, speaks of 'modern governance' (1993), 'social-political governance' (1999; see also Lawson, 2000, with 'socio-political governance') and 'self-governance' (Kooiman and Van Vliet, 2000). The latter uses the concept of 'communicative governance', also (Van Vliet, 1993). In the view of Pierre and Peters, the term 'governance' in Europe refers to 'new governance': ideas of the involvement of society in the process of governing. By contrast, in the USA, the term 'retains much of its original steering conception' (2000: 7).

Rhodes (1997) and Saward (1997) also use the term 'new governance'. Toonen (1990) speaks of 'co-governance'; Greca (2000) of 'institutional co-governance'; Huxham (2000) of 'collaborative governance'; Hupe and Meijs (2000) of 'hybrid governance'. Earlier, Kickert (1997) spoke of 'public governance' and Rhodes (1992) of 'local governance'.

In addition, some authors give a broad definition, which they then differentiate into a number of *models of governance*. Under that heading Pierre and Peters (2000), for instance, distinguish between three scenarios: 'reasserting control'; 'letting other regimes rule'; and 'communitarianism, deliberation, and direct democracy'.

In fact, it seems possible to classify these varying meanings given to the term 'governance' into five categories. First, there are authors using the label in order to assign a certain historical phase – that is, the contemporary one – in the evolution of Western government. After the eras of planning (the 1960s and 1970s) came the era of the market (the 1980s). Since then, government has realized it cannot act alone, but nor can it expect the market to provide the solution to all problems. That is why government engages with other parties in society. This is, concisely and in domestic terms, the essence of the argument here; that is why we now live *in the age of governance*. In this context, Richards and Smith (2002) speak of the transition from the Weberian to the postmodern state. Second, authors like Stoker (1991), Rhodes (1997), or John (2001) use the term governance to refer to a specific, 'third way', of 'steering', that is, via networks. Third, the term is used as a more or less neutral umbrella, under which some variants are distinguished, like *models* of governance (Pierre and Peters, 2000) or *modes* of governance (Kooiman, 2003). Fourth, governance is used as a label to conceptualize the multi-dimensional character of 'government-in-action' (for instance: O'Toole, 2000a). Authors like Lynn and his associates (Heinrich and Lynn, 2000; Lynn et al., 2001) use the term as a basis for developing an analytical framework for studying the 'logic of governance'. With what we call the 'Multiple Governance Framework' in the present book, we aim at a similar objective; see Chapter 6. Such meta-theoretical frameworks enable researchers to specify their leading questions and illuminate the differentiation of the kind of acts 'governing as governance' (Kooiman, 2003) is consisting of. Finally, with the adjective 'good' added – or not – the term governance may function as a norm for the behaviour of actors in contemporary public administration. The World Bank (2007), for instance, employs 'governance indicators' to rank the quality of government, society and its relations in countries on a world scale. Such indicators as 'voice and accountability', 'political stability and absence of violence', 'government effectiveness', 'regulatory quality', 'rule of law', and 'control of corruption' are used.

Implementation research and governance

Among these many definitions of governance circulating, the one formulated by O'Toole, in our view, shows an appropriate balance between comprehensiveness and specificity; and is therefore used in this book. The conceptualization of governance is designed 'to incorporate a more complete understanding of the multiple levels of action and kinds of variables that can be expected to influence performance' (O'Toole, 2000a: 276). Governance has consequences for the way the object of implementation research is defined. Implementation research can be placed under the heading of governance research, but in doing so it has to be broadened. Then new connections, with other fields and sub-fields in the social sciences, also need to be put into the picture. In some of them, like public management, converging movements can be observed. Lynn and his colleagues, for instance, practise such 'governance research' (see Lynn et al., 1999, 2001). In broad outline their project constitutes an effort to synthesize influences on government performance of several sorts and from several levels. As both a participant in that project and an implementation researcher, O'Toole is positive about the consequences of the former for the latter, because the project referred to is 'taking account of the standard concerns of implementation researchers and integrating these with other kinds of related analyses' (2000a: 278). In his view, 'implementation per se has moved to the background, in favour of attention to concerted action across institutional boundaries on behalf of public purpose' (ibid.).

Multiple loci, layers, and levels

The widened heading for implementation research has several consequences. First, with the distinction between government and governance, the difference between structures and processes, between institutions and behaviour, and between actors and activities has become important. In fact, the distinction between locus and focus is at stake here, referring to the separate character of the *what* and the *how* of scholarly attention.[5] In the diversity of political-societal relations within a (national) political-administrative system, a variety of *loci* can be observed. For instance, looking at what civil servants in public bureaucracies 'at the street level' are doing, Lipsky (1980) leaves aside what takes place in the Washington departments. Hanf and Scharpf (1978), on the contrary, pay attention to the external relations between both public and private organizations. It is obvious, therefore, that not all implementation researchers are focusing on the same locus, while exactly that variety needs to be incorporated into the analysis of implementation and governance.

Second, explicit attention is given to the layered character of the political-administrative system. Instead of the antagonistic top/bottom distinction, a variety of institutional relations is addressed, both vertical and horizontal ones. For the loci of the formal, legitimate political-administrative institutions, including representative organs with a certain territorial competence, we would like to reserve the term *administrative layers*. In a federal system, for example, these layers involve the federation, the states, the counties and municipalities. In a 'decentralized unitary state' like The Netherlands, apart from the 'functional' water boards, there are three territorial administrative layers: the *Rijk*, the provinces, and local government, each with a certain degree of autonomy. A specific public policy may be both formed and implemented at one and the same political-administrative layer. Many policies, however, while following their policy intentions–policy outputs trajectory, encounter a variety of such layers. At each of the layers there are official competences and there is legitimate politics at work. It depends on the legal framework of the specific public policy whether just implementation or, in fact, 'policy co-formation' can be observed.

Third, the act of management is taken seriously, more or less a new feature in implementation research (often presented as 'public management research', see the discussion in the next chapter). The term then refers to 'the set of conscious efforts to concert actors and resources to carry out established collective purposes' (O'Toole, 2000b: 21). Here we are talking about the realm of action. Our supposition is that in all of the loci in political-societal relations, action of a varied character takes place. Action may involve designing institutions as well as managing implementation. Research of such different activities means specifying *levels of analysis*. Consequentially, the acknowledgement of this multiplicity implies a contextual approach, both in research and in practice.

Multiplicity demands contextualization

The broadening of the perspective on implementation to a multi-disciplinary, multi-level and multi-focal exercise looking at a multiplicity of actors, loci and layers clearly should be welcomed. Hence, questions of implementation can be reframed in terms of 'performance via governance in the delivery of policy results' (O'Toole, 2000a: 281). Nevertheless, some things remain the same: 'Explaining – and ultimately improving – the way policy intention influences policy action is the research agenda, by whatever name' (O'Toole, 2000a: 283).

Interestingly, however, in his introduction written with Majone to the 1979 edition of *Implementation*, Wildavsky (Pressman and Wildavsky, 1984: 164) made an observation that can be seen as entirely relevant to this new perspective:

> If implementation is everywhere, as one of the authors suggested in another connection, is it *ipso facto* nowhere? ... No doubt this is why students of implementation complain that the subject is so slippery; it does depend on what one is trying to explain, from what point of view, at what point in its history.

It means, perhaps even more than before, that contextualization is needed. The consequences for the agenda of implementation research are explored further in Chapter 8.

It would be excessively repetitive in a chapter that has simply introduced the book as a whole, and explored some key definitional problems, to add 'conclusions' here. The essential process of siting the scholarly examination of implementation in the wider context of academic studies of the policy process is continued further in the next chapter.

Notes

1 See Parsons (1995: 27) for a list of the key texts on the study of public policy.
2 In an appendix to his book on politics, values and public policy Fischer (1980) points to some early examples of comparative research aiming at establishing causal linkages between dependent and independent variables of policy models. He mentions Rae and Taylor (1971), and, for a critical review of the literature, Jacob and Lipsky (1968). He also refers to Hammond and Adelman (1978) for an illustration of the integration of social scientific data about policy variables and normative judgements about the variables elicited from the political environment. As a 'post-positivist', Fischer is critical of the extent to which what he calls 'the scientific approach' – formal modelling – can contribute to integrating empirical and normative judgements.
3 Compare Popper's statement (1959) on the preliminary character of all scientific knowledge.
4 For a relatively early use of the term, see Wittrock (1983).
5 Although we can no longer trace where and when, it was Robert Golembiewski who introduced this distinction to us.

2

POSITIONING
IMPLEMENTATION STUDIES

Contents

Introduction

It has become conventional wisdom to see implementation studies as emergent in the 1970s. Hargrove then (1975) wrote of the 'missing link' in the study of the policy process while Pressman and Wildavsky's influential *Implementation* was published in 1973. The reaction of one of us to Pressman and Wildavsky's claim that they could find next to no literature on implementation was to draft a short paper for his colleagues headed by a quotation from Molière's *Le Bourgeois Gentilhomme*: 'Gracious me! I have been talking prose for the last forty years and have never known it.' While not at that stage being able to claim 40 years' experience of academic practice, earlier work had involved trying to reinforce long-standing concerns in public administration with ideas from organization theory in the implementation part of the policy process (Hill, 1972). Obviously, implementation was a central concern, although that word was seldom used. Pressman and Wildavsky's bibliography, ostensibly demonstrating the absence of an implementation literature, did not contain such classic American works as Blau's *The Dynamics of Bureaucracy* (1955), Kaufman's *The Forest Ranger* (1960) and, above all, Selznick's *TVA and the Grass Roots* (1949).

Van Meter and Van Horn, in another of the seminal contributions to the modern implementation literature, were similarly critical of Pressman and Wildavsky's omissions:

> While we share Pressman and Wildavsky's concern that far too little attention has been paid to the question of policy implementation, their criticism of the literature is unnecessarily harsh and shortsighted. Our argument is put simply: there is a rich heritage from the social sciences which is often overlooked by those purporting to discuss the policy implementation process. This literature includes theoretical and empirical work in several disciplines, including sociology, public administration, social psychology and political science. While most of these studies do not examine specifically the policy implementation process, close inspection reveals that it takes little imagination to comprehend their relevance. (1975: 452–3)

Hargrove, obviously stung by such comments, argued in a later paper:

> It could be argued that I misstate the problem. In fact, there is plenty of theory around to be applied to cases. One could cite organization theory in general or, more specifically, the rich literature of public administration. However, very little of this work deals with the contemporary problems of policy implementation which preoccupy political scientists and analysts. (1983: 280)

He went on to claim that the new implementation theory addresses problems not faced in the older public administration literature.

Of course, we could leave it there and launch immediately into a discussion of the implementation literature that has developed since the 1970s. That was a time when academic work in the social sciences was exploding, and when there were all sorts of efforts to apply social scientific ideas to the policy process. However, we think it worthwhile briefly to look back in time. We consider that to do so helps us to develop a clear view about the literature on implementation, and particularly on the difficulties that have been encountered in advancing the 'implementation perspective'.

Harald Saetren's careful review of the history of implementation studies (2005), like the comments above, challenges the simplistic account of the birth of the sub-discipline but of course acknowledges that a great deal depends upon the extent to which studies are identified as about 'implementation', with that word explicitly used. We will not here follow him into an elaborate examination of different literatures, particularly those such as education policy studies where the focus on the substance of the policy concerned dominates. There researchers are not interested in connecting up their work with the concerns of analysts of politics or public administration in general. Rather, in this chapter, we explore connections between implementation studies and other work, dating from both before and since the 1970s, which examine questions pertinent to that subject without using the term 'implementation' or making explicit connections with implementation theory. Within that literature, authors express concerns that are very central to controversy within implementation theory: about the rule of law, accountability and the roles of civil servants within the policy process. The place of these concerns in the sub-discipline within which implementation studies have been explicitly located, public administration and its modern variant public management, is then briefly examined. In the next section we look at institutional theory in political science and sociology, which has concerns that overlap with those of analysts of implementation research. This section is followed by some observations on postmodern perspectives, which develop the viewpoint of those institutional theorists who question the feasibility of systematic generalization about the policy process. Overall, this mixture of topics offers an account of a range of work that in one way or another 'talks' about implementation without explicitly using the term or developing the analytical approach to that topic that we will be exploring in the rest of the book.

Concerns about implementation: historical origins

Clearly, some of the earliest human activities must have involved the setting of objectives. It is pointless to speculate to what extent achievements identifiable today arose out of purposive activity, just as it is difficult to make assumptions about the relationship between actions and preceding objectives when we observe the behaviour of others. Where analysis does become possible is where (a) individuals secured actions from others and (b) left information that enables us to infer that they were setting goals for these actions. The evidence we have of the earliest collective actions comes from the relics that have survived. We can observe some extraordinary achievements – stone circles, pyramids, palaces, and so on – that must have been products of collective action, and in many cases there is evidence that this action was on behalf of some dominant individual or group.

There is nothing in the basic definition of implementation that ties it, as the modern literature does, to the idea of *public* policy. That fact suggests that the study or analysis of implementation should be seen as a part of the study of organizational behaviour or of management. That chimes in with a very modern view that the management of public policy should be regarded as no different from the management of any other activity (see Dunsire, 1995, and Gray and Jenkins, 1995, for discussions of this view). We return to this below. There is obviously something to be said for seeing the study of public policy implementation as being simply the study of the management of organized behaviour. We must therefore consider what might make public policy implementation different.

Again it is helpful to explore this issue in historical terms, confronting the question: Under what circumstances may we identify some implementation activities that were different from simple private efforts to manage collective endeavours? What then seems to be the case is that there were, from very early times, some sustained activities over a long period or a broad geographical area that were led by people who sought to exercise some overall system of government. At this stage, little progress can be made with any analysis of implementation without grappling with the two topics very central to political science – authority and the state. The evidence we have of the earliest 'states', 'kingdoms' or 'empires' consists of the relics they left behind. Where there are no written records, these are the remains of constructions, as has already been noted. With these, we know only of the implementation successes of these very early political systems (although we may perhaps infer failure too from the fact that many remarkable achievements were ultimately left to decay). Later, written records are available, of varying but increasing sophistication, which enable us to identify accounts of organizational achievements. A significant amount of Greek and Roman literature is about the implementation problems confronting those who sought to organize societies and engage in war.

Much of this early material tends to be read as concerned with explaining the 'power' of rulers or the effectiveness of quasi-democratic systems. We cannot easily make interpretations about the relationships between objective setting and the carrying out of those objectives. Systems of rule can be perceived to have been set up, to have survived for a period and then to have been modified or undermined. Wars were conducted with inevitably varying degrees of success. Cities came and went, trading systems operated with mixed achievements. Perhaps the most interesting phenomena were those that must have required sustained co-ordination over long periods of time. Systems for the control of water – to prevent flooding, provide irrigation, and so on – have attracted particular attention. These have been seen as explaining 'empires' (Wittfogel, 1963), but the questions about how they were achieved are equally interesting. Similarly the extension of power systems across great tracts of territory, where it could take months to send a punitive expedition against rebels, has long attracted the interest of scholars. (Above all, the rise and fall of the Roman Empire involved a complex sequence of 'implementation problems'.)

It is not our intention here to offer an elaborate historical analysis of implementation. We have already noted that what we see of the activities of the distant past depends very much upon what has survived. It should also be noted that those who have left us records of these activities were largely those in dominant roles, or closely allied to such people. Much less easily recognizable are the many implementation successes that depended upon bottom-up forms of collective action. The history of 'empires' tends to be very much the history of those who controlled them.

The study of power in these early states has of course generated a literature that seeks to explain the puzzles about how control was exercised. We know quite a lot about the various ways in which naked power was exercised; a topic that we could translate into the language of implementation studies in terms of bloody reprisals for implementation failure. We can trace a variety of complex devices – the use of spies, eunuchs, foreigners, and so on – to try to ensure the loyalty of subordinates over whom it was very difficult to exercise direct supervision. There is much evidence of the use of approaches to power that depended upon a feudal system of some kind in which a sort of hierarchy of opportunities for gain was operated. These can perhaps be seen as power systems that allowed for implementation deficit. So long as the ruler got the taxes and the military support when it was needed, other control over local events could be traded down the hierarchy. Tax farmers, for example, profited if they could collect a surplus over what their ruler required, and were punished if they achieved a deficit. The criterion for implementation success was simple.

There has also been an enormous interest in the extent to which it was possible to legitimize rule. Here of course we are in the realm of the literature about Max Weber's systems of authority (1947). It is appropriate to be in Weber's 'company' as we jump forward from speculation about very early systems of power. If we look at implementation in terms of Weber's three types of authority, we can dismiss one type – charismatic authority – as essentially involving no concept of separation between goal setting and sustained independent action and as being ephemeral in nature unless 'routinized', transforming it into one of the other types. On the other hand, we cannot so readily move on from the concept of traditional authority. After all there have been long periods – in European history from the early Middle Ages until even the nineteenth century, almost throughout recorded Chinese history and in much of the history of the Islamic world – in which extensive policy implementation occurred. That was legitimated largely in terms of adherence to goals set by religious leaders or absolute rulers (or both in concert). During this long period of traditional authority the modern notion of the state began to emerge with some very explicit assertions of rights to rule – over territories much more explicitly defined – and thus clearer expectations of implementation success.

Over a period between about the fourteenth and the twentieth centuries, legitimizing ideologies within states gradually took on three new characteristics. One of these involved assertions of *the idea of the nation state* – seeing collective action as legitimized by notions of shared racial, cultural or linguistic characteristics. This is not particularly pertinent to the study of implementation, except inasmuch as it provided a context for the other two developments. These were the emergence of the idea of the *rule of law* and the *development of democracy*. These ideas need careful consideration for the implications they have for the way we think about implementation. They are in various respects connected, but can be analyzed separately as they raise rather different themes for this discussion.

The rule of law

The issues concerning the rule of law are important for the study of implementation because implicit in that concept is the notion that citizens should be able to predict the impact of the actions of the state upon their lives and secure redress when affected by illegitimate actions. Wade (1982) suggests that the 'rule of law' has four aspects:

1   'Its primary meaning is that everything must be done according to the law', which when applied to the powers of government means that 'every act which affects the legal rights, duties or liberties of any person must be shown to have

a strictly legal pedigree. The affected person may always resort to the courts of law, and if the legal pedigree is not found to be perfectly in order the court will invalidate the act, which he can then safely disregard' (ibid.: 22).

2   'The secondary meaning of the rule of law ... is that government should be conducted within a framework of recognized rules and principles which restrict discretionary power' (ibid.: 22).

3   Disputes about the law should be settled by a judiciary that is independent of government (ibid.: 23).

4   The 'law should be even-handed between government and citizen' (ibid.: 24).

The particular way those principles are enunciated by Wade may have characteristics that are peculiar to the Anglo-Saxon countries, but the general thrust of the principles is accepted wherever it is claimed that governments operate within the 'rule of law'. As a Swiss/French text puts it: 'The law constitutes the source of legitimation *par excellence* for all public actors' (Knoepfel et al., 2007: 65). For the purposes of this discussion it is what Wade calls the primary meaning that is important. It implies that there should be some connection between policy implementation and the statutes that authorize it. This provides one of the foundations of the concerns of the top-down approach to implementation, which will be given much further consideration later in this book.

The importance of the 'rule of law' as a basis for legitimate rule is explored in Weber's third type of authority: 'rational legal'. Weber argues (in a text originally put together in the early years of the twentieth century): 'Today the most usual basis of legitimacy is the belief in legality, the readiness to conform with rules which are formally correct and have been imposed by accepted procedure' (1947: 131). He goes on to distinguish order derived from voluntary agreement from one that is imposed – but calls this distinction 'only relative'. The first of the ideas that he sees as central to the 'effectiveness' of legal authority is:

> That any given legal norm may be established by agreement or by imposition, on grounds of expediency or rational values or both, with a claim to obedience at least on the part of the members of the corporate group. This is, however, usually extended to include all persons within the sphere of authority or of power in question – which in the case of territorial bodies is the territorial area – who stand in certain social relationships or carry out forms of social action which in the order governing the corporate group have been declared to be relevant. (ibid.: 329)

In that rather convoluted argument, of course, lies the concept of the state. The second idea is that 'every body of law consists essentially in a consistent system of abstract rules which have been intentionally established' (ibid.: 330).

The remaining ideas go on to emphasize other aspects of the system by which this body of rules is established, in which we see glimpses of Weber's emphasis on the importance of bureaucracy. There is no suggestion that democracy is essential for the rational legal order. On the contrary, elsewhere, Weber says of France: 'Without this juristic rationalism, the rise of the absolute state is just as little imaginable as is the Revolution' (Gerth and Mills, 1947: 94). In Weber's approach to the concept of the 'rational legal order' there are two notions that need separating. One of these is the idea that obedience is to an identifiable body of rules. This is clearly very like the key principle embodied in the idea of the rule of law. In this sense the 'rationality' is embodied in the structure of the rules, wherever they come from. The other is that Weber is concerned to stress the importance for their legitimacy of the way the rules are made – although he does not invoke the idea of democracy – in terms of the extent to which they are the product of the work of a body of officials working in a systematic and impersonal way. This supposition Weber seems to hold valid for bureaucracies in general, both in their private sector and public sector variants. In short, the idea of the rational legal order and the idea of bureaucracy are closely linked together. This is the controversial aspect of Weber's work. While a body of rules could be created in a variety of different ways, and could even be developed and renegotiated through 'bottom-up' processes, the bureaucratic model is essentially hierarchical and by implication the rules are dominated by principles dictated from the top of that hierarchy, and are conservative and very stable.

The arguments about Weber's ideal-typical model of bureaucracy are not our concern here, but it is important to recognize the extent to which one of the roots of the concern about implementation as a controlled and predictable process comes from a widespread belief in the need for this. Weber was not so much prescribing (although that is a matter of dispute) as identifying bureaucracy as taken for granted in the organization of government in the early twentieth century.

In the examination of Weber's 'rational legal' and 'bureaucratic' ideal-types by sociologists in the mid-twentieth century, questions were raised about the limits to control through bureaucratic models. That examination closely paralleled discussions in management theory about the case for formal organization along what are often called Fordist lines, based upon the very strict organization of motor assembly lines influenced by the management theory of F.W. Taylor (1911).

With the development of the social sciences in the 1940s and 1950s, two developments in organization theory – one stimulated by the work of Max Weber, the other by work that questions the formal management model (see particularly Mayo, 1933) – began to come together. Sociologists, using Weber's work (or their understanding of it) as their starting point, set out to show the importance of patterns of informal relationships alongside the formal ones. Social psychologists, on the other hand, sought to explore the conflict between human needs and the apparent requirements of formal organizations. Drawing on this work, administrative theorists sought to update the old formal prescriptive models with more flexible propositions based upon this new understanding of organizational life (McGregor, 1960; Argyris, 1964; Herzberg, 1966).

There are two related issues emergent from this literature – whether the formal prescription of behaviour from the top is feasible, and whether it is desirable. We will see in later chapters the various ways in which these emerge in discussions of implementation. In the context of the 'rule of law', under discussion here, an interesting related debate emerged about administrative discretion. The issues concerned are about the extent to which the behaviour of public officials can and/or should be precisely prescribed by laws, or conversely about the extent to which officials need to use their discretion to interpret and under some circumstances modify the impact of the law. In Britain, the roots of that debate seem to lie in concerns about delegated legislation, that is, basic framework laws that can be amplified by subsequent regulations. A particular target of critics of this legislation has been what have been nicknamed 'Henry VIII clauses', after the arbitrary rule of that monarch, which give very wide scope to ministers to amplify original legislation. In many respects the arguments about delegated legislation relate to the law-making process, and thus to issues of the relationship between the legislature and the executive. Hence, they are not so much about the absence of the rule of law as about the capacity for a government to make laws without going through rigorous parliamentary procedures. However, they have been seen, by legal philosophers like Dicey (1905), as symptomatic of the development of collectivism, giving government powers that cannot easily be controlled by citizens through legal processes. In that sense, the issues regarding what we may call discretionary policy-making become linked with wider issues regarding discretion in the implementation process, when the amplification of a law occurs a long way away from the legislative process, perhaps by a low-level official.

The more modern attack on discretion by legal theorists has largely been led by an American, K.C. Davis. According to Davis: 'A public officer has discretion wherever the effective limits on his power leave him free to make a choice among possible courses of action and inaction' (1969: 4). Davis argues that rule structures within which discretion is exercised should be drawn as tightly as possible: 'Our governmental and legal systems are saturated with excessive discretionary power which needs to be confined, structured and checked' (ibid.: 27). Later in the same book, he asserts that

> We have to open our eyes to the reality that justice to individual parties is administered more outside courts than in them, and we have to penetrate the unpleasant areas of discretionary determinations by police and prosecutors and other administrators, where huge concentrations of injustice invite drastic reforms. (ibid.: 215)

Other legal theorists (Jowell, 1973; Dworkin, 1977; Galligan, 1986; Baldwin, 1995) have explored the variety of ways in which Davis's aspiration is difficult to achieve, given the need for public officials to deal with situations that are inherently difficult to regulate precisely in advance. Dworkin (1977) distinguishes between strong discretion, where the decision-maker creates the standards, and weak discretion, where standards set by a prior authority have to be interpreted. Galligan (1986) is similarly concerned to analyze discretion in this way, identifying that decision-makers have to apply standards to the interpretation of facts. These distinctions may seem very academic, but they are important in administrative law for distinctions between decisions that are within an official's powers and ones that are not.

This debate, largely carried out between lawyers, is important for the study of implementation in highlighting the issues that emerge, in relation to complex policies, about control over implementation processes. These are issues that have been recognized as particularly evident once government becomes active in trying to regulate economic activities and provide welfare benefits and services. In these circumstances laws have to deal with complex situations and with contingencies that are hard to anticipate in advance.

These issues have also been given attention by sociologists of law, in ways that are particularly relevant for a scholarly theme important for the study of implementation, that of 'street-level bureaucracy' (see Mashaw, 1983). This topic is explored further later in this book, with particular reference to the work of Michael Lipsky (see Chapter 3, pp. 51–3). Kagan (1978) distinguishes between styles of rule application. In his study *Regulatory Justice*, looking at rule application in regulatory agencies, he makes a distinction between the emphasis on adherence to rules and the emphasis on the realization of organizational ends. On the basis of these dimensions, he distinguishes between the judicial mode, legalism, unauthorized discretion and retreatism as modes of rule application. The first one he calls 'the preferred pattern of rule application in American regulatory agencies' (Kagan, 1978: 91). On the basis of Kagan's work, other sociologists of law have made elaborations of and adaptations to his distinction. Knegt (1986) speaks of three styles of rule application: a bureaucratic style, a 'political' style and a pragmatic style (see also Aalders, 1987; Van Montfort, 1991).

Some analysts of public administration (Ringeling, 1978; Van der Veen, 1990) distinguish between various sources of what they call 'policy discretion', such as the character of the rules and regulations involved; the structure (labour division) of the implementing organization; the way in which democratic control is exercised; and work circumstances in the narrow sense, particularly interaction with clients.

There has been a tendency for each category of street-level bureaucracy to have its own kinds of studies concentrating on that specific (semi-) profession. In studies of the police, for instance, J.Q. Wilson (1968) was one of the first to discover patterns in the way police officers use their discretion. He speaks of the watchman style, the legalistic style and the service style. Van der Torre (1999: 19) argues that 'police styles' are connected with regulations or policy programmes that have to be implemented. He defines a 'police style' as 'the range of values, norms and view of a group of police officers that forms the basis of the patterns in their behaviour'. He distinguishes between 'pragmatists', 'pessimists', 'law enforcers' and 'social workers'.

Conceptual contributions like the ones presented here have enriched the scholarly theme of street-level bureaucracy and therefore implementation studies. They elaborated the insight that public servants working at the street level have a relative autonomy, while on that level a specific 'logic of implementation' can be observed. Street-level bureaucrats see themselves as decision-makers, whose decisions are based on normative choices, rather than as functionaries responding to rules, procedures or policies (Maynard-Moody and Musheno, 2000). Enhancing street-level discretion may, under certain conditions, be more functional for the implementation of those policies than curbing it (for an example, see Maynard-Moody et al., 1990).

As a specific category of public servants, street-level bureaucrats have a lot in common, as Lipsky has indicated (Chapter 3, pp. 51–3). Nevertheless considerable attention has been given in the sociological literature and elsewhere to the relevance of expertise. While there is a general sense in which any 'agent' with a delegated task carried out in conditions that his or her superior cannot totally comprehend or control is an 'expert', much of the debate concerns those highly expert functionaries who are often described as 'professionals'. This is an issue that has secured much modern attention. A widespread popular view on this subject is embodied in a widely quoted aphorism written by Bernard Shaw in his play *The Doctor's Dilemma* in 1911: 'All professions are conspiracies against the laity.' In a pure market system that 'conspiracy' is a problem that the laity have to confront alone, but states have seldom been prepared to leave them on their own in this respect. However, the new dimension introduced by the active state is the use of professionals in the implementation of public policy. In an influential book published in 1970, an American, Eliot Freidson, attacked the medical profession, elaborating Shaw's argument, and alleging that publicly provided health services particularly enhance the power of doctors by placing them in a monopoly situation. We do not subscribe to this simplistic statement of the issues. There has been a vast literature exploring them further (for an overview, see Moran and Wood, 1993). However, the 'conspiracy' view of professionalism does highlight a general question that has to be addressed in the study of implementation: Does the involvement of professional decision-making in policy implementation processes undermine the prospects for top-down control over the process? It should be noted that this theme is present also in 'public choice' analyses of the power of public servants, where a more general perspective is provided which sees bureaucrats as essentially exploiters of monopoly power in their own interests (see Dunleavy, 1991, for a review of this work).

The discussion of discretion and the related issues about professions started from the concern of lawyers about control over implementation processes. Inasmuch as lawyers recognize limits to the use of top-down control, their remedy is that discretionary activities should be carefully hedged within a framework of rules and that there should be scope for adjudicative procedures that enable discretion to be challenged in a court or a tribunal. The sociological contribution here adds, in particular, scepticism about the feasibility of this. However, there is something else lying in the background of this whole discussion, that is, the extent to which the best way to ensure the rule of law lies in the maintenance of a democratic political system. When this is introduced into the discussion, two key questions emerge. First, to what extent does the real problem of unregulated discretion lie in the fact that public officials may be carrying out actions not authorized by their elected 'superiors'? And second, to what extent may such control (given the discussion above about complexity) need to be exercised by more complex democratic mechanisms than simply top-down control by the legislature? This leads us to the next section.

The implications of the idea of democracy

Without democracy – except inasmuch as there are concerns about the predictability of implementation as embodied in the concerns about the rule of law discussed in the previous section – issues about control over public policy implementation are much the same as those that concern the owners and managers of private organizations. While the latter may want to avoid having their goals modified or subverted by their staff, they face no problems of accountability extending beyond their own ranks. There are of course some examples of private organizations with quasi-public faces – with obligations to shareholders or members. Some of the remarks below about democratic accountability will also apply to them.

The simplest ideas of democracy involved direct participation of citizens in the running of their communities or organizations – as allegedly practised in ancient Greek cities and to some extent in more recent times in the smaller Swiss cantons and some of the New England towns. Implicit in the idea of direct democracy is the absence of a split between policy formation and implementation. In practice, however, even the members of the most participative small organizations soon find that there are circumstances in which they have to delegate tasks. Nevertheless we may follow the broad drift of the concerns of democratic theorists that, beyond a certain very limited size, self-governing communities have to develop indirect approaches to representation, and argue that this issue also applies to control over implementation.

We therefore have to see the concerns of the political philosophers with the nature of representative government as very crucial for the setting of the modern implementation agenda. Page (1985) offers an analysis of this issue in his discussion of what has already been identified above as a closely related issue: the relationship between bureaucracy and democracy. He suggests that three ways of democratizing bureaucracy have been identified:

1   The 'representative bureaucracy' view that 'a system is more democratic when the socio-economic and ethnic backgrounds of top government officials resemble those of the nation as a whole' (ibid.: 163–4). This is a view that has been explored in influential studies of the social composition of the civil service (see Kingsley, 1944; Aberbach et al., 1981).

2   The 'pluralistic approach', with 'democracy in public decision-making ... guaranteed by the absence of centralized political authority'. Officials have to take part in 'bargaining and negotiation, partisan mutual adjustment with a variety of groups' (Page, 1985: 164). (This is a view central to pluralist theory – see Truman, 1958; Dahl, 1961; Bentley, 1967 – and to the more complacent view of 'incrementalism' as stated in the early work of Lindblom, 1959, 1965, and Braybrooke and Lindblom, 1963.)

3   The 'institutional' view, in which 'democratic "control" exists to the extent that representative institutions participate in policy-making' (Page, 1985: 164). This perspective focuses attention upon the mechanisms that link politicians with the

administration. It has perhaps been the dominant perspective in British studies of public administration (see, for example, Hennessy, 1989) and is found as a central concern of a variety of American studies that explore the influence of the President and Congress (see, for example, Cater, 1964; Cronin, 1980; Nathan, 1983).

It will be evident from various words in the extract from Page that his concern is with activities involving the 'top' of bureaucracy and 'policy formation'. He is reviewing a considerable literature that has been concerned with the extent to which public officials may be seen as a 'power elite' who may undermine democratic control over policy formation. We can, however, usefully take our lead from his taxonomy inasmuch as the issues about implementation are closely related to these. The third of Page's categories is what may be seen as the dominant or taken-for-granted view, until the careful examination of implementation in the modern age, that the top policy formers (even if they include senior civil servants) *should* 'control' the implementation process. At the same time we do find – in various forms and varying in importance from country to country – echoes of the other two categories in models of control over policy implementation. The first is seen in approaches of implementation in which there is a high concern about grass-roots participation, and in a curious way pre-democratic models of local implementation often embodied a version of this ideal. This can be seen, for instance, in the role given to appointed magistrates in English local administration. The second model, which is particularly important in American discussions of democracy, has also had an impact upon the way implementation processes are conceptualized in the United States.

It is generally correct to say that large-scale government and democracy have evolved side by side. However, there have been differences between countries in the rates of growth of these two phenomena, and of course in the actual forms either large-scale governmental organization or democracy has taken. Two nations in the Western world are often contrasted in these respects: Germany, where complex governmental institutions were developed before democracy; and the United States, where democracy developed at a time when government activities were still very limited in scale. Other nations may be seen as somewhere between these two extremes.

There is a sense therefore in which, while a key German preoccupation has been how to inject democratic control into the management of government, the American concern has been how to develop efficient government despite democracy. That contrast, at least as viewed from the American side, is brought out very clearly in Woodrow Wilson's famous essay that attempts to draw a distinction between politics and administration (1887). Wilson saw the need to reform American administration; he belonged to a school of political theorists and activists who saw political interference in the minutiae of administration as a source of inefficiency and corruption. He argued:

The field of administration is a field of business. It is removed from the hurry and strife of politics; it at most points stands apart even from the debatable ground of constitutional study. It is a part of political life only as the methods of the counting-house are part of the life of society; only as machinery is part of the manufactured product. (Reprinted in Woll, 1966: 28)

Yet he ended that paragraph:

But it is, at the same time, raised very far above the dull level of mere technical detail by the fact that through its greater principles it is directly connected with the lasting maxims of political wisdom, the permanent truths of political progress.

Hence Wilson is trying to find an ideal path between his admiration of the efficiency of Prussian administration and his hostility to the political environment in which that was developed:

Prussia's particular system of administration would quite suffocate us. It is better to be untrained and free than to be servile and systematic. Still there is no denying that it would be better yet to be free in spirit and proficient in practice. (ibid.: 26)

Some years after Wilson's essay, Max Weber, in his writings on German politics, addressed some of the same issues (see particularly his 'Politics as a Vocation' in Gerth and Mills, 1947: 77–128). He saw the need to stimulate a lively 'politics' in Germany to give a sense of a democratic direction to an administration that would otherwise just go its own way. On the other hand, he regarded German bureaucrats as impersonal and objective servants of the state and was fearful of demagoguery and of the emergence of a class of politicians who would be, like their American counterparts, living *off* (or perhaps we would today rather say 'from') politics rather than *for* politics.

Wilson was an early example of an important group of writers on American politics engaged in a quest for greater rationality in government (see, *inter alia*, Dewey, 1927, 1935; Simon, 1945). His idea that there should be a clear split between politics and administration is echoed in much modern work that is concerned about the subversion of the goals of top-level decision-makers – the President, Congress, the Executive, the federal government, and so on – in the implementation process. He was both identifying an important problem regarding administrative accountability and recognizing that the United States faced a set of institutional arrangements that made political problem solving very difficult. It took another 90 or so years after Wilson had struggled with this issue for American political scientists to lay the foundations of implementation studies. Between the 1880s and the 1970s in many walks of life – most of all in the organization of production – a rational model of implementation had come to be seen as essential to national achievement. This influence upon the development of implementation studies is explored further in Chapter 5.

There is a strange contradiction within American politics that, despite a set of institutional arrangements that very often render them impotent, politicians stress their capacity to do anything they want and express their commitment to rational problem-solving both in statements about what they will do and in their appointments of a multitude of rationally oriented experts (note here the enormous importance of think tanks, policy research, and so on, see Heinemann et al., 1990).

Woodrow Wilson's rationalism has attracted a great deal of criticism.[1] The alternative view on his politics/administration dichotomy is that this is a distinction that bears little relation to the reality of political and administrative behaviour. When this view is advanced with particular reference to the United States, two approaches to the original determination of the political and institutional structure of that society are invoked. One of these is what is described as the Madisonian insistence on the division of powers:

> Fearful of the oppressive potential of centralized power, the Founding Fathers devised a political system to prevent factions from overrunning minorities that makes such collective action nearly impossible. The separation of powers, the federalist structure of government, and the different constituencies of elected officials served to institutionalize a system of checks and balances designed to guard against the worst abuses of power. While this system has been fairly successful in stymieing serious threats to democratic rule, it has also been the source of institutional incapacity. (Ferman, 1990: 40)

The other approach is associated with another significant figure in the early history of the United States, Andrew Jackson. He was President between 1829 and 1837 and is seen as a key figure in the development of the spoils system, under which there are very considerable opportunities for a successful politician to introduce his or her supporters into a wide range of public offices. While this system has been much curbed since the mid-nineteenth century, through the efforts of people who shared Woodrow Wilson's disapproval of it, it remains as a way in which politics may be infused into administration.

What is important about Woodrow Wilson's perspective, shared with many other 'progressives' in the United States (Waldo, 1948), is the way his ideal division influenced thinking about the management of government, and thus about implementation, in the United States and elsewhere. The main burden of his critics is that his aspirations were unrealistic, in the face of deeply embedded institutional arrangements. His response to that comment might be to agree that the difficulties in achieving administrative reform would be considerable, but to argue that is not a reason not to try. In this sense he, and the many who have followed his lead, assert the desirability of top-down politically inspired domination.

Another line of criticism, then, is to suggest that there are different approaches to accountability that may be either more practical or superior (or both). These involve, to go back to the other approaches identified by Page, either pluralism (Madisonian democracy) or representative bureaucracy (Jacksonian democracy). Again, Wilson would doubtless argue that these were democratic mechanisms designed for an age when the activities of government were simpler. Hence those who adopt versions of these approaches need to advance ways of dealing with the problem of accountability that take into account organizational complexity. In many ways the dominant view until very recently has been to accept the case for top-down – organizational – accountability. Alternatives have only begun to emerge with an increased awareness of organizational inefficiency.

Public administration and public management

Woodrow Wilson features as one of the founders of the study of public administration as the discipline – perhaps some would say: multi- or inter-discipline – within which implementation studies are explicitly located, as indicated in Chapter 1. In that sense there is no need to explore that particular connection elaborately here. Public administration as an academic subject is seldom explicitly defined other than as the study of what public administrations do. Note therefore Peters and Pierre saying 'The principal activity of public administration is implementing laws' (2003: 1). Then, however, they immediately go on to say 'but there are also a range of other important activities carried on in these public organizations. One is the bureaucracies make policy, and in essence make law' (ibid.). In this view thus implementation is a sub-set of activities within public administration, but – as was stressed in Chapter 1 and then revisited in the discussion of Wilson's dichotomy – there are hazards implicit in making clear distinctions within policy processes as a whole.

Given the broad definition of public administration as a discipline we could perhaps leave it there, were it not for the modern introduction of another disciplinary label, 'public management'. Is this just a new heading for the study of public administration? The fact that it has emerged in the context of challenges to traditional bureaucratic ways of running the public sector supports that view. It has involved the introduction of new managerial techniques into the public sector and claims that management is essentially the same whether the organization is public or private (implying therefore a case for a business school takeover of the education of public officials). Going more widely still, we have all the issues about the delegation of public sector tasks to the private sector. In that sense then, the shift in terminology may be seen as changes in the language driven by political and ideological motives.

However, various writers have suggested that the study of public management is more than the study of public administration under a new name. While Laurence Lynn's writings on public management (1996a, 2003, 2006) acknowledge the substantial overlap between the subjects of public administration and those of public management, one issue he highlights is the extent to which public management is more prescriptive. This is relevant to our task in this book, because the issues about prescription loom very large in many presentations of the case for implementation studies (a topic that is central to our next chapter).

It should be added that both the ideological roots of public management as a discipline and the prescriptive agenda are explicit in the many discussions of the topic which use the term 'new' in front of public management, speaking thus of a 'bureaucratic reform agenda' (Hood, 1991: 3). What is embodied in these roots and agenda has considerable relevance for implementation studies. It involves new approaches to policy delivery which are likely to fully or partially replace the governmental-bureaucratic mode. Accordingly, these approaches pose issues for the concerns about the rule of law and about democracy which we discussed above. We will not explore this topic further here, but will return to it in a number of places later in the book.

Lynn also draws more subtle distinctions between public administration and public management, stressing issues about the *practice* of management in the public sector. Particularly relevant to the study of implementation is his observation about the modern evolution of public management:

> The newer behavioural approach to public management has tended to become more action-oriented and prescriptive. As such it says both more and less about public management than traditional conceptions. Briefly, the older view is that public management is the responsible exercise of administrative discretion. The newer conception adds to this what Roscoe Martin called 'the craft perspective', that is, a concern for decisions, actions and outcomes, and for the political skill needed to perform effectively in specific managerial roles. However, by emphasizing the strategic political role of public managers *within given political and administrative settings*, the newer conception is concerned more with the immediate, pragmatic concerns of managers at executive levels of governmental organizations. (2003: 16)

Hence we find Lynn echoing the issues about discretion and the rule of law discussed in our earlier section when he talks of 'the concept of public management as the responsible exercise of discretion' (ibid.).

Elsewhere he, with his colleagues Carolyn Heinrich and Carolyn Hill, puts that same point in a way which more explicitly highlights the prescriptive perspective as concerned with 'the discretionary actions of actors in managerial roles subject to formal authority' (2000a: 239). Those last two words seem to link this very specifically with the 'top-down' approach to implementation (see the discussion of this in the next chapter). In the article from which that quote comes, an agenda is set out for public management research which has much in common with approaches that have been developed for the study of implementation.

Other authors characterize the distinction between public administration and public management in a rather less precise way than Lynn, seeing it particularly as involving differences in approach to the examination of policy processes. Gray and Jenkins suggest: '[P]ublic management has, to a considerable extent, redefined the focus, language and theoretical basis of the study of the public sector, drawing on literatures and ideas often external to traditional public administration' (Gray and Jenkins, 1995: 78).

Since one of the present authors wrote a book long ago called *The Sociology of Public Administration* (1972) seeking to introduce new analytical approaches into the then very descriptive British public administration literature, we do not agree that a new terminology was needed to effect this change. However, our next section highlights some aspects of the change, identified by Gray and Jenkins, particularly applicable to the study of implementation, in looking at theory with roots in developments in sociology and economics as well as in political science.

Institutional theory

The issues explored at the end of the previous section raise questions about the extent to which implementation processes need to be placed in their constitutional and institutional contexts. This is a theme by no means neglected by mainstream implementation theorists, whose work will be examined in the next two chapters. (That is particularly true of some of the more recent contributors to the literature, whose work will be considered in Chapter 4.) However, a body of theory about the impact of institutions upon the policy process developed during the last decades of the twentieth century can be seen as having a distinct impact upon thinking about implementation.

That body of theory has manifestations within other disciplines as well as political science. In economics, an institutional perspective developed that challenged the relatively context-free way in which classical economics analyzed market relationships, pointing out the importance of seeing these exchanges within structures with their own rules and expected practices (Coase, 1937; Williamson, 1975). But it was within sociology that a concern developed about the impact of institutions that is particularly pertinent for the study of implementation. In some respects institutional analysis is fundamental for the discipline of sociology, raising questions about the extent to which human actions are structurally determined. It is then given an emphasis that is particularly important for organizational activities, and thus clearly important for the analysis of implementation.

A distinction is made, in much of this sociological work, between 'organizations' and 'institutions'. A key influence here is Selznick, who argues:

> The term 'organization' … suggests a certain bareness, a lean no-nonsense system of consciously coordinated activities. It refers to an expendable tool, a rational instrument engineered to do a job. An 'institution', on the other hand, is more nearly a natural product of social needs and pressures – a responsive adaptive organism. (1957: 5)

This distinction emphasizes the social world within which organizations have been created, drawing attention both to the impact of the external environment and to the way people bring needs and affiliations into organizations that shape the informal social systems that develop there. Selznick explains this perspective very clearly in his classic study of one of Franklin Roosevelt's important policy initiatives, *TVA and the Grass Roots* (1949):

> All formal organizations are moulded by forces tangential to their rationally ordered structures and stated goals. Every formal organization – trade union, political party,

army, corporation etcetera – attempts to mobilize human and technical resources as means for the achievement of its ends. However, the individuals within the system tend to resist being treated as means. They interact as wholes, bringing to bear their own special problems and purposes; moreover the organization is embedded in an institutional matrix and is therefore subject to pressure upon it from its environment, to which some general adjustment must be made. As a result, the organization may be significantly viewed as an adaptive social structure, facing problems which arise simply because it exists as an organization in an institutional environment, independently of the special (economic, military, political) goals which called it into being. (ibid.: 251)

While later sociologists have seen Selznick's approach as too deterministic, the general thrust of his argument remains pertinent. Later work has emphasized the need to see institutions as 'cultural rules' (Meyer and Rowan, 1977) and to identify the way in which 'structural isomorphism' occurs so that organizations working in similar 'fields' tend to develop similar characteristics (DiMaggio and Powell, 1983). W.R. Scott has played a key role in developing institutional theory in a systematic way, writing about three 'pillars' of institutions:

- regulative, resting upon 'expedience' inasmuch as people recognize the coercive power of rule systems;
- normative, resting upon social obligations;
- cognitive, depending upon taken-for-granted cultural assumptions. (1995: 35)

This sociological work attacks the issues of policy implementation from a rather different direction to that of the political scientists. It is concerned with questions not about how public policy develops but about how organizations work, including, therefore (as, for example, in the case of the Tennessee Valley Authority), what happens within organizations with responsibilities for the implementation of public policy. Not surprisingly, therefore, this work has something to say about why organizations may be unreceptive to efforts to change their practices and why they may not collaborate very well with each other (see Aldrich, 1976; Benson, 1982). Similarly, individuals whom we will find very important for the study of implementation, namely street-level bureaucrats (see the discussion of the work of Michael Lipsky, Chapter 3, pp. 51–3), have also been the focus of attention of organizational sociologists exploring issues of compliance within organizations (see particularly key contributions by Gouldner, 1954; Merton, 1957; Etzioni, 1961).

Within political science, institutions tend often to be taken for granted (as organizations). That is evident in the traditional emphasis upon the prerogatives of those who formulate policy and in the concerns about the 'rule of law'. In the period when behaviourist approaches to political analysis were dominant, there was some tendency to lose sight of the importance of institutional structures. But then a group of theorists emerged who combined the older concern about structures with a recognition, influenced by the institutional school in sociology, that questions had to be raised about how institutions work in practice. Of particular importance here is the work of James March and Johan Olsen (1984, 1989, 1996). March and Olsen explain their view of the importance of the institutional approach as follows:

> Political democracy depends not only on economic and social conditions but also on the design of political institutions. The bureaucratic agency, the legislative committee, and the appellate court are arenas for contending social forces, but they are also collections of standard operating procedures and structures that define and defend interests. They are political actors in their own right. (1984: 738)

Others of the institutionalist school of thought have made similar points (see, for example, Hall, 1986). Such observations suggest that an examination of a policy process – and accordingly of an implementation process – needs to be seen as occurring in organized contexts where there are established norms, values, relationships, power structures and 'standard operating procedures'. Those structures may be handled in systematic work on implementation as independent variables, influencing outputs and outcomes of implementation as dependent variables. However, much of the work in the institutionalist tradition is also concerned to look at how those structures were formed and to elucidate the extent to which they impose explicit constraints and the circumstances in which they are subject to change. The revision or reinterpretation of the rules ('meta-policy-making') is important. In that sense here there is a set of issues regarding the implementation of meta-policy – the issues entailed in changing structures and the implications of structural changes for substantive policy changes (see Dror, 1986; Hupe, 1990).

There are also issues (particularly examined in the institutionalist work of Skocpol, 1995) regarding the extent to which a policy change at one point in time creates institutions that may serve as a barrier or conduit to change at a later point (this is sometimes described as historical institutionalism). As March and Olsen say: 'Programs adopted as a simple political compromise by a legislature become endowed with separate meaning and force by having an agency established to deal with them' (1984: 739 – drawing here upon Skocpol and Finegold, 1982).

The focus here, however, should not simply be upon the institutions of government. Rothstein suggests, from a study of the development of Swedish labour market policy that examines the way trades union interests were built into the policy process, that '[i]n some, albeit probably rare, historical cases, people actually create the very institutional circumstances under which their own as well as others' future behavior will take place' (1992: 52). Similarly, analyses of health policy have been concerned to look at the way decisions about the structuring of health services put doctors in a position in which their future collaboration would be important for the implementation of new policies (Alford, 1975; Ham, 1992).

Clearly this institutional approach to the study of the policy process involves interpretation. It does not suggest that outcomes can easily be 'read off' from constitutional or institutional contexts. Immergut sets this out in a games analogy as follows: 'Institutions do not allow one to predict policy outcomes. But by establishing the rules of the game, they enable one to predict the ways in which policy conflicts will be played out' (1992: 63).

This rules/game distinction is also found, although with a different terminology and a further distinction, in Kiser and Ostrom's specifications of three related but distinct 'worlds of action': 'The *operational level*, referring to the world of direct action. The *collective choice level*, concerning the world of "authoritative decision-making". The third is the *constitutional level*, explaining "the design of collective choice mechanisms"' (1982: 184).

This distinction is explored further in Chapter 6, where we relate it to the concept of governance. What is worth noting here, however, is the suggestion that institutional analysis may lay so strong an emphasis upon specific configurations of institutional situations and actors that what it offers is an account of past events, from which little generalization is possible. This is the direction some of the things March and Olsen had to say about the institutional kind of approach seem to be leading:

> [T]he new institutionalism is probably better viewed as a search for alternative ideas that simplify the subtleties of empirical wisdom in a theoretically useful way.
>
> The institutionalism we have considered is neither a theory nor a coherent critique of one. It is simply an argument that the organization of political life makes a difference. (1984: 747)

Going even further down this problematical path, March and Olsen have given us, from their earlier work with Cohen, a memorable expression to typify an extreme version of the institutional approach: 'the garbage-can model'. They say, in a later reference to their own idea, almost as if distancing themselves from it:

> In the form most commonly discussed in the literature, the garbage-can model assumes that problems, solutions, decision-makers, and choice opportunities are independent, exogenous streams flowing through a system (Cohen, March and Olsen, 1972). They come together in a manner determined by their arrival times. Thus, solutions are linked to problems primarily by their simultaneity, relatively few problems are solved, and choices are made for the most part either before any problems are connected to them (oversight) or after the problems have abandoned one choice to associate themselves with another (flight). (March and Olsen, 1984: 746; see also March and Olsen, 1989)

Such a perspective suggests a policy process in which policy formation cannot be distinguished from implementation (a theme that will certainly be explored further in later chapters). What it also suggests is that the policy process is merely a flow of reactions to events and the reactions of other actors. Kingdon (1984) has picked up this theme in comparing the policy process to chance events in the early history of evolution, with policy ideas floating around as in 'primeval soup'. Following that road further, any attempt to generalize is likely to be left behind. Researchers on the policy process are being required to take a position like a purist a-theoretical historian, determined to let the facts speak for themselves without any principles to help organize attention or lessons to draw from the study. Accounts of events will be stories – told as accurately as is feasible (although that feasibility itself is a topic of some dispute among historiographers and other social science methodologists). It will offer a strong emphasis upon unique situations, dealing with the inspiration of key figures or with chance reactions to events.

Clearly the extreme position described in the last few paragraphs is not typical of the institutional school, but much institutional analysis of the policy process has pushed it in an intuitive and interpretative direction. There are others who are prepared to take that position further; their perspective is examined in the next section.

Postmodernist theory

'Postmodernism' has become a term frequently employed. Although more often it is linked with architecture or literature, the term is used in relation to public administration. The distinction between 'postmodern' and 'postmodernist' is important. With the first term, reference is made to contemporary phenomena, like the widespread use of electronic communication in a 'global village', the rise of multinational conglomerates in the mass media industry, or the birth of so-called 'bourgeois bohemians' as a new cultural elite (Brooks, 2000). While some of *what* we observe is very 'up to date' and therefore can be called 'postmodern', the qualification 'postmodernist' refers to a certain, particularly artistic, *way* of approaching reality. An example of the latter is presenting a regular *pissoir* as a work of art and exhibiting it as such in a museum, as Marcel Duchamp did. Characteristic of this way of looking is especially a casual breaking away from the norms and conventions seen as standard hitherto. A cultivation of eclecticism as 'anything goes' deliberately replaces the distinction between what is seen as 'done' and 'not done'; between 'high' and 'low' culture.

How, then, are both these terms used in public administration? First, the term 'postmodern' is applied with an eye on what is contemporary. Clegg (1990), for instance, gives his book on modern organizations the subtitle 'organization studies in the postmodern world'. Zuurmond (1994), describing the ways in which new information technology transforms working procedures in municipal social services departments, speaks of the rise of an 'infocracy'. On the other hand, Lash (1988), for instance, speaks of 'postmodernism as a regime of signification', and Frissen (1999) calls his book on politics, governance and technology 'a postmodern narrative on the virtual state'. In fact, given the substance of this narrative, it could rather have been called 'postmodernist'.

Essentially two dimensions are relevant here: a scientific and a normative, or political, orientation. One can look at postmodern phenomena while having a more positivist epistemological stance, in whatever variant, or a more interpretative/hermeneutic one, also with possible variants. This scientific stance is independent of the answer to the question of whether or not one actively propagates forms of direct, participative democracy.

A variety of scholarly attention to postmodernity can be observed. In Zuurmond's study of 'infocracy' mentioned above and, for instance, in the study by Pröpper and Steenbeek (1999) of citizens' participation in Dutch policy processes, the analysis is systematic, giving these studies a standard descriptive-analytical character. Both Zuurmond and Pröpper and Steenbeek focus on contemporary phenomena in public administration, using a more or less positivist approach.

In her article on 'the listening bureaucrat' Stivers states: 'The experience of listening involves openness, respect for difference, and reflexivity' (1994: 364). These notions seem to refer directly to the kind of thought and concepts developed by French postmodernist philosophers like Baudrillard (1973, 1981) and Lyotard (1979). It is interesting that Stivers uses the notions as part of a plea for greater participation between public servants and citizens in political-administrative processes: 'Thus public officials can be good listeners (they can be responsive) by encouraging citizens' responsibility to listen to one another and solve disputes' (1994: 368). In their *Postmodern Public Administration*, Fox and Miller (1995) have a similar message. This also goes for some of the contributions to *Telling Tales*, which has as a subject 'work done by evaluators at the crossroads of evaluation and narrative' (Abma, 1999: 6). Bevir and Rhodes (2000) show that the use of a 'narrativist' method or approach is not necessarily connected with making an explicit plea for more democratic participation 'from the bottom'.

An author like Yanow (1993, 1996) is interested in a critical exposure of the values and language of administrators. Van Twist (1994) also focuses on that language, while he approaches the study of public administration as an art; more specifically, an art of telling convincing stories. Between what happens in the material world, and on the level of words, language and stories, there are connections, but for analysts of public administration it all comes down to aiming at 'verbal renewal'. In contrast to Yanow's, Van Twist's perspective on public administration, generally supportive of the status quo, seems that of a consultant.

Although authors like Zuurmond, Pröpper and Steenbeek, Van Twist, Yanow and Stivers share attention for *the postmodern condition*, they differ as far as the nature of their specific attention is concerned. This is shown in Table 2.1.

Table 2.1 Scholarly attention to the 'postmodern condition'

Stance on democracy	Epistemological stance	
	Positivist	Interpretative
Neutral	'Infocracy'	'Verbal renewal'
Deliberative democracy	'Interactive policy-making'	'The listening bureaucrat'

In their attention to contemporary phenomena in public administration, the contributions in the first column may be called 'postmodern'. As far as the interpretativist contributions referred to in the second column entails a change in the way in which public administration is usually approached and studied, they can be called 'postmodernist'. This change particularly concerns the view that systematic testing of ideas is irrelevant. The differentiation made is important, because interpretativism and postmodernism cannot be equated. Aiming at 'telling stories', postmodernist scholars generally are interpretativists. On the contrary, however, not all interpretativist scholars are postmodernists. Different from the latter, mainstream interpretativists remain adherent to the standard norms of social science, particularly as far as methodology is concerned (for example, Roe, 1994).

The kinds of contributions presented have functions for our subject matter. First, they direct scholarly interest to phenomena that are highly contemporary and therefore justify attention. Second, although most of these studies are not highlighting the nuts and bolts of implementation in the narrow sense, they broaden the conceptual perspective on public policy-making in general.

Conclusion

The discussion at the beginning of this chapter suggested that there have been concerns to secure successful implementation ever since people sought to co-opt the efforts of others to undertake complex tasks. But to acknowledge that is simply to say that the analysis of implementation is the analysis of human organization under another name. There are merits in taking that view, and in not seeking to construct a separate intellectual activity alongside organizational sociology. It certainly reminds us of the need to recognize the many ways in which implementation is studied without that word being used. This has led this chapter in two different directions. One of these involved the examination of two themes that provide very important contexts for the study of public policy implementation: concerns that activities of governments should be in conformity with the rule of law and ideas about democratic control over those activities. The other direction was to stress how the exploration of aspects of human organization – particularly in the literature on institutions – gave rise to work that throws light upon implementation processes carried out by scholars – many of them sociologists – uninterested in and indeed sometimes unaware of the implementation literature. Issues about implementation were the subject of extensive debate and scholarly activity long before anyone wrote about 'implementation studies' *per se*. There is a literature that both precedes and parallels the modern work on implementation.

Issues about the rule of law and about democracy have, however, been particularly significant preoccupations in modern discourse about government and politics. It is clear that this discourse has to be set in context with other issues about 'modernity', particularly the concerns about the size, scope and complexity of human activities in modern societies and about the aspirations of the state to influence and control those activities. In that sense we must also site the roots of the contemporary concerns about implementation in the extent to which public policies are being developed that are very often difficult to translate into action.[2]

In observing government efforts, we can observe the growth of complex activities on which governments have been reluctant to be extravagant and which are subject of substantial resistance by powerful groups. This is particularly true of social policy, the area (outside of defence policy) where twentieth-century growth was most significant. In other words: What characterizes public policy development is a level of complexity never attempted before. Where implementation deficit would have been tolerated in low-level activities, which the central state was happy to delegate to local implementers and leave them to go their own ways most of the time, it could not do so where it had made central commitments or even political mandates to achieve new social goals (compare Poor Law administration with modern social security, health care and social care programmes).

In Chapter 5, we will explore the way in which concerns of the kind outlined above contributed to the development of implementation studies. It will then be shown how new models of governance – developed after the 1970s – have reshaped the agenda.

Notes

1 It is perhaps not irrelevant that he became an American President and the dominant figure in the post-First World War settlement in Europe, which gave rise to a set of institutional divisions along alleged national 'self-determination' lines that people are still fighting about.
2 That statement is as true of war as of peace, and it must be noted in passing that there is a literature on the art and science of war that stands quite apart from the literature on public administration. What characterizes war is an enormous extravagance in the use of people and materials so that implementation inefficiencies are compensated by the amount of effort going in ('overkill' – often in the literal sense). It is also probably often the case that the high level of goal consensus means that levels of efforts to frustrate policy implementation are much lower (except of course those of the enemy).

3

THE TOP-DOWN/BOTTOM-UP DEBATE

Contents

The discovery of the 'missing link'

The previous chapter challenged the view that implementation studies started in the 1970s when Erwin Hargrove (1975) wrote of the 'missing link' in the study of the policy process and Jeffrey Pressman and Aaron Wildavsky wrote a highly influential book with the main title of *Implementation* (1973). Nevertheless it is clear that a distinct kind of approach to the study of implementation did emerge at that time. Efforts to develop government interventions to address social problems of various kinds were rapidly increasing, and there was awareness that these interventions were often ineffective. This was a period in which a substantial growth in studies concerned to evaluate policy could be observed (see Rist, 1995). In the course of this activity it was recognized that it might be problematical, in evaluation studies, to treat the administrative process between 'policy formation' and 'policy outcomes' as a *black box* irrelevant to the latter (as in policy analysis models such as that developed by Easton, 1965).

The often quoted sub-title of Pressman and Wildavsky's book expresses this new concern perfectly: 'How Great Expectations in Washington are Dashed in Oakland; or Why It's Amazing that Federal Programs Work At All, This Being a Saga of the Economic Development Administration as Told by Two Sympathetic Observers who Seek to Build Morals on a Foundation of Ruined Hopes'. There is an expression here of the frustration felt by many Americans about the failures, or limited successes, of the War on Poverty and Great Society programmes of the late 1960s.

That frustration was translated into a concern to look at the implementation part of the policy process as well as, or even perhaps, rather than, the initial parts of it.

As noted in the last chapter, the assumption made by the new students of implementation that their subject had been neglected can be challenged. This was the central argument in the previous chapter. To some extent, it was merely the case that political scientists began to use a new concept 'implementation' in policy analysis and administrative studies. Nevertheless it is perhaps true that until the end of the 1960s there had been a tendency to take it for granted that political mandates were clear and that administrators would do what their political bosses demanded of them. In formal statements of constitutional law, implementers, like civil servants, have often been entirely ignored. Furthermore, the neglect of the examination of administrative processes can be partly attributed to the difficulties involved in looking into the 'black box', after parliamentary processes, particularly in a secretive administrative culture like the British one. We will also find at least one implementation theorist (Hjern, see pp. 53–4) who suggests that implementation studies should be seen as distinctly different from studies of public administration (although in doing so he consigns to the 'public administration' category many of those whose work will be discussed here).

In this chapter and the next one we will look at the implementation literature that has emerged since the early 1970s. In this one, we highlight some of the pioneering contributions. This analysis would become tediously repetitive if we were to try to do justice to the work of everyone who had something to say on this subject. Although the choice of whose work to highlight is necessarily, to a certain extent, an arbitrary one, here it is influenced by our view of who had something rather different to say as the debate between implementation scholars emerged. We have left out some figures who undoubtedly made important contributions during the development of the debate (notably Williams, 1971, 1980; Derthick, 1972; Hargrove, 1975, 1983; Berman, 1978; Dunsire, 1978a, 1978b). In emphasizing what we see as the main contributions, we will try to ensure that other significant but rather similar efforts are at least referenced.

In providing this account of the literature, we have inevitably been influenced by our views of what are the key issues when implementation is studied now and by some of the concerns we want to explore in the rest of the book. In presenting the various key contributions we will highlight the way they approach what we see as the main problems regarding the study of implementation. These particularly concern the issues about the relationship between policy formation and its implementation as discussed in Chapter 1. The discussion on these matters took the form of a lively debate, in the early years of implementation studies, that has been described as one between the 'top-down' and the 'bottom-up' perspective. This chapter will highlight the work of the major exponents of these two positions. Then the next chapter will look at how scholars have sought to synthesize the two perspectives or to move away from that debate. We present this first chapter as brief accounts of key authors, in broadly chronological order. While we highlight key issues in their arguments and point out ways in which they differ from each other, we do not aim to provide a critical commentary. Clearly those very familiar with the literature, or eager to move on to our more substantive recommendations, may want to skip this chapter. However, it seems to us that it is appropriate to give readers a general map of the literature at this stage.

While the top-down/bottom-up debate was heavily influenced by the question of how to separate implementation from policy formation, that was only part of a wider problem about how to identify the features of a very complex process, occurring across time and space, and involving multiple actors. It will be seen that writers on implementation vary in the way they respond to that complexity. In the social sciences methodological questions about how to handle complexity have preoccupied many theorists. We have no intention of trying to review the various approaches to those questions here, but simply need to recognize that similar alternative approaches occur in the implementation literature. We find that some authors have been eager to reduce the number of variables to be given attention to a limited number seen as critical, while others have built models that try to take into account all identifiable variables. The difficulties with either of these approaches have influenced an alternative view that systematization and generalization are impossible and that the only approach possible is to provide an accurate account of specific implementation processes.

Clearly the last category of scholars offers a critique of those who seek to try to develop a general theory of implementation and are, therefore in a sense, if we look for synonyms for 'implementation', trying to develop a theory of 'doing' or *a theory of action*. For that reason there is a need to ask whether there are certain limiting conditions within which specific approaches to the study of implementation will be applicable. We have in mind here two considerations of this kind, which we will find many of the implementation theorists struggling with:

- variations between policy issues, or types of policy issues; and
- variations between institutional contexts, which may include questions about the extent to which generalizations apply outside specific political systems or national contexts.

The classical top-down authors

Jeffrey Pressman and Aaron Wildavsky: The founding fathers

As indicated above, the American scholars Jeffrey Pressman and Aaron Wildavsky (1984; 1st edn 1973) tend to be celebrated as the 'founding fathers' of implementation studies (see, for example, Goggin et al., 1990; Parsons, 1995; Ryan, 1995). Notwithstanding some backing away from that perspective by Wildavsky in a second edition produced after Pressman's death (see the comment below), the overall approach of their book places them quite explicitly with the other authors whom we will typify here as 'top-down' in approach. Their book's subtitle, quoted above, surely indicates that.

As we showed in Chapter 1, for Pressman and Wildavsky, implementation is clearly defined in terms of a relationship to policy as laid down in official documents. They say, 'A verb like "implement" must have an object like "policy"', and go on: 'policies normally contain both goals and the means for achieving them' (Preface to the first edition, reprinted in the third edition, 1984: xxi). Much of the analysis in their book, a study of a federally mandated programme of economic development in Oakland, California, is concerned with the extent to which successful implementation depends upon linkages between different organizations and departments at the local level. They argue that if action depends upon a number of links in an implementation chain, then the degree of co-operation between agencies required to make those links has to be very close to 100 per cent if a situation is not to occur in which a number of small deficits cumulatively create a large shortfall. They thus introduce the idea of 'implementation deficit' and suggest that implementation may be analyzed mathematically in this way.

This particular formulation has been seen as responsible for a pessimistic tone in much implementation literature, since it suggests that purposive action will be very difficult to achieve wherever there are multiple actors. Bowen (1982) points out that such a formulation disregards the extent to which the interactions between these actors occur in contexts in which they rarely concern simply 'one-off' affairs; rather, these interactions are repeated and accompanied by others. Hence it is perhaps more appropriate to use game theories which analyze repeated games rather than probability theory. In which case it can be seen that collaboration becomes much more likely and that recommendations can be made about ways to strengthen that possibility.

Pressman and Wildavsky's original work takes very much a 'rational model' approach. Policy sets goals; implementation research is concerned with considering what then makes the achievement of those goals difficult. However, by the second edition (as indicated above), Wildavsky had begun to have doubts about that model. It is of more than biographical interest to note that Wildavsky's new collaborator, with whom he wrote a new last chapter called 'Implementation as Evolution', was an Italian, Giandomenico Majone. It seems reasonable to assume that experience of the contrast between rigid law making and flexible implementation in the Italian administrative system would lead to scepticism about the 'rational model'. The title of that new chapter indicates its alternative view, seeing the relationship between policy formation and implementation as an interactive process. The chapters added in the 1983 edition reflect Wildavsky's further elaboration of that alternative view. In those chapters implementation is approached in terms of learning, adaptation and exploration.

Donald Van Meter and Carl Van Horn: System building

The contribution to the literature by the American scholars Donald Van Meter and Carl Van Horn consists in moving forward from the more general approach of

Pressman and Wildavsky to offer a model for the analysis of the implementation process (1975). They refer to Pressman and Wildavsky's work alongside a variety of other empirical studies (particularly Kaufman, 1960; Bailey and Mosher, 1968; Derthick, 1970, 1972; Berke et al., 1972). At the same time they argue that '(w)hile these studies have been highly informative, their contributions have been limited by the absence of a theoretical perspective' (Van Meter and Van Horn, 1975: 451).

In developing their theoretical framework Van Meter and Van Horn describe themselves as having been 'guided by three bodies of literature' (1975: 453):

- organization theory, and particularly work on organizational change – here they recognize the importance of the concerns about organizational control in socio-logical work influenced by Max Weber, including Crozier's classic French study of bureaucratic resistance to change (1964) and Etzioni's analysis of forms of compliance (1961);
- studies of the impact of public policy and particularly of the impact of judicial decisions, such as Dolbeare and Hammond's study of the factors that influenced responses to US Supreme Court rulings on school prayers (1971); and
- some studies of inter-governmental relations, in particular, the work of Derthick (1970, 1972) and, of course, Pressman and Wildavsky.

Van Meter and Van Horn's presentation of their theoretical perspective starts with a consideration of the need to classify policies in terms that will throw light upon implementation difficulties. Their approach is comparatively simple. They suggest that there is a need to take into account the amount of change required and the level of consensus. Hence they hypothesize that 'implementation will be most successful where only marginal change is required and goal consensus is high' (1975: 461). They present this, however, in terms of an interrelationship, suggesting, for example, that high consensus may make high change possible, as in a wartime situation. We will see that a number of subsequent theorists have tried to get beyond these very basic propositions about the characteristics of policy, although with only limited success.

Van Meter and Van Horn go on to suggest a model in which six variables are linked dynamically to the production of an outcome 'performance'. The model is set out in Figure 3.1. They clearly see implementation as a process that starts from an initial policy decision: '(p)olicy implementation encompasses those actions by public and private individuals (or groups) that are directed at the achievement of objectives set forth in prior policy decisions (1975: 447). That process is presented as going through a series of stages, with the arrows in Figure 3.1 pointing forward or sideways and not back to the policy. Accordingly Van Meter and Van Horn argue that 'it is vital that the study of implementation be conducted longitudinally; relationships identified at one point in time must not be extended causally to other time periods' (ibid.: 474). Hence theirs is clearly a 'top-down' approach. Nevertheless, when they stress concerns about consensus and compliance they recognize the importance for these of participation in the policy formation by 'subordinates' (ibid.: 459). The contrast here with some of

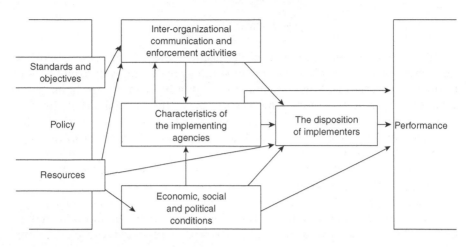

Figure 3.1 A model of the policy-implementation process
Source: Van Meter and Van Horn (1975: 463)

the bottom-up approaches that we will look at later is that this is participation at a prior policy-formation stage.

The six variables (surely they are in fact clusters of variables) identified in Figure 3.1 are:

- policy standards and objectives, which 'elaborate on the overall goals of the policy decision ... to provide concrete and more specific standards for assessing performance' (ibid.: 464);
- the resources and incentives made available;
- the quality of inter-organizational relationships (we find in their discussion of this, as in so much of the American literature on implementation, an extensive discussion of aspects of federalism);
- the characteristics of the implementation agencies, including issues like organizational control but also, going back surely to inter-organizational issues, 'the agency's formal and informal linkages with the "policy-making" or "policy-enforcing" body ' (ibid.: 471);
- the economic, social and political environment; and
- the 'disposition' or 'response' of the implementers, involving three elements: 'their cognition (comprehension, understanding) of the policy, the direction of their response to it (acceptance, neutrality, rejection) and the intensity of that response' (ibid.: 472).

Van Meter and Van Horn's comparatively straightforward model provided a valuable starting point for studies of implementation processes. Their model aims to direct the attention of those who study implementation rather than provide prescriptions for policy-makers. Our own exploration of how to research implementation in Chapter 7 broadly follows the map of the variables they provide.

✳✳

for study
not I.

Eugene Bardach: Fixing the game

In 1977, another American, Eugene Bardach, wrote an influential book on implementation called *The Implementation Game*, reviewing early contributions to the literature and adding case-study material of his own. In this book we see a top-down perspective embracing recognition of the inevitability of interference with pre-set goals. Hence Bardach provided both ideas that were to influence the top-down writers, who devoted extensive attention to measures to try to protect those goals (authors who are discussed in the next two sub-sections), and ammunition for the bottom-up theorists, who were to argue for a rather different approach to goal setting.

Bardach suggests that implementation processes need to be perceived as involving 'games', and he outlines the wide variety of the games that may be played. Hence his advice to the 'top' consists of two sets of recommendations. One of these concerns the need for great care in the 'scenario writing' process, so as to structure the games in the right way to achieve desired outcomes. In Hogwood and Gunn's work, discussed below (pp. 49–51), we see a typical example of advice on scenario writing. The other prescription from Bardach is that attention needs to be given to 'fixing the game'. This involves two related usages in the notion of 'fixing', in colloquial American: as mending (as in 'I had the car fixed') and as something rather close to cheating (as in the notion of 'Mr Fixer'). Crucially these are linked through the celebration, in the early part of the book, of the work of a Californian politician, Frank Lanterman, who devoted the last part of his political career to the promotion of mental health reform in his state. Essentially Lanterman was not satisfied to be the promoter of a reform measure; he followed it through with day-to-day involvement in its implementation, working to remove practical obstacles to change, to influence appointments and to promote additional legislation where necessary.

Hence, we see in Bardach's work the very clear exposition of a view that implementation is a 'political' process, and that 'successful' implementation from a 'top-down' perspective must involve a very full 'follow-through'. In this sense he is critical of the 'wounded' rationalism voiced in Pressman and Wildavsky's apparent anguish about the capacity of Oakland to frustrate Washington.

In a much later work, *Getting Agencies to Work Together* (1998), Bardach returns to the perspective on implementation he developed earlier. Here we see a strong emphasis on the informal, with street-level workers being seen as 'craftsmen', often with a commitment to their work, who must be brought together when collaboration is required, not so much by formal devices as by the encouragement of a shared approach to problem solving.

Paul Sabatier and Daniel Mazmanian: Process modelling

The next contribution from the top-down perspective comes from two more American scholars Paul Sabatier and Daniel Mazmanian (Sabatier and

[handwritten marginal note: Most top-down theorist that start of unwaing their adopt stance]

Mazmanian, 1979 and 1980; Mazmanian and Sabatier, 1981 and 1983). We will return to Sabatier's later work in the next chapter, since having taken a very robust top-down stance in this early publication he moved away from that position. Much of this account of Sabatier and Mazmanian's is based upon Sabatier's own characterization of it in a later work (Sabatier, 1986). The starting point for them is, as for Van Meter and Van Horn, the expectation of analyzing the implementation of a 'top' level policy decision and then asking:

1   To what extent were the actions of implementing officials and target groups consistent with that policy decision?
2   To what extent were the objectives attained over time, i.e. to what extent were the impacts consistent with the objectives?
3   What were the principal factors affecting policy outputs and impacts, both those relevant to the official policy as well as other politically significant ones?
4   How was the policy reformulated over time on the basis of experience? (Sabatier, 1986: 22)

We see here a very clear distinction being made between policy formation and policy implementation, but at the same time a recognition of a feedback process. The phenomena identified in the fourth question would presumably be the starting point for a new implementation study. *[handwritten: accountability]*
   The factors impacting upon the implementation process are then seen as falling under three headings:

*   factors affecting the 'tractability of the problem';
*   'nonstatutory variables affecting implementation'; and
*   the 'ability of the statute to structure implementation'. (Sabatier and Mazmanian, 1980: 544)

[handwritten marginal note: non-imp]

While it is the last group of factors that are crucial for Sabatier and Mazmanian's advice to those seeking to control the implementation process, it is important to observe that their approach does not fail to recognize the factors in the other two lists that are likely to make successful implementation difficult. The problem is that it is the interactions between these (which includes variables likely to determine political support) and the efforts to 'structure implementation' that may be crucial for the implementation process.
   We see here then both a methodology – involving identifying factors that will cause difficulties and factors that may be controlled – and recommendations to the 'top' about the steps to be taken to try to control implementation. They have a great deal in common with the list produced by the next theorists we will consider.

Brian Hogwood and Lewis Gunn: Recommendations for policy-makers

The approach to implementation of two British writers Brian Hogwood and Lewis Gunn derives to a large extent from a lecture to civil servants that Gunn published in 1978. The pragmatic approach of that work is also reflected in the title of their book in which we see these ideas developed: *Policy Analysis for the Real World* (1984). In a discussion of the alternative perspective of two other British writers to be discussed below, Susan Barrett and Colin Fudge (1981c), Hogwood and Gunn defend their 'top-down' view on the ground that those who make policy are democratically elected.

It has already been noted that Hogwood and Gunn, like Sabatier and Mazmanian, offer propositions that can be read as recommendations to policy-makers. These are that policy-makers should ensure:

- that circumstances external to the implementing agency do not impose crippling constraints;
- that adequate time and sufficient resources are made available to the programme;
- that not only are there no constraints in terms of overall resources but also that, at each stage in the implementation process, the required combination of resources is actually available;
- that the policy to be implemented is based upon a valid theory of cause and effect;
- that the relationship between cause and effect is direct and that there are few, if any, intervening links;
- that there is a single implementing agency that need not depend upon other agencies for success, or, if other agencies must be involved, that the dependency relationships are minimal in number and importance;
- that there is complete understanding of, and agreement upon, the objectives to be achieved, and that these conditions persist throughout the implementation process;
- that in moving towards agreed objectives it is possible to specify, in complete detail and perfect sequence, the tasks to be performed by each participant;
- that there is perfect communication among, and co-ordination of, the various elements involved in the programme; and
- that those in authority can demand and obtain perfect obedience (a précis of Hogwood and Gunn, 1984: 199–206).

Just as Sabatier and Mazmanian avoid the charge of naïvety about such an activity by their recognition of factors that are hard to control, Hogwood and Gunn site their propositions in the context of an argument about the unattainability of 'perfect implementation'. The list above sets out the conditions necessary for the realization of that. The concept of 'perfect implementation' derives from the work of Christopher Hood (1976). He suggests:

> One way of analyzing implementation problems is to begin by thinking about what 'perfect administration' would be like, comparable to the way in which economists employ the model of perfect competition. Perfect administration could be defined as a condition in which 'external' elements of resource availability and political acceptability combine with 'administration' to produce perfect policy implementation. (ibid.: 6)

Hood goes on to develop an argument about the 'limits of administration' (his book title) that focuses not so much on the political processes that occur within the administrative system as on the inherent limits to control in complex systems. This is similarly the concern of a two-volume contribution to the subject by another British writer, Andrew Dunsire (1978a, 1978b). The approach involves the use of an abstract model of the problems to be faced by persons attempting top-down control over the administrative system. It obviously offers a way to help researchers to identify characteristics of real implementation processes. Like the economic concept from which it is derived, it postulates a model against which to measure reality. Hence, while it, like perfect competition, seems to be a purely analytical concept, in practice it carries the normative connotation that there is an ideal to which the 'top' should try to make the real world correspond.

The bottom-up challenge

Michael Lipsky: Street-level bureaucracy

Michael Lipsky's analysis of the behaviour of front-line staff in policy delivery agencies, whom he calls 'street-level bureaucrats', has had an important influence upon implementation studies. We present him here as in many respects the founding father of the 'bottom-up' perspective. He first presented his ideas in an article in 1971, interestingly even before his American compatriots Pressman and Wildavsky published their book. Lipsky's influential book, however, was not published until 1980.

Lipsky is widely misrepresented simply as the writer who demonstrates how difficult it is to control the activities of street-level bureaucrats. If that was actually what he had to say, he could merely be seen as someone reinforcing the top-down control-oriented perspective, albeit – along the lines of Sabatier and Mazmanian's 'factors affecting the tractability of the problem' or Hogwood and Gunn's limits to 'perfect implementation' – stressing the difficulties. In those terms he is co-opted in support of the political Right's argument for market solutions to distribution problems, to circumvent the capacity of suppliers to control public monopoly services.

In fact, however, what Lipsky says is rather different, indeed much more subtle. Certainly he argues that 'the decisions of street-level bureaucrats, the routines they establish, and the devices they invent to cope with uncertainties and work pressures, effectively become the public policies they carry out' (1980: xii). He goes on, however, saying that this process of street-level policy-making does not involve the advancement of the ideals many bring to personal service work to the extent that might be hoped. Rather, the process induces practices that enable officials to cope with the pressures they face:

> [P]eople often enter public employment with at least some commitment to service. Yet the very nature of this work prevents them from coming close to the ideal conception of their jobs. Large classes or huge caseloads and inadequate resources

combine with the uncertainties of method and the unpredictability of clients to defeat their aspirations as service workers. (Lipsky, 1980: xii)

Lipsky argues that, therefore, to cope with the pressures upon them, street-level bureaucrats develop methods of processing people in a relatively routine and stereotyped way. They adjust their work habits to reflect lower expectations of themselves and their clients.

> [They] often spend their work lives in a corrupted world of service. They believe them-
> selves to be doing the best they can under adverse circumstances and they develop
> techniques to salvage service and decision-making values within the limits imposed
> upon them by the structure of work. They develop conceptions of their work and of
> their clients that narrow the gap between their personal and work limitations and the
> service ideal. (ibid.: xii)

Thus, Lipsky handles one of the paradoxes of street-level work. Such workers see themselves as cogs in a system, as oppressed by the bureaucracy within which they work. Yet they often seem to have a great deal of discretionary freedom and auton-omy. He speaks of the street-level bureaucrat's role as an 'alienated' one (ibid.: 76), stressing such classic features of alienation as that work is only on 'segments of the product', that there is no control over outcomes, or over 'raw materials' (clients' circumstances), and that there is no control over the pace of work. Lipsky also emphasizes that street-level bureaucrats face uncertainty about just what personal resources are necessary for their jobs. They find that work situations and outcomes are unpredictable, and they face great pressures of inadequate time in relation to limitless needs. On the whole, control from the top to combat the alleged failures of street-level staff involves the intensification of these pressures.

There is a sense, therefore, in which Lipsky is providing a variant on the Marxist dictum: 'Man makes his own history, even although he does not do so under conditions of his own choosing.' Street-level bureaucrats make choices about the use of scarce resources under pressure; contemporary fiscal pressure upon human services makes it much easier for their managers to emphasize con-trol than to try to put service ideals into practice. In a sense he makes 'heroes' of street-level bureaucrats, because while they are caught in situations that are fun-damentally tragic – in the original sense – they still try to make the best of it.

Why regard Lipsky as a key figure for the development of the 'bottom-up' per-spective on implementation studies? First, his emphasis on the crucial nature of the street-level bureaucrat role is used by others as a justification for methodolog-ical strategies that focus upon that work, rather than upon the policy input. Later we will see this point being developed by Richard Elmore. Second, and more importantly, he is suggesting that the preoccupation of the top-down perspective with 'how great expectations in Washington are dashed in Oakland' is really beside the point. This is because, for him, the implementation of policy is really about street-level workers with high service ideals exercising discretion under intolerable pressures. Therefore attempts to control them hierarchically simply increase their tendency to stereotype and disregard the needs of their clients. This means that different approaches are needed to secure the accountability of implementers, approaches that feed in the expectations of people at the local level (including, above all, the citizens whom the policies in question affect). This is an issue that Lipsky addresses in his last chapter. We will see later that it is one that others have tried to address. It is this shift of normative concern away from questions about how those at the top can exert their wills that above all characterizes the 'bottom-up' kind of approach to implementation.

Benny Hjern: Implementation structures

Benny Hjern is a Swedish scholar who developed his approach to the study of implementation while working on studies of European employment and training programmes at a research institute in Berlin. While we have singled out Hjern here, it is important to recognize that his ideas were developed in close collaboration with others, particularly David Porter, Kenneth Hanf and Chris Hull. Crucial for the development of Hjern's methodology was the fact that the policies he and his colleagues were studying depended upon interactions between several different organizations. It should be noted that this issue was central to Pressman and Wildavsky's pioneering work, too. We will find it also as a theme in much of the work of those, discussed in the next chapter, who aimed to synthesize the top-down and bottom-up approaches. Note, for example, the work of Elmore and also of Scharpf. The latter was an influence upon Hjern's thinking; the difference between them being that Hjern took Scharpf's emphasis upon the importance of networks in a distinctively 'bottom-up' direction. It is also relevant that at the time Hjern developed his theoretical approach, sociological studies of organizations were beginning to come to grips with the fact that the emphasis on formal boundaries of organizations might provide a misleading account of the way people actually construct working relationships since they often do not respect those boundaries (Aldrich, 1976; Benson, 1977).

Hence Hjern and his colleagues saw activities as within 'implementation structures' formed from 'within pools of organizations' and 'formed through processes of consensual self-selection' (Hjern and Porter, 1981: 220). They used a methodology that, while starting from an identified pool of relevant organizations, 'snowballed' to collect a sample of respondents who were working together. In this way they constructed empirically the networks within which field-level decision-making actors carried out their activities without predetermining assumptions about the structures within which these occurred.

Hjern, however, must not simply be seen as a theorist arguing for a bottom-up methodology. In an article reviewing Mazmanian and Sabatier (1981) he argued: 'The aim of the exercise for Mazmanian and Sabatier is to help federal and state politicians to better control public administration. This is not perforce to ensure effective implementation' (1982: 304). Is Hjern suggesting here that there is a definition of 'effective' implementation that can be independent of any issue about control, or is he just challenging the top-down approach to the latter? He goes on to argue that traditional implementation work of that kind is trapped 'in the public administration notion of stable and sequential relationships between politics and administration'. Hjern and Hull argue that this work involves 'policy output analysis' (1982: 107) and that the effective study of implementation must be 'organization-theory inclined' in a way that does not privilege any specific actor or set of actors.

This is more than an argument about methodology. Hjern and Hull go on to argue that:

> Once we are clear about who participates how and with what effect in policy processes, then we can begin to think about how politics and administration could and should be (re-)combined in the policy process. In this sense implementation research continues political science's long tradition of constitutional analysis – and as empirical constitutionalism can hopefully fructify that tradition. (ibid.: 114)

Here Hjern and Hull suggest that implementation research can tackle the issues raised by Lipsky when he, at the end of his book, raised questions about new mechanisms of accountability linking street-level bureaucrats and the public. Unfortunately they left the issue there, promising some new work dealing with the philosophical issues about public accountability that has not materialized. It leaves as the core of their contribution the challenging of the '"single-authority, top-down" approach to political organization' (ibid.: 107).

Susan Barrett and Colin Fudge: Policy and action

Susan Barrett and Colin Fudge, two British scholars who entered the debate in the early 1980s, strongly commend Hjern's 'implementation structure' approach. In their discussion they, like Hjern and his associates, draw upon developments in organization theory that involve challenging hierarchical perspectives on the way organizations work. They particularly emphasize the notion that much action depends upon compromises between people in various parts of single organizations, or related organizations. One organization theorist whose work they find particularly pertinent is Anselm Strauss. Barrett and Fudge make use of his notion of 'negotiated order'. Quoting Strauss that 'wherever there are social orders, there are not only negotiated orders but also coerced orders, manipulated orders and the like' (1978: 262), they go on to pose the following questions:

> First, why, in what circumstances, and with what assumptions are the various modes of action utilized? Second, is there a relationship between the utilization of the different modes and the differential power relations between the interacting parties? If there is, what is the nature of that relationship? And third, are there connections between the different modes of action? (Barrett and Fudge, 1981b: 264)

This emphasis upon 'action' in Barrett and Fudge's work is related – as the title of their edited book *Policy and Action* suggests – to policy, with the two seen as linked 'dynamically'. Hence 'policy cannot be regarded as a constant. It is mediated by actors who may be operating with different assumptive worlds from those formulating the policy, and, inevitably, it undergoes interpretation and modification and, in some cases, subversion' (ibid.: 251). Elsewhere they indicate, as have others (see Hill, 2005: 6–10), that policy is a problematic concept, offering the interesting suggestion that one way of looking at policy is as 'property'. Different actors may make different claims as to its true features.

This analysis brings Barrett and Fudge to a distinct position on the normative assumptions embedded in the traditional 'top-down' literature. They argue that there is a tendency in the top-down implementation literature to depoliticize the policy–action relationship. Their alternative view emphasizes the continuing political processes occurring throughout implementation. In effect, this suggests that it is very difficult to separate implementation from policy formation.

Barrett and Fudge argue that, as, for example, for Pressman and Wildavsky in their original formulation, 'if implementation is defined as putting policy into effect, then *compromise* by the policy-makers would be seen as policy failure' (1981b: 258). They then offer a formulation like that provided by Hjern (see pp. 53–4 above) namely, that 'if implementation is seen as "getting something done", then performance rather than conformance is the main objective and compromise a means of achieving it' (1981b: 258).

We have here then a clear rejection of the normative assumption embedded in the top-down approach. Susan Barrett's concern with the normative aspects of the implementation debate continued to the end of her life. In an article published in 2004, she wrote of

> a renewed need to address the central paradox of control and autonomy in achieving desired performance/outcomes. How to balance the requirement for public accountability with consumer responsiveness, respect for difference and local autonomies, creativity and so on. How to avoid performance becoming conformance with targets at the expense of broader goals? (Barrett, 2004: 260)

Such a perspective poses problems for methodology. In fact, Barrett and Fudge do not address methodological issues, except inasmuch as they endorse Hjern's network analysis approach. However, if it is not possible to separate policy formation from implementation, there is a difficulty in setting the limits for an implementation study. And even more seriously: How can effectiveness be assessed in 'getting something done' or a compromise be judged as achieving something as opposed to throwing away an objective, without reference to at least someone's policy goals?

In some respects, Barrett and Fudge must therefore be seen as making a case against the study of implementation *per se,* or as the first of the theorists who reject, in more or less postmodernist terms, the case for more than individual qualitative case-study analysis.

Conclusion

As mentioned in the introduction to this chapter, the debate between the protagonists of the top-down and bottom-up perspectives has moved (as will be shown in the next chapter) on to efforts to synthesize the approaches, picking out key ideas from each. The methodological elements in the debate were not, in themselves, particularly contentious. The same was true of those elements in the debate that concerned the most realistic way to perceive implementation processes. Authors began to argue that mixed approaches might be used or that the right approach might depend upon the issue. The normative debate could not so easily be resolved, embodying as it did alternative stances on democratic accountability.

BU= problem of accountability

4

IMPLEMENTATION THEORY

<hr>

Contents

<hr>

Introduction

The goal of this chapter is to address the variety of contributions to the implementation theory debate that followed on the initial arguments between the protagonists of the top-down and bottom-up perspectives. We offer here a discussion of a literature in which there have been interesting developments; although no distinct flow towards a scholarly consensus. Therefore we present the theoretical insights around a number of themes recurring in the literature.

In the following section we start with the ways in which authors have sought to define and develop implementation research through a synthesis of the original top-down and bottom-up types of approaches. That leads us on to one of the main complications about doing this: the difficulties in separating policy formation and policy implementation. We examine theoretical approaches that suggest ways of doing empirical work across that so-called boundary (third section). This takes us to a discussion of the implications of the fact that issues about the formation/implementation distinction (as levels in the policy process, see the definitional point made on this in Chapter 1, pp. 15–6), are complicated by the existence of separate politico-administrative layers (see ibid.) (fourth section). This is highlighted in relation to federalism, a key complication for implementation research in the United States. It goes beyond that 'special case' of layers, however, to be a problem for the analysis of modern governance in general. We show that issues particularly related to the latter have been given attention in forms of network theory. This can be seen as carrying forward the original concerns of the 'bottom-up' theorists (fifth section).

In contrast to the *complexity* of approaches that emphasize networks or blur the policy formation/implementation boundaries, another group of theorists has sought to *simplify* implementation analysis. Partly in reaction to the complexity introduced by the former contributions, these authors sometimes return to the control preoccupations of the top-down theorists. Their focus is thus much more on the management of single organizations or of inter-organizational relationships uncomplicated by disputes over policy formation prerogatives. This work is the concern of the sixth part of this chapter. Next, we look at a topic that cuts across the debates explored so far, prompted by a matter of fact question: Why should people expect to be able to generalize about policy implementation when what is being implemented can vary very considerably? Hence we observe efforts to use policy typologies to explain differences in the characteristics of implementation processes (seventh section). Before arriving at a conclusion we explore how authors deal with the various ways citizens and other stakeholders relate to public policies (eighth section).

The search for a synthesis

It has become commonplace for more recent authors on implementation to suggest that the original debate should not distract us, for example:

> The *top-down* and *bottom-up* perspectives were useful in drawing attention to the fact that both top and bottom play important roles in the implementation process, but in the long run the battle between the two approaches was not fruitful. (Winter, 2006: 154)

As the first part of that statement indicates, there remains a case for exploring the two types of approaches to tease out the elements in implementation for teaching purposes. Dichotomies, moreover, offer convenient formulations for examination questions – so long as students realize they are then expected to arrive at judicious middle positions. However, a continued awareness of the debate, and especially the bottom-up challenge, remains important. This is particularly so because of the continued tendency of everyday statements about implementation – from politicians, the media and so on – to be formulated in uncompromising top-down terms. They see the problem of implementation as simply about achieving compliance: the 'delivery' of explicit and unambiguous policy (see Peck and 6, 2006, Chapter 1, for a discussion of the problems regarding this).

Normative or empirical, process or output

Hence the publications of authors who have explicitly explored the top-down/bottom-up distinction in search of a synthesis remain relevant. A particularly useful contribution of this kind is an essay published by Paul Sabatier in 1986. We have already identified Sabatier as a key figure in the establishment of the 'top-down' perspective on implementation. In the 1986 essay, Sabatier is willing to concede some of the methodological strengths of the bottom-up type of approach: its effective incorporation of the study of networks; its strength in evaluating other influences on policy outcomes than government programmes and its value when a number of different policy programmes interact. Hence Sabatier suggests that choice of methodology might depend upon whether there is or is not a 'dominant piece of legislation structuring the situation' (Sabatier, 1986: 37; he has followed this up in later work, see particularly Sabatier, [1999] 2007).

A similar concern to adopt an open-minded approach to methodology is expressed by Richard Elmore, making a plea for the use of mixed methods. In his 'Organizational Models of Social Program Implementation' (1978), Elmore takes a cue from an influential decision-making, or policy formation, study of the Cuban missile crisis (Allison, 1971). He suggests that, in the study of complicated events, it can be valuable to triangulate accounts. This means using different theoretical models to try to achieve a satisfactory explanation of what happened. He thus contrasts 'implementation as systems management', 'implementation as bureaucratic process', 'implementation as organization development' and 'implementation as conflict and bargaining'.

In fact, those responses just deal with the methodological issues. Also Sabatier's essay does not deal satisfactorily with the critique of his original normative assumptions by the 'bottom-uppers'. He argues that they overemphasize 'the ability of the Periphery to frustrate the Center' (1986: 34). What the bottom-up critique does, however, is precisely to question this language of intentions and consequences. Lane (1987) provides a more neutral stance on the normative issue here. He questions the search for an integrated theory of implementation by drawing attention to what he sees as a problem embodied in the meaning of the word. He suggests that implementation is seen both as involving notions of an 'end state or policy achievement' and 'a process or policy execution' (Lane, 1987: 528). A similar point is made by Winter who says: 'the concept "implementation" is often used to characterize both the implementation process and the output – and sometimes also the outcome – of the implementation process' (Winter, 2005: 159). Winter urges us to concentrate on output.

While the dichotomy Lane is making has much in common with the top-down/bottom-up distinction, it does not exactly parallel it. Perhaps it rather highlights the normative as opposed to the methodological distinction in the top-down/bottom-up dichotomy. This dichotomy has a resemblance to the one that Hjern and Hull make between 'policy output analysis' and 'organization-theory inclined' work, see p. 54. Lane goes on to emphasize two alternative considerations in relation to his dichotomy: responsibility and trust. He argues that the 'responsibility' concerns are about the 'relationship between objectives and outcome' (Lane, 1987: 542) while the 'trust' concerns refer to 'the process of putting policies into effect' (ibid.: 542). Lane argues that top-down models are particularly concerned to emphasize the 'responsibility side', while bottom-up models 'underline the trust side' (ibid.: 543). He then argues:

> An implementation process is a combination of responsibility and trust ... Without the notion of *implementation as policy accomplishment* there is no basis for evaluating policies and holding politicians, administrators and professionals accountable. On the other hand, *implementation as policy execution* rests upon trust or a certain amount of degrees of freedom for politicians and implementers to make choices about alternative means for the accomplishment of goals.
>
> ... Implementation theory has thus far been the search for some pattern or way of structuring the process of implementation in such a manner that there will be a high probability of policy accomplishment. This has resulted in a controversy between those who believe in control, planning and hierarchy on the one hand, and on the other those who believe in spontaneity, learning and adaptation as problem-solving techniques. A reorientation of implementation theory would be to inquire into how accountability is to be upheld in the implementation of policies and how much trust is in agreement with the requirement of accountability. (ibid.: 543)

Like Lane, Rothstein also explores issues about legitimacy and trust; themes that, he claims, have been rather neglected by implementation researchers. He goes on to point out that 'Without citizens' trust in the institutions responsible for implementing public policies, implementation is likely to fail' (1998: 100). This is an important point, which perhaps helps us to understand some of the differences between the dominant American implementation literature, involving very high expectations in a relatively low trust context, and some of the rather different European contributions.

Stressing, as noted above, that the state must act even when it does not know what will work, Rothstein argues that 'Successful policy implementation is often a question of so organizing the implementation process as to accommodate the need for flexibility and the uncertainty in the policy theory' (1998: 113). He goes on to stress that the greater these are, 'the stiffer the demands on organization and legitimacy' (ibid. 113).

What we have in the work of Lane and Rothstein (interestingly both Swedish) is a particular concern with the normative arguments between the top-down and bottom-up perspectives. The way they highlight this comes down to a need to recognize, as in much applied social science research, issues about 'whose side you are on' as an influence upon the way issues and problems are framed.

Implementation as translation or change

At the same time highlighting the methodological and normative issues still leaves unresolved questions about the different picture of the implementation process provided by the two types of approaches. That is, the top-down portrait of a probability of reasonably straightforward translation of policy into action and a bottom-up emphasis upon change so that action ultimately bears little resemblance to initial policy. In fact, these are empirical questions that can be tackled by various methodologies. After all, did not Pressman and Wildavsky's portrait of action in Oakland suggest that it was very different to 'expectations' in Washington? It is only when proponents of either perspective go to the extremes of dogmatism *either* about the feasibility *or* the impossibility of compliance with policy expectations, that there is really an issue here.

For example, Sabatier is particularly critical of those like Barrett and Fudge who tend to obliterate the distinction between policy-formation and implementation. He argues:

> First, it makes it very difficult to distinguish the relative influence of elected officials and civil servants – thus precluding an analysis of democratic accountability and bureaucratic discretion, hardly trivial topics. Second, the view of the policy process as a seamless web of flows without decision points ... precludes policy evaluation ... and the analysis of policy change. (1986: 31)

This is, of course, an assertion of the case for the politics and administration dichotomy discussed in Chapter 2. If, however, those Sabatier criticizes are right about real processes, his alternative imposes an artificial distinction. In other words, his (normative) concern with accountability (and he is not alone here) seems to obscure his judgement on what actually happens.

A similar problem seems to occur in a much more recent work, Peck and 6's discussion of policy delivery (2006). As noted above, they castigate those who see delivery as essentially straightforward, and then concede the importance of the normative and methodological elements in the bottom-up view. They go on to dismiss a version of the bottom-up tradition that they attribute to Bovens and 'Hart's discussion of 'policy fiascoes' (1996) which they describe as 'fatalist':

> for whom 'bottom-up' meant a claim that there are so many unanticipated and unintended consequences of trying to pursue a policy in practice, so many difficulties in getting any policy put in place or, indeed, in salvaging anything beneficial from the process, that the role of the commentator is little more than to document the cussedness of organisational outcomes. (Peck and 6, 2006: 10)

Peck and 6 dismiss this view on theoretical and *empirical* grounds. We emphasize the latter word, since that seems a dogmatic proposition. Surely an important area for political enquiry in the modern world, as Bovens and 't Hart illustrate with examples in their book, is situations in which any relationship between intentions and actions is very attenuated indeed.

Rather than offer our favourite examples to illustrate this last point, since this is a review of theory, we prefer to highlight something that has happened in the development of implementation research that relates to that point. This is the elaboration of complex theoretical approaches that go beyond the notion of the distinct division between policy formation and implementation, particularly embodied in the top-down approach. We do this in the next section.

Where does implementation begin?

In the light of his criticisms of Barrett and Fudge cited above it is interesting to note how Sabatier went on to elaborate a model of implementation that in many respects fuses implementation analysis with exploration of other parts of the policy process. Winter suggests Sabatier 'actually moved the focus of analysis towards policy change and formulation and away from implementation' (Winter, 2006: 155). Sabatier argues that the approach he had earlier adopted with Mazmanian 'did not provide a good conceptual vehicle for looking at policy change over periods of a decade or more'. As a reason he states that it 'focused too much on the perspective of program *proponents*, thereby neglecting the strategies (and learning) by other actors' (1986: 30). His later works endeavour to rectify this error.

Therefore, after that 1986 essay Sabatier shifted his attention to the development of his 'advocacy coalition' approach (see particularly Sabatier and Jenkins-Smith, 1993), offering a more holistic view of the policy process. In the lead essay for an edited collection *Theories of the Policy Process* ([1999] 2007), Sabatier challenges the 'stages heuristic' within which the examination of implementation tends to have been embedded. He argues that a policy process consists of the following:

- a multiplicity of actors (both individual and corporate), each of which have different interests, values, perceptions and policy preferences;
- a time span of a decade or more;
- within a policy domain there are normally dozens of different programmes involving multiple layers of government;
- a variety of debates about the policy involved, partly of a highly technical character and held in different fora;
- the high stakes involved give rise to 'politics' and power political behaviour in and around a policy process.

While each of these elements also interact over time, Sabatier speaks of 'an extremely complex set' (2007: 3). This takes Sabatier much closer to the bottom-up perspective, because the 'advocacy coalition' can be seen as comprising actors from all layers. There remains, however, a question about the extent to which the concept of 'coalition', like the concept of network to which it has obvious links and on which we say more below, can tend to mask the significance of conflict within the policy process.

In the last part of the 1986 essay, Sabatier outlines what he sees as the way forward, involving the 'advocacy coalition framework', adopting:

the bottom-uppers' unit of analysis – a whole variety of public and private actors involved with a policy problem – as well as their concerns with understanding the

perspectives and strategies of all major categories of actors (not simply program proponents). It then combines this starting point with the top-downers' concerns with
the manner in which socio-economic conditions and legal instruments constrain
behavior. It applies this synthesized perspective to the analysis of policy change over
periods of a decade or more. (1986: 39)

There is of course a dilemma here; a problem for implementation studies
about steering a course between the Scylla of a rigorous but narrowly conceived study and the Charybdis of a study that reflects the lengthy and complex character of a policy process but therefore may become both broad and
shapeless. These are important points to which we will have to return in later
parts of this book.

What Sabatier actually is struggling with is the difficulty of making a distinction between policy formation and policy implementation. Others are less
worried about doing this. Dennis Palumbo and Donald Calista's *Implementation
and the Policy Process* (1990), while an edited collection within which there is
no entirely unified stance, aims to 'place implementation in the broader policy-making process' (ibid.: xii). Although this leaves open the possibility that
implementation and policy formation are analyzed separately, the view that
this should not be done is taken by some of the contributors to the book. The
main concern of the volume is set out in Palumbo and Calista's own essay. Here
they argue:

There is no doubt that implementation research has finally laid to rest the politics-
administration dichotomy. Early implementation research fostered this view when it
assumed that implementers were supposed to simply carry out previously made policy directives. More recent research demonstrates that implementation is a legitimate
part of the policy-making process – a part that can be neither diminished empirically
nor de-legitimized normatively. (ibid.: 14)

This position particularly rests upon the argument that 'implementers are
involved in every stage of the policy cycle' (ibid.: 15), a case that partly involves
producing evidence – certainly long present in British literature on the role of
the civil service – that bureaucrats contribute to policy design (Chapman,
1970). It is reinforced by an argument that policy design is seldom initially
clear and that renegotiation of details with the multiplicity of actors affected
by that policy is an accepted part of the policy process. Huber and Shipan
(2002) also explore this issue. A bit misleadingly they use the expression 'deliberate discretion' to describe this filling in of policy detail within policy formation processes, rather than – as in Davis' usage (see p. 25) – to describe a
street-level phenomenon. An even more explicit case of disregard of the policy
formation/implementation distinction is provided by a British study of the
impact of Margaret Thatcher (Marsh and Rhodes, 1992) entitled *Implementing
Thatcherite Policies*. It starts with an exploration of implementation theory
but in fact is largely concerned with ideological influences upon initial policy
formation.

Layers in policy processes

In Palumbo and Calista's book, an essay by Ferman explores the phenomenon of the complexity of the relationship between policy formation and implementation as a particular facet of federalism. She asserts that 'implementation politics is an integral part of the American political system as envisioned by the Founding Fathers' (Ferman, 1990: 50). Thus she highlights the divisions in the American system, stressing the connections between fragmentation between legislature and executive and that between the federal government and the states. Ferman argues that:

> the factors that contribute to the gap between policymaking and implementation are manifestations of the Madisonian system of American politics and government. The implication of this finding for implementation theory is that we should view implementation in a very different light – implementation is another check in the American system of government. (ibid.: 39)

Hence, she argues that Thomas Madison's 'victory' in creating a system of government in which centralized power was prevented, created different demands and incentives for policy-makers and implementers and thus two different 'types of politics' (ibid.: 40). Ferman's emphasis on this last point is interesting. On the one hand, she accepts the evidence for a 'gap between policymaking and implementation'. On the other, she argues that this can be seen as a legitimate check upon executive or legislative power. An alternative position, such as that embodied in some of the bottom-up work (particularly that of Hjern and of Barrett and Fudge) would be to emphasize the extent to which negotiation between actors on various layers in practice closes that gap.

Issues of American federalism were fundamental for Pressman and Wildavsky's (1973) classic work. Part of their thesis about implementation could be swiftly dismissed from a bottom-up point of view with the assertion that Washington's will was not carried out in Oakland because the implementation chain they observed was embedded in a federal system of government. We find then Goggin, Bowman, Lester and O'Toole (1990), probably the most sophisticated of the theorists who endeavour to model the implementation process highlighting aspects of inter-governmental relations in their model.

Aiming for rigour

The aim of Goggin and his colleagues is to further a 'more scientific' (1990: 18) approach to the study of implementation. To that end they set out what they call a *'communications model'* for the analysis of implementation, with a very strong emphasis upon what affects the acceptance or rejection of messages between layers of government. They develop an extensive list of hypotheses on this theme. The case studies Goggin and his colleagues use are in many respects preoccupied by federal/state relations in the United States. The cases all concern federal Acts that depend very much upon implementation at state level. Indeed, they may even be seen as about issues that under some interpretations of the American Constitution would be regarded as no business of the federal government at all. Quite appropriately Goggin et al. are critical of earlier American studies for their disregard of activities on the layer of the separate states. More significantly, they discuss national policy as 'federal messages' (Chapter 3); a usage that seems to highlight the fact that there is a problem about assuming a capacity to command from the federal government layer.

The concern of Goggin and his colleagues to cope with problems related to political-administrative layers in a federal system has a significant effect upon their methodology. It makes the specification of variables rather difficult and generates large numbers of elaborate hypotheses. They are struggling with the tension between a need to satisfy the practical demand for propositions about implementation success or failure and the complex nature of the phenomena with which they are concerned.

Clearly Goggin et al.'s *Implementation Theory and Practice* is a careful and elaborate attempt to specify a scientific framework for implementation studies. It escapes from the static nature of earlier studies that have difficulty in handling feedback between implementation and policy formation, as well as from the rigidity of top-down efforts to specify particular 'rules' for those who want to control implementation. Yet, as has already been suggested, it focuses on one particular aspect of implementation, that is, communication between layers of government (with particular reference to the version of this issue which arises in American federalism). Because of this, it may be asked to what extent the book of Goggin et al. offers a comprehensive and universally applicable theoretical approach to the study of implementation.

Elaborating the federal dimension

Robert Stoker (1991) deals explicitly with issues of the implementation of federal policy in the United States. Stoker identifies as a crucial flaw in the American top-down literature the extent to which it is concerned with failures to exert federal authority in a system of government that was designed to limit that authority. He highlights as the leading expression of that view what he calls the 'disability thesis'. This 'thesis', as suggested by Ferman in the essay quoted above, entails a view that the 'U.S. government is disabled by design' (1990: 50). Stoker therefore contrasts two alternative approaches to the solution of implementation problems, which to a large extent parallel the normative aspects of the top-down and bottom-up views. Taking his lead from Lindblom (1977), he labels these approaches 'authority' and 'exchange'. Compare here Lane's distinction between 'responsibility' and 'trust' (discussed above). The authority approach involves suggesting ways to simplify or circumvent the barriers to compliance. The exchange approach requires the achievement of co-operation.

Stoker's emphasis on the importance of the division of powers within federalism and his endorsement of the case for limitations upon government power, leave little doubt about where he stands on the case against trying to solve implementation problems through the exercise of authority. What, however, is important about his analysis is that he also sees shortcomings in the exchange approach. He recognizes, like Barrett and Fudge, the way this confuses policy formation and implementation. While that comment does not in itself invalidate the exchange approach, Stoker goes on to stress how that approach leads to an analysis in which what results from an exchange process is seen as inevitable, regardless of the interests or moral ends that may be involved. He suggests that this is to disregard the extent to which co-operation needs to be seen as a device to handle conflicts rather than one which can only succeed if they are eliminated. Hence Stoker argues:

> The flaw in the disability thesis, and the implementation literature that reflects it, is that it may be possible to manipulate the conditions of the implementation process to encourage co-operative responses to conflicts of interest. This possibility has received scant attention in the literature. (p. 50)

Hence, as a third alternative to 'authority' and 'exchange' Stoker sees 'governance' as an activity in which 'reluctant partners' are induced to collaborate. In this sense he takes up an argument from C. Stone (1989) that it is important to give attention to 'power to' accomplish collective goals as opposed to 'power over' recalcitrant others. This leads him on to an exploration of the extent to which different 'implementation regimes' can arise, or be created.

This intense debate about federalism is thus very largely one about the absence of a fit between levels in the process of policy production, in respect of the policy cycle, and layers within the national politico-administrative system in the United States (see the discussion of this distinction in Chapter 1, pp. 15–6). It is important to recognize that the federal/state relationship in the United States may often be more appropriately viewed as one in which a collaborative policy formation (sub-) process rather than an implementation (sub-) process is occurring. And that lesson needs to be carried on into the analysis of other federal systems, and even into that of systems characterized by different inter-governmental relations (note discussions of the 'implementation' of European Union directives). Issues of securing the collaboration of 'reluctant partners' are by no means absent from such other, possibly simpler, constitutional structures of inter-governmental relations. It is important, for example, to note:

- many central/local government relationships in which the latter lay claim to a measure of autonomy;
- the factors analyzed by Lipsky, discussed in Chapter 3, that convey a measure of actual autonomy to street-level bureaucrats.

These are recognized by Stoker himself: making a contrast between the 'centralized', 'shared' and 'diffuse' distribution of public authority in different constitutional or institutional contexts. Hence, while Stoker makes a particularly important contribution to arguments about federalism, his work must be seen as also making a contribution to the normative arguments about co-ordination and control that preoccupy so much of the implementation literature.

Networks: broadening the horizontal dimension

The concern with the complexities introduced into the study of implementation by federalism and inter-governmental relations in general, as well as the recognition of the importance of 'governance', connects with a wider concern to see the implementation process as involving complex networks. Such networks may spread horizontally, between organizations of equivalent power and stature as well as between organizations that are, in some respects, related vertically.

Of course a concern with networks is embedded in much of the work described in this chapter and in Chapter 3, in both the top-down literature (in Pressman and Wildavsky's concern with linkages) and in the work of those with a bottom-up perspective (particularly that of Hjern and his associates). That concern is clearly taken forward in the important synthesizing contribution by Goggin and his associates.

By the early 1980s, issues of networks had become very important both for political science and for organizational sociology. The theoretical roots of the approach lie in inter-organizational theory and the interactive perspective on public policy (Hufen and Ringeling, 1990; Kickert et al., 1997). While it is in some respects invidious to single out any particular theorist, there is nevertheless one figure who seems particularly important for the introduction of these ideas into the study of implementation: the German scholar, Fritz Scharpf. It was an essay of his, published as far back as 1978, that particularly emphasized that:

> [I]t is unlikely, if not impossible, that public policy of any significance could result from the choice process of any single unified actor. Policy formulation and policy implementation are inevitably the result of interactions among a plurality of separate actors with separate interests, goals and strategies. (1978: 347)

Scharpf develops an approach to the study of policy formation and implementation processes in which issues of co-ordination and collaboration are given central attention, through the identification of the need for specific types of coordination and the examination of the empirical factors 'facilitating or impeding' this. What this means is a focus upon the nature of the networks that may be formed, as well as upon the resource dependencies and exchanges that facilitate the process.

As noted above, the network approach has become important in both political science and sociology (see Knoke, 1990; Smith, 1993; Klijn, 1997; or Koppenjan and Klijn, 2004, for reviews of the literature). Smith argues that:

> The notion of policy networks is a way of coming to terms with the traditionally stark state/civil society dichotomy .... State actors are also actors in civil society, they live in

society and have constant contact with groups which represent societal interests. Therefore the interests of state actors develop along with the interests of the group actors and the degree of autonomy that exists depends on the nature of policy networks. (Smith, 1993: 67)

Some scholars, particularly in Britain (see Jordan and Richardson, 1987), have explored the extent to which it is possible to identify both a variety of policy networks and stronger variants of this phenomenon, which have been called 'policy communities'. Networks may cohere into communities and communities may disintegrate into networks. There may be some issues where communities are more likely than networks and vice versa.

Kickert, Klijn and Koppenjan say:

Until recently the concept 'policy network' had often been negatively evaluated. It was seen as one of the main reasons for policy failure: non-transparent and impenetrable forms of interest representations which prevent policy innovations and threaten the effectiveness, efficiency and democratic legitimacy of the public sector. (1997: Preface, p. xvii)

They go on to indicate that they do not agree with that view. We do not need here to take sides in that argument. What is important is, as Scharpf states in his essay, that a realism about networks requires us to recognize two points. First, that networks may be crucial for the sort of 'implementation deficit' that Pressman and Wildavsky were so concerned about. And, second, that effective implementation, as suggested by Hjern and his colleagues, may depend upon the development of collaborative networks. Certainly, the British network literature recognizes that they may be very important for successful policy formation and implementation and it suggests that governments have sought to foster policy networks and policy communities. Smith (1993), drawing on Jordan and Richardson (1987), identifies four reasons for this:

- Networks facilitate a consultative style of government.
- They reduce policy conflict and make it possible to depoliticize issues.
- They make policy-making predictable.
- They relate well to the departmental organization of government.

The British network literature has shown little interest in implementation *per se*. Implicit in much that has been said about networks, however, is a view related to implementation. That view entails that much of the discontinuity between policy formation and implementation perceived as problematic by the top-down theorists, is seen as eliminated through the continuity of the relationship that exists between the government and its specific partners in a policy network (such as the agriculture or the health policy network). We do not need to examine the evidence for such a view here. The point is that this is a theoretical approach which does not see implementation in terms of the realization or non-realization of hierarchically determined goals, but rather as embedded in a wider policy process negotiated through networks.

Network management

In the discussion of network theory in the last section concerns about complexity emerge in various forms. Koppenjan and Klijn speak of 'complex problems' as 'increasingly resolved in a setting of mutual dependencies' (2004: 5). The expression 'wicked problem' is used in the same context with Koppenjan and Klijn arguing:

> Complex and highly undetermined types of interactions characterize wicked problems. This strategic uncertainty is not easy to reduce and can never be completely eliminated. In a complex society characterized by network formations and horizontalization, actors have discretion to make their own choices. Unexpected strategic turns are an intrinsic characteristic of interaction processes surrounding wicked problems. (ibid: 7)

There is an ambiguity here. In some respects it is being suggested that complexity is an inherent feature of modern societies. On the other hand, it is indicated that this is particularly the case in respect of wicked problems, implying that there may be simpler problems where this is not the case. This point is made more explicitly by Sabatier and Weible when discussing the Advocacy Coalition Framework (ACF), which we have noted above as having much in common with the network approach. They describe the ACF as 'developed ... to deal with "wicked" problems' (Sabatier and Weible, 2007: 189).

In this respect there is an emphasis not so much on the inevitability of networks, as on the need for a network approach for the management of some (argued to be frequently evident) kinds of policies. The efforts of theorists to distinguish different kinds of policies are explored later in the chapter.

For Koppenjan and Klijn, then, network 'management' is particularly required where there is:

- problem complexity;
- lack of consensus;
- institutional complexity.

In a similar sense, Exworthy and Powell (2004) write of 'implementation in the "congested state", the world of governance or multi-level government'. Adapting Kingdon's analysis of policy agenda setting (1995), they suggest that implementation models need to recognize the relationship between 'big windows' at national level and 'little windows' at local level. Decisions rest upon the successful integration of three streams (another concept from Kingdon):

- a policy stream concerned with goals and objectives;
- a process stream dealing with 'causal, technical and political feasibility' (Exworthy and Powell, 2004: 266);
- a resource stream, using that concept to embrace, of course, finance but also other resources.

Network theory contributes both to a recognition of the need for new ways to formulate the issues about implementation and to highlighting the difficulties about the policy-formation/implementation distinction. It may go further than Exworthy and Powell's model of streams, which postulates organizations with relatively pre-determined characteristics that need to be co-ordinated, to take a more open view.

Kickert, Klijn and Koppenjan (1997; see also Klijn and Koppenjan, 2000; Koppenjan and Klijn, 2004) offer a particularly cogent exposition of the importance of issues of networks for the policy process. Their central assumption is 'that policy is made in complex interaction processes between a large number of actors which takes place within networks of interdependent actors' (Klijn and Koppenjan, 2000: 139). The actors involved are mutually dependent because they need each other's resources to achieve goals (Scharpf, 1978; Benson, 1982; Rhodes, 1988). Patterns of interaction emerge around policy problems and resource clusters. So policy networks can be defined as a (more or less) stable pattern of social relations between interdependent actors, which take shape around policy problems and/or policy programmes (Klijn and Koppenjan, 2000). In time, rules are developed in the network that regulate behaviour and resource distribution. In this way, networks influence the regulations, in which the rules and resource distribution are gradually shaped, solidified and altered (Giddens, 1984). Policy networks thus form a context in which actors act strategically.

Series of interactions take place around policy and other issues, which can be called games (Crozier and Friedberg, 1980; Rhodes, 1981; Scharpf, 1997a). Series of games thus form policy processes. During a game, actors operate within the established resource distribution and set of rules. The existing, ambiguous rules are interpreted (March and Olsen, 1989; Klijn, 1996). Actors select strategies based on their perceptions of the nature of the problem, their desired solutions and those of the other actors. Different actors have different perceptions.

In this perspective, co-operation is a necessary condition in policy networks to achieve satisfying outcomes. However, this does not mean it is established without conflict, since there is a tension between interdependency and the diversity of goals and interests. This tension needs to be solved in any policy game. To achieve co-operation, steering is needed. So network management is focused on the improvement of co-operation between involved actors (O'Toole, 1988). Two types of steering strategies can be distinguished: process management and network constitution. Process management has as its aim the improvement of interaction between actors in policy games, taking the structure and composition of the network as given. Network constitution aims at changing the network. Since this means institutional change, these strategies are time-consuming (Klijn and Koppenjan, 2000).

Because co-operation between actors is central in the policy network approach, explanations for the 'success' or 'failure' of policy processes (do not forget the normative dimension of these qualifications) are based on the extent of co-operation achieved. Explanations are found on the one hand in process variables, like the degree to which actors are aware of their mutual dependencies; the degree to which interactions are balanced favourably or unfavourably with perceived outcomes of the interaction; and the degree to which game management is foreseen. On the other hand, success or failure are explained by the structural characteristics of the network, such as the degree to which actors possess veto power because of indispensable resources and the degree to which actors in a game belong to the same network. The latter means that they also interact with each other and that they have developed reciprocal rules (Klijn and Koppenjan, 2000).

In policy networks, actors are relatively autonomous; they all have their own objectives. There may be no central, co-ordinating actor. However, the government may take that role and then its special advantages need to be examined. The point here is that given other actors with degrees of autonomy as well, it may be inappropriate to evaluate process and outcome in terms of the objectives of one actor.

Furthermore, initial problem definitions or objectives, even when established collectively, change during the interaction processes. One of the problems that has been identified in respect of network theory is that networks may be fluid in nature. Yet it is difficult to theorize about the circumstances under which they form, mutate or break up. Dowding (1995) thus argues that the policy network approach may be doing no more than using an indicative 'metaphor'. In this respect, those seeing network management as an appropriate approach to problem solving may simply be arguing that solutions are more likely *if* networks can be established.

Finally, it is important to note how, in general, the network approach, many of whose advocates are not particularly interested in implementation *per se*, tends to involve an emphasis upon the ways in which policy formation and implementation are intertwined. Then, more specifically, those who are concerned with network management see the process as one of seeking to solve 'wicked' problems through flexibility 'upstream'. Hence many of the examples in Koppenjan and Klijn's (2004) book concern large and complex 'wicked' problems where what is involved is a very elaborate policy process (for example, major environmental problems – flood control, pollution reduction, etc.). In these cases the analysis is largely about stages 'upstream' from implementation – such as widening the circle of those who are involved in problem solving (in other words, policy formation as a combination of policy formulation and decision-making; or even agenda setting). Then, in fact, the ultimate implementation issues are scarcely addressed. In a sense these will be simpler (at least as far as the politics is concerned): how to build dams once the case for dams has been accepted, etc.

Managing performance: redefining the vertical dimension

Clearly within the category of theorists discussed in the last section there are both authors who largely want to integrate the analysis of implementation with the study of policy formation and others who nevertheless aspire to engage in the detailed examination of implementation performance, while recognizing organizational complexity. While we highlighted how the approach adopted by

Goggin and his colleagues tends to open up the whole problem posed by American federalism for our topic, they were nevertheless concerned (through elaborate modelling) to separate out the vertical policy formation issues from more downstream issues about influences on implementation.

Implementation and performance

One of Goggin's co-authors, Laurence J. O'Toole, Jr, has been particularly concerned with this topic, recognizing the importance of both vertical and horizontal relationships within networks. In a review of implementation literature published in 1986, he showed how few recommendations were emerging on implementation in multi-actor contexts, and how often actors had been offered quite conflicting 'proverbs'. He returned to that theme in an article published in 1993, drawing heavily upon his studies of wastewater privatization (see also O'Toole, 1989a and b). O'Toole's work later in the 1990s took him even more deeply into complex implementation situations when he carried out studies in Hungary, as that country emerged from Communism (1994, 1997). We find him here arguing that the implementation process was complicated by the fact that the country was engaged in a process of 'constitutional choice' (1994: 516), and that therefore theories about policy implementation 'as developed in the West are of limited use' (ibid.: 493).

That work by O'Toole, and perhaps also his earlier work on wastewater privatization, raises questions about the ambition of implementation theory to handle complicated change processes. At the end of the 1990s, O'Toole became involved in work with the much more specific objective of trying to model inter-organizational processes, and particularly the management of networks, in such a way as to facilitate quantitative empirical research (see below).

Another theorist who draws upon network theory, and particularly game theory, but sets out to do this in ways that facilitate a focus upon implementation performance, is René Torenvlied (1996a, 2000). What is important about his work is that he adopts a comparatively parsimonious approach when mathematically modelling the respective impacts of policy-makers and implementers. He expounds, in his 1996 article, an approach that sees the prediction of outputs as a function of, on the one hand, the extent of consensus on the part of policy-makers and, on the other, of choices between two options on the part of implementing agencies. Torenvlied describes the latter as wanting to minimize two 'types of utility loss', that is: 'preference loss and reputation loss'.

> Agencies are torn between the decided outcome and their policy position. A deviation from the decided outcome induces a reputation loss to an agency. A deviation from the agency's policy position induces a preference loss. Both types of loss sum to a total utility loss. (Torenvlied, 1996b: 31)

In more down-to-earth language: Implementing agency choices demand consideration of the costs both of failure to do what is required of them and of failure to do what they want to do.

Torenvlied's approach – accompanied by algebra and geometry that may be alien to those not trained in mathematics or economics – involves setting up bases for making formal assumptions about self-interested choices. As such, although he tests his ideas with empirically derived data, his modelling may seem to be a long way from the empirical study of the real world. Nevertheless, from a theoretical point of view, it does seem valuable to try to establish ways of formulating propositions about the behaviour of the key actors in implementation relationships. What is interesting is that Torenvlied questions what is a central assumption for most theory about networks: the significance of bargaining (see his discussion and test of this approach in his article with Thomson, *Torenvlied and Thomson* 2003).

Torenvlied's quest for parsimony can also be found in an article by Meier. The latter warns:

> If policy implementation is as complex as contemporary theory portrays it with numerous policy instruments affected by myriad variables interacting over several levels of government and conditioned by radically different environments (or policy types), then I despair that we will ever make much progress. (1999: 6)

Hence Meier suggests: 'Any policy implementation scholar who adds a new variable or a new interaction should be required to eliminate two existing variables' (ibid.: 6). He has subsequently joined with O'Toole in the analysis of the management of implementation networks, aiming to single out key variables (O'Toole and Meier, 1999; Meier and O'Toole, 2001).

Specifying contexts

Another author critical of the complexity of much earlier work is Richard Matland. His comment on a literature review by O'Toole (1986) that identifies a large number of key variables, is: 'A literature with three hundred critical variables doesn't need more variables: It needs *structure*' (Matland, 1995: 146). Matland is also critical of Sabatier for his shift away from a specific attention to a policy, to one for a policy field. The former argues:

> A policy field followed over many years can change so radically that it bears little resemblance to its initial form. If implementation research is to retain a meaningful definition, it should be tied to a specific policy rather than to all actions in a policy field. (ibid.: 152)

Central to Matland's argument is a view that instead of simply producing lists of variables to be taken into account, implementation theorists must specify 'the conditions under which these variables are important and the reasons we should expect them to be important' (ibid.: 153). He suggests that these conditions must be derived from a coherent approach to the concept of 'successful implementation'. Perhaps another way of putting this is to argue that there needs to be a clearly specified 'dependent variable'. Matland sees disagreements about the concept of successful implementation as very fundamental for the top-down/bottom-up argument, with the former much more likely to want to use specific outcomes as the dependent variable while the latter 'prefer a much broader evaluation' (ibid.: 154).

Matland refers to a discussion of this topic by Ingram and Schneider (1990) which looks at the top-down/bottom-up debate as an argument about how discretion should be assigned to implementers. Ingram and Schneider distinguish:

- the strong statute approach, with the whole policy design task tackled at the top (as highlighted in Davis' attack on discretionary power (see Chapter 2, p. 28);
- the 'Wilsonian Perspective' (1990: 77), picking up on Woodrow Wilson's concern about efficient but unpoliticized administration (see pp. 29–31), in which clear goals are set but administrative agencies have discretion on the organization of administration;
- the 'grass roots approach' (1990: 79) in which street-level staff and even 'target populations' have discretion over 'all the elements of policy logic';
- the 'support building approach' (1990: 81) in which policy content is bargained between top and bottom.

While this seems a useful way of conceptualizing how policies are actually made, the peculiar feature of this analysis is that it is all set out in terms of questions about how they *should* be made. The political realism of other authors who suggest ways discretion emerges as a result of struggles over policy goals, is entirely disregarded and these alternatives are presented as choice options for the 'top'.

The approach actually adopted by Matland largely avoids that problem by noting a variety of plausible definitions of successful implementation:

- compliance with statutes' directives;
- compliance with statutes' goals;
- achievement of specific success indicators;
- achievement of locally specified goals;
- improvement of the political climate around a programme.

In relation to these, there are decisions to be made about the extent to which the values of those who design policy are to be accorded primacy over those of others. Crucial then to this argument is the question whether or not policy goals have been explicitly stated in some official policy document. If this is the case, Matland argues:

> then, based on democratic theory, the statutory designers' values have a superior value. In such instances the correct standard of implementation success is loyalty to the prescribed goals. When a policy does not have explicitly stated goals, the choice of a standard becomes more difficult, and more general societal norms and values come into play. (1995: 155)

Defining goals, however, may be problematical. There does not seem any intrinsic reason why rigorous implementation studies cannot be based on alternative goals to those of the 'statutory designers'. Nevertheless that does not detract from Matland's central point about the distinction between clear and unclear goals. Perhaps a more serious deficiency is that his essentially top-down position seems to exclude the possibility that implementing agencies themselves make choices (compare here, for example, Torenvlied's approach to modelling implementation behaviour, discussed above, pp. 72–3).

Matland goes on from that last point to argue that there is a tendency for top-down theorists to choose relatively clear policies to study while bottom-uppers 'study policies with greater uncertainty inherent' in them (1995: 154). Rothstein seems to take a similar stance when describing implementation research as 'to a great extent ... misery research, a pathology of the social sciences, if you will' (1998: 62). The echo of the famous Pressman and Wildavsky subtitle about the frustration of expectations is obvious. Rothstein suggests that there are three problems embodied in that view of implementation research. The first is a tendency for research to focus on programmes that fail. The second is that even when that is not the case, there nevertheless tends to be an interest in programmes of considerable complexity with high ambitions in the face of limited knowledge. The third problem is that 'implementation research has taken an excessively mechanistic and rationalistic view of the process of implementation' (1998: 64).

Matland then suggests a need to focus on two factors that have a key impact upon implementation: ambiguity and conflict. These two concepts perhaps rather tend to interact, and can obviously be related back (as he acknowledges later in the essay) to issues about goal conflict. Nevertheless Matland is pointing us towards an important issue in separating different kinds of implementation studies. In particular, in treating ambiguity and conflict as intrinsic features of policy rather than as phenomena that good policy designers should try to eliminate, Matland gets away from a specific contradiction embedded in top-down recommendations. That contradiction entails that those who design policies are being urged to control the very things that they are least likely to be able to control, or perhaps want to control.

We will come back to Matland in Chapter 8 because he uses this argument to stress the importance of policy differences for implementation analysis. Where Matland has responded to the simplification problem with a theoretical model, Winter, in two reviews of this topic published in influential public policy and public administration handbooks, has adopted a more pragmatic response (2003, 2006). Winter argues that 'looking for *the* overall and one for all implementation theory' is a 'utopian' objective which is not feasible, and may even inhibit the creativity that comes from diversity (Winter, 2006: 158). He says therefore that we should look for partial rather than general implementation theories.

From that point of view, Winter sees implementation research as able to address concrete issues, of a kind that an obsession with all encompassing theories will tend to inhibit. He argues that there needs to be an emphasis on exploring the determinants of policy outputs: 'I suggest that we look for behavioural *output* variables to characterize the *performance* of implementers ... The first aim of implementation research then should be to explain variation in such performance' (ibid.).

Winter concedes that in some circumstances it may be possible to go on to the more difficult task of explaining outcomes. Crucial here is that he suggests no attempt is made to explore the much more slippery and contestable notion of goal-achievement. Goals are contestable and change over time. Work that focuses upon goals gets into questions about what 'the real goals' in a policy process are, and often gets tangled up with debates about what they should be. Variation in performance can be identified without engaging with these issues. This meets, in a pragmatic way, one of the points raised by network theory about the complexity introduced by the negotiation of goals.

Differentiating policy types

Looking for ways to be more specific about the 'concrete issues', Winter suggests Randall Ripley and Grace Franklin (1982) give particular attention to the relevance of policy type for the policy process. They classify policy types into:

- distributive
- competitive regulatory
- protective regulatory
- redistributive.

Many scholars have sought to develop policy typologies (see Parsons, 1995: 132–4). Ripley and Franklin's classification owes a great deal to earlier work by Lowi (1972), although it lacks one category: 'constituent policy' (concerned with the design of institutions) and it divides regulatory policy into two categories. The latter distinction is one between 'competitive regulatory' policies which 'limit the provision of specific goods and services to one or a few designated deliverers' (Ripley and Franklin, 1982: 72) as with the granting of airline routes or television channels, and 'protective regulatory' policies controlling potentially harmful activities. Essentially the classification is designed to help the elucidation of the factors that influence implementation success. The essential argument here is summarized in Table 4.1. Implicitly this suggests that under the question of whether some kinds of policy may be harder to implement than others lie issues of the probability of conflict and outside interference.

The actual classification used is open to challenge. The distributive/redistributive distinction implies, illogically, that distributive situations are ones in which the state gives without having to derive an income from someone or somewhere while, with redistributive ones, there are both winners and losers. Obviously this distinction really rests on the extent to which the losers can readily identify themselves; that is the extent to which the source of distributed resources is obscure. Significantly, Ripley and Franklin partly acknowledge this illogicality by indicating that they confine their redistributive concept to shifts of resources from advantaged to disadvantaged groups, while recognizing that the reverse does apply. They justify this in terms of ideological perceptions in the United States (we would want to say 'dominant ideology').

Table 4.1   Ripley and Franklin's exploration of the impact of policy type on implementation

Policy type	Likelihood of stable implementation routines	Degree of stability of actors and relationships	Degree of conflict over implementation	Degree of opposition to bureaucratic implementation decisions	Degree of ideology in debate over implementation	Degree of pressure for less government activity
Distributive	High	High	Low	Low	Low	Low
Competitive regulatory	Moderate	Low	Moderate	Moderate	Moderate to high	Moderate to high
Protective regulatory	Low	Low	High	High	High	High
Redistributive	Low	High	High	High	Very high	High

Source: adapted from Ripley and Franklin (1982), Table 8.1, p. 193.

The basis for the distinctions between the distribution and redistribution types on the one hand and regulation on the other can also be challenged on the grounds that regulatory activities also have winners and losers. Again as with the distributive/redistributive distinction, there is a presumption that Ripley and Franklin's classification is at times influenced more by what they want to say about implementation difficulty than by logic. 'Affirmative action', for instance, they give as an example of a redistributive policy rather than a 'regulatory policy'. Finally, it should be noted that it has been commented that in actual policies the various types are often mixed (Ingram and Schneider, 1990: 69). However, this is in many ways simply an extension of the earlier ground for criticism. Where the types are logically grounded, empirical variety could be handled.

Ripley and Franklin and others are raising important questions about the extent that policy type makes a difference, and connect this significantly to the extent to which an intense and conflictual 'implementation politics' is likely to emerge with some policies. Nevertheless there are grounds for questioning whether the typology they derive from Lowi is satisfactory for a systematic analysis of this issue. Rather what is needed is an examination of the relatives strengths of those who directly benefit from a policy, those who are disadvantaged by it as direct 'targets' and those 'third parties' for whom there will be indirect positive or negative effects (an approach to implementation analysis used by Knoepfel and his colleagues, 2007). Policy typologies do no more than help draw our attention to the identities of these parties.

Including responses of affected actors

The concern with policy characteristics also draws attention to 'the question of how different ways of organizing public administration affect the prospects for carrying out programs successfully' (Rothstein, 1998: 7). This shifts attention from policy characteristics *per se* to the fit between those characteristics and the approach adopted for implementation. Rothstein explores issues about the conditions under which policies may be designed to minimize implementation problems. This leads him to look at the issues of policy taxonomies, with in his case a particular concern to explicate those policies for which the simple 'universalist' targeted model for the delivery of public policies (particularly social benefits) can be argued to be the most appropriate. When this is not possible, he recognizes, as have most of the more modern implementation theorists, that admonishments to policy designers to have clear objectives and work with valid causal theories are often unrealistic. He notes that 'the state must take measures even when certain knowledge is not to be had' (ibid.: 75).

Hence Rothstein stresses that the best ways to organize policy implementation depend on 'the type of *task* the organization must carry out' (ibid.: 90). Here he is building on a substantial body of organization theory (particularly contingency theory; see Burns and Stalker, 1961; Woodward, 1965; Hickson et al., 1971; Greenwood et al., 1975). That formulation seems to assume that policymakers choose their own implementation organization framework. An alternative view is implicit in Exworthy and Powell's analysis of the needs for separate 'streams' to be connected in the implementation process (discussed above). Their empirical work is on policies where inter-organizational collaboration is needed where, they argue, separate organizational 'silos' inhibit effective action. Their observation may be generalized to suggest that there may be many ways in which there is a lack of fit between policy objectives and the organizational arrangements necessary to fulfil them.

Rothstein identifies as a central concern of the 'top-down' literature the notion of 'responsibility drift' (1998: 93) as policies are implemented in complex networks. He recognizes the Hjern solution of control through networks as vulnerable to leaving policies liable to capture by special interests. We have already noted Rothstein's preference for simple targeting. The issue here is: What should happen when this is impossible? What he sees as important in these cases is (like Lipsky, see pp. 51–3) the development of street-level accountability systems.

Rothstein's concern with implementation theory is largely prescriptive – in two senses. First, as noted earlier where his approach was likened to that of Lane, he aims to resolve the top-down/bottom-up argument about accountability. Rothstein does so by drawing attention to the multiplicity of ways policies may be legitimated. Second, he wants policy formulators to learn from implementation analysis that, where policies cannot be kept simple, attention must be given to the structuring of the relationship 'between the partially autonomous *producer* and *the citizen*' (1998: 115). In advancing these prescriptive arguments he draws our attention to some of the complexities in the accountability relationship that have to be addressed when we endeavour to describe and study the implementation process.

Conclusion

In this chapter we have explored the development of theoretical work on implementation since the top-down/bottom-up debate that so dominated discussions of implementation after Pressman and Wildavsky's seminal work. In a way, the array of insights gained since then still appears to have some of the characteristics of that fundamental debate. In conformity with the bottom-up perspective, some authors stress complexity. Others, however, aim for ways to achieve simplicity, echoing top-down control concerns. In the first edition of this book the development of implementation theory was explored by means of the examinations of the work of the key contributors, divided into sections using their names as headings. While still endeavouring to ensure that the key figures do not go unmentioned, this chapter has now been organized in terms of themes.

Considering it important to focus particularly upon the way in which there are issues running through the recent literature on implementation, we identified seven such themes. This range relates to the clusters of variables we presented in the first edition of this book as result of a systematic scan of articles. Apart from the search for a synthesis beyond the 'classic' dichotomy indicated above, we have identified issues of whether policy formation and implementation can be separated; of the interaction between levels in the policy process and politico-administrative layers; of the incorporation of networks; of a need to focus upon the management of implementation performance; of the ways in which policy content makes a difference, and of ways authors recognize varying stakes concerning a specific policy.

One theme running through the chapter is the extent to which authors are seeking to prescribe. Central to the top-down/bottom-up debate has been a difference of view, either about who should be in control or about how control should be achieved. With later writers it is possible to detect differences in the extent to which they want to develop an approach to the study of implementation, implying a stance in respect of that normative or prescriptive argument.

5

IMPLEMENTATION AND GOVERNANCE

Contents

Introduction

Some contemporary observers of social change speak of the 'fate of the state' (Van Creveld, 1996), 'phantom states' (Derrida, 1993) or even of the 'end of the nation state' (Ohmae, 1995). The 'information society' (Drucker, 1995) or 'network society' (Castells, 1996) has no ideological, institutional or political centre attributed to it. Guéhenno went one step further when he gave his book the title *La Fin de la Démocratie* (1993). Talking of postmodern politics, Smith sees a 'political system disorientated, deficient and out of sorts with itself' (1994: 137). An alternative is presented by some writers in the form of the rise of the 'virtual state' (Frissen, 1999; Rosecrance, 1999).

In the context of such 'postmodern' perspectives, a phenomenon like the implementation of public policy looks a bit out of date. If the flourishing period of the national state is over, is there still something like 'implementation' to be observed and studied? Do new forms of governance affect how we examine matters of implementation, and make them less or more relevant? These questions are central in this chapter. In order to position implementation theory and research in its societal context, the chapter's focus is on developments in both the practice and study of public administration after the Second World War. The first part of the chapter examines, side by side, what in the successive periods has happened in the real world and the academic responses to it. We aim to do justice to these responses, but, of course, complement them with an interpretation and judgement of our own. Under the heading of 'Assessment' in the second part of the chapter the linkages between the study of implementation and the practice of public administration are further explored.

Structure of the chapter

When one wants to give a historical account of a period of more than sixty years within a framework of one book chapter, a certain degree of subjectivity is unavoidable. Next to readability, however, proceeding systematically can be seen as a norm. Aiming at reconciling both, in the historical description given in the next sections we use the following leading questions, each referring to a dimension of the relations between the study of implementation and the practice of public administration. What is, societally, expected from government? What kind of ambitions does government have? And which issues are prevailing on the agenda of the study of public administration in the period concerned? The answers to these questions are given within a distinction between three phases. The first is identified as the era of great expectations from society, leading to a broad interventionist role practised by government (the 1950s, 1960s, 1970s; with its origins in the 1930s). The second was the period of both government retrenchment and government looking at itself as being a business corporation (the 1980s and 1990s). Then in the third, and current phase, it seems that governments in various countries have become aware of their own role again, and particularly of the special character of that. They are expressing this awareness in a selective (= neo-) interventionism.

In the following three sections, developments in the practice of public administration and implementation of public policy are sketched for each phase. The account of these cannot be comprehensive or universal in their coverage. Our focus is in particular upon developments in the United States, the United Kingdom and The Netherlands. This selection – obviously related to the locations of the authors – can be justified by the fact that it offers a valuable contrast, given the somewhat different system characteristics of the countries involved (see Esping-Andersen, 1990; Hupe and Meijs, 2000; Hall and Soskice, 2001). The descriptions of public administration in practice form the background for a sketch of developments in implementation theory and research that can be interpreted as characteristic of each phase. After these primarily descriptive sections, an overall assessment of the social history of the practice and study of public policy implementation is made. The chapter ends with some concluding remarks.

The age of interventionism

Great expectations, results perceived as disappointing: the 1930s to the 1980s

With his 'New Deal' the American President Franklin Roosevelt, in the early 1930s, offered policies to face the social consequences of a major economic crisis. Public works were undertaken, employment programmes were developed, social policy measures were enacted (Weir et al., 1988; Skocpol, 1995). It was in this period that many talented individuals sought to liberate American administration from the constraints of American politics (Schlesinger, 1960; Leuchtenburg, 1963). Government, in particular federal government, promoting social welfare, took on an active role. When the Second World War started, the high level of government activity stretched to sectors of society that were formerly seen as completely private. After the war, government expenditure declined for obvious reasons, but in the Truman and Eisenhower years the general confidence in the public sector remained relatively high (Reichard, 1988). In 1961, President Kennedy attracted 'the best and the brightest' to Washington to participate in federal government (Halberstam, 1972). Johnson, his successor, undertook his 'Great Society' project, aiming at the reduction of income and class inequalities. He declared a 'war on poverty' (Zarefsky, 1986).

As in the Depression in the 1930s, the Second World War led to efforts to liberate administration from the constraints of politics. In the war period, American society scarcely had to face the demands of total mobilization so desperately imposed upon the European nations. For Americans an understanding of the inefficiency of the governing system came perhaps even more from the anxieties of the 'cold war' (the fear that the Soviet Union would overtake them) and difficulties in Vietnam. It also came in a recognition for some that the war against poverty at home (which had not been fought very effectively by Roosevelt in the 1930s) needed to be fought more efficiently again in the 1960s and 1970s. It was explicitly out of this 'war' that implementation studies emerged.

Thanks to American Marshall Aid, Western European countries like The Netherlands were, after the Second World War, rapidly put on their feet again. In a material sense The Netherlands was rebuilt. Alongside financial aid, American influences were visible in the way the rebuilding took place. Industrialization, planning and consumption were key elements in the underlying thinking of policy-makers, which was explicitly macro-economic. A similar kind of 'thinking-from-the-top' was expressed in rural and urban planning. Despite the socio-cultural and political segmentation called 'pillarization' (Lijphart, 1975), all actors in the public domain accepted the necessity to 'roll up their sleeves' to reconstruct the country. The organized employers offered stable employment in exchange for moderated wage demands from employees, while both wanted government to invest in the physical and social infrastructure of the country. With differences along lines of religious denomination as far as specific variants were concerned, there was consensus about the need to extend social security into a comprehensive system. The steadily developing economic prosperity made such an extension possible, while the Keynesian axiom of keeping up purchasing power provided the rationale (Cox, 1989). The creation of a nationwide net of motorways, processes of suburbanization and the large-scale introduction of American household gadgets had direct consequences for the lifestyles of various social layers. From 1958 on there has been a rise in the number of middle- and lower-class students entering higher education (Schuyt and Taverne, 2000); a process that was called 'external democratization'. Many of these students fulfilled the demand of the ministries – increasing until deep into the 1970s – for academically trained civil servants to make public policies at the various domains of the extending 'Verzorgingsstaat' (zorg = care; verzorging = taking care of) (Van der Meer and Roborgh, 1993).

While the United Kingdom did not, like The Netherlands, suffer invasion, it experienced total mobilization in face of that threat. During the war it also began to prepare for peace. In particular, Beveridge set out the principles for what was generally seen as a decent social security system. After the war, while developments had much in common with those in The Netherlands, administrative change was less fundamental. Although the Labour government elected in 1945 saw a need to continue many of the approaches of wartime administration to effect social change after the war, it saw less need to change the way that government itself was organized. Despite the fact that the United Kingdom's role in the world was much changed, the fact that the country had not been occupied and that it was one of the victors perhaps made it reluctant to re-examine traditional approaches to public administration. In any case, the practice of public administration in the UK has traditionally been rather distinctive. Unlike the USA, with its strong Constitution, but also unlike continental Europe, public administration and government in the United Kingdom are linked within a framework of administrative law that is to a large extent not formalized. Referring to the values that have been attributed to the British civil service, Gray and Jenkins state that these

> represent an ideal and perhaps idealized world where the administrative practice is set in a traditional structure of parliamentary accountability. This almost Weberian model of administrative structures – hierarchical, neutral, salaried, pensioned and rule-bound – was perhaps not often analysed as such but was seen as an adequate and necessary model for the UK political system. (1995: 77)

Gray and Jenkins go on to observe that the practice of British public administration took place for a substantial period in a consensus regarding both the context of political–administrative relationships and its underlying basic values. Young speaks of the 'mandarin world of Whitehall, in which skepticism and rumination [are] more highly rated habits of mind than zeal or blind conviction' (1989: 155). Dunsire characterizes the values leading the practice as equity, justice, impartiality and conspicuous uprightness, with liberty and participation relegated to representative organs. He speaks of a 'paternalist, statist canon, with emphasis on collective action and faith in bureaucratic rationality and professional autonomy' (1995: 28).

In the 1960s and 1970s, challenges emerged to the 'gentlemen amateurs' in Westminster and Whitehall (Fulton Committee, 1968; Thomas, 1968), which led to incremental changes. Gray and Jenkins (1995) mention a focus on strategic planning in local government and the National Health Service, the introduction of rational techniques of budget reform and an increased emphasis on the strategic management of the public services. According to these authors, rather than questioning the fundamental links between political and administrative structures, the role of government and the value basis of the public service, these reform efforts remained within the accepted consensus. The reform objectives were not a smaller state, but better service delivery. Nevertheless, Gray and Jenkins observe in retrospect that 'the argument that the state was badly managed was common' (ibid.: 79).

Implementation research and social engagement

By the time the Second World War began, according to Kettl, the study of public administration in the USA had acquired 'remarkable prestige and self-confidence' (2000: 10). Many prominent public administration theorists came to Washington to help manage the war. Afterwards, in the light of the war experience, argues Kettl, such a simple administrative principle as the separation between administration and politics (see Chapter 2) seemed shallow. Some time after the war the rise of graduate programmes of public affairs at American universities could be observed. In these programmes the strict separation between politics and administration was replaced by a mixed focus.

Robert McNamara, Secretary of Defense in both the Kennedy and the Johnson administrations, invited the Rand Corporation to introduce the 'Program Planning Budgeting System' (PPBS) into his department. As a follow-up, this system was introduced by President Johnson into other departments as well. Thus a demand arose for what are called 'policy analysts': civil servants academically trained in the application of policy analysis techniques, and producing analyses for the formation of public policies. Harvard, transforming its Littauer School of Public Administration into the John F. Kennedy School of Government, was one of the first universities to offer a 'public policy program'. Berkeley, too, founded a 'Graduate School of Public Policy' (Kickert, 1996). 'Contrary to the traditional public administration more oriented as it has been towards the "nuts and bolts" of the practice of management in government, the new "public policy analysis" relies more on the "hard" analytical sciences' (Kickert, 1996: 130).

It was against this background that Pressman and Wildavsky in 1973 carried out their study *Implementation*. Curious about what had happened in Oakland to the good intentions expressed in Washington, these authors formulated a distinctive approach for what would be called implementation research (see

Chapter 3). As has been made clear above (Chapters 3 and 4), an ongoing stream of studies followed, growing into a scholarly field of its own. Whether there was – seen from 'the top' – disappointment about the outcomes of policy implementation or – observed at 'the bottom' – concern about the operational problems experienced in the implementation part of policy processes, normative and methodological stances were seldom treated as needing distinct identification and elaboration. At the same time, in either instance, the social engagement of the implementation researcher was often great.

The study of public administration in Great Britain, Rhodes states (1996b), has long been insular, dominated by an institutionalist tradition characterized by an interest in administrative engineering but a distaste for theory. Dunsire speaks of an 'old style of purely narrative-descriptive academic writing about public administration' (1995: 33). Hogwood points out the specific British feature that apart from the study of public administration there is the discipline of social administration or social policy. Before the rise of academic interest in public policy in the 1970s, there was already a substantial literature on social policy. Much of that was 'descriptive of current provisions or the development of each set of provisions, and often with an explicit or implicit normative support for the maintenance or further development of welfare provisions' (Hogwood, 1995: 60). Hogwood observes that, although there are older British examples of public policy studies, from the mid-1970s British authors begin to adapt or incorporate insights from American writers, and develop their own case studies (ibid.: 62). The impact of this, as far as the study of implementation is concerned, was the elaboration of British contributions to theory influenced both by the Americans and by developments in Germany and Sweden (the work of Hjern and of Scharpf, for example, discussed in Chapters 3 and 4). In Chapter 3, significant British contributions from both a 'top-down' and a bottom-up' perspective were examined (see the discussion of the work of Hogwood and Gunn pp. 49–50 and Barrett and Fudge pp. 54–5 respectively). One of the current authors was heavily involved in this British work (Barrett and Hill, 1981).

Nevertheless, in the United Kingdom, the links between the study of public policy and the practice of public administration did not become as close as they became in the late 1960s in the USA and, slightly later, in The Netherlands (Kickert and Van Vught, 1995). Although the study of public policy is institutionalized in public administration and political science studies, the interdisciplinary drive behind the policy orientation of the 1960s did not take hold in Britain (Hogwood, 1995: 70). Whitehall civil servants remained sceptical about formal policy analysis, stating that much of what they do is policy analysis in itself. At the same time training by social science academics of public servants particularly working in local government and the National Health Service fulfilled a demand for a policy focus. After all, the call for a more 'bottom-up' approach to implementation came from the School for Advanced Urban Studies at the University of Bristol, an academic unit heavily engaged in the study of *local* government. According to Hogwood (1995: 69), this can be no coincidence.

The age of the market and corporate government

Private versus public: the 1980s and the 1990s

There have been many attempts to explain the way public administration changed in the phase of government retrenchment that occurred in the 1980s and 1990s. It would be going well beyond the brief of the current book for us to attempt to add to them (for an overview, see Pollitt and Bouckaert, 2004). This development, usually labelled now as 'New Public Management', acquired in due course a more or less global character, and saw some of its most extreme manifestations in New Zealand. Its emergence, however, was seen initially as very much linked to two determined right-wing politicians, Margaret Thatcher and Ronald Reagan, acquiring power. Thatcher became Prime Minister of a Conservative government in Britain in 1979. Across the public sector, large structural changes were initiated: in central government, local government, the health service and the public utilities (Dunsire, 1995). The so-called 'Next Steps' agencies were established in central government. Dunsire describes them as involving 'the relatively wholesale adoption of structural separation of political responsibilities from executive responsibilities, the former remaining with ministers assisted by small 'policy' departments, the latter divested to new executive agencies each with its chief executive and required to produce mission statements and performance targets in a 'framework document' (1995: 24; see also Gains, 1999). Business methods were introduced into government, changing both external (privatization, contracting out) and internal relationships (performance measures). This created a 'genuine clash of cultures' between the world of Whitehall as described above and an 'almost Cromwellian impatience with the status quo' (Young, 1989: 155). Referring to the work of Fry (1984), Dunsire speaks of a 'gulf between the mandarins' rooted understanding that their job was to advise on policy; and the new Prime Minister's idea that their job was to execute policy and to manage their departments efficiently' (1995: 27).

Gray and Jenkins (1995) explain the drastic changes in the political agenda that took place in the United Kingdom in the 1980s in terms of the failure of the efforts to control the economy in the previous decade. The rejection of the old solutions for the management of the state was followed by a search for new methods of control, accompanied by a changing political ideology that broke with the existing consensus. In Gray and Jenkins' view, this focus on management and control, particularly of resources, also explains the political rejection of policy analysis in the mid-1970s. They observe: 'Faced with deepening crises of public expenditure the prime policy goal of government in the United Kingdom and elsewhere became the control of public finances' (1995: 87). In all parts of the public sector, at various levels and in different modes, changes accompanying the realization of this primary goal were initiated. Gray and Jenkins indicate that confronting the public sector with market concepts like costs, prices and performance measurement implied the creation of different relations of accountability and, in fact, power relations, at the expense, for instance, of professional groups. Not only were these new labels introduced into the vocabulary, but they also changed the practice of administration. Rhodes (1996b) speaks of an integrated and sustained attack on what was perceived as the 'failure' of traditional government and administration.

John Major, succeeding Margaret Thatcher in 1990, added new elements to the ideology and practice of corporate government when he stressed 'giving more power to the citizen'. With his 'Citizen's Charter' he aimed at setting standards for the quality of public service in terms of prompt action, delivery dates, courtesy, with the final possibility of an entitlement of citizens to compensation payments (HMSO, 1991). Referring to the work of Richards (1992), Dunsire (1995: 31) stresses the new patterns of legitimation that were being introduced here:

> Empowering the 'consumer' of public services creates new forms of controlling also the middle and lower ranks of public bureaucracy, while at the same time it disempowers the 'citizen' as participant in collective decision making at the macro-level. The Charters do not compensate for the loss of power by representative institutions, or the 'democratic deficit.'

Having been administrators during the period of the steady growth of public expenditure that gave birth to the modern welfare state, public servants in the 1980s and 1990s became 'managers'. Among other things this implied that a specific public task might be fulfilled via a contract: a system of 'management of outputs' emerged. The delivery of the public services became perceived as the production process of such outputs. What we call 'implementation' was thus taking place at a distance from a centre of government, even more invisible than it was for the directors of the former policy programmes. The difference was furthermore that the public 'administrator-turned-public-manager' now had a legitimation for not being interested in the internal process of implementation. It was only the results that counted. If the outputs deviated from what had been agreed upon, this had consequences for the contract and hence, in some cases, for the financing of the organization involved. 'Policy' and 'implementation' were being disconnected. The couplings, particularly in the form of contracts, were loose.

A year after Margaret Thatcher became British Prime Minister, Ronald Reagan won the American presidency. His predecessor, President Carter, had earlier declared war on Washington 'red tape' and created the President's Reorganization Project. It was a debacle (Wamsley, 1990a). In his first inaugural address President Reagan stated: 'In this present crisis, government is not the solution to our problems. Government is the problem' (20 January 1981). While it was more difficult to change the machinery of public administration in the United States than it was in Britain, the criticism of 'Big Government', articulated by the head of government himself, did not remain without effect. Although the material consequences in terms of (re-)privatization of government offices and services became visible slowly at a later stage – and perhaps with a more mixed character than hoped for by its originators – it seems less the effect on existing policies that was overwhelming than the influence on potential policies. It was especially the rhetorical side of the market ideology that was valued highly, both in politics and in administration. The breaking of a general post-war consensus gave room to forces aiming at 'reinventing government' (Osborne and Gaebler, 1992) in a rather fundamental way. Fundamental by effect, though simple in essence, the core of the retrenchment philosophy was that the mode of operation seen as usual for business corporations, and also the norms and values related to the private sector more generally, should similarly apply in the public sector. At all layers of government, and almost on a global scale, public officials embraced an 'away with us' attitude (Ringeling, 1993).

At the core of this development was the fact that government reduced its own service delivery capacity to a minimum and, instead, preferred contracting out operational activities. Milward and his collaborators observe that

> even though health and human services are funded by public agencies, the distribution of these funds is controlled and monitored by non-governmental third parties, who themselves determine which agencies to subcontract with for the actual provision of services. (1993: 310)

Just as in private businesses, the functions of the headquarters of an organization became primarily focused on retaining 'system integration skills' (Peters, 1990: 13). Milward (1996) describes the degree of separation between a government and the services it funds as a measure of the 'hollowness' of the state, indicated by the number of layers between the source and the use of funds to secure outputs. On various policy domains, on different layers of government and in numerous countries, similar examples of this 'hollowing out of the state' can now be observed.[1]

'Government is broken' remarked President Clinton after reading the eight hundred recommendations to improve federal government that were contained in Vice-President Gore's report *From Red Tape to Results: Creating a Government that Works Better and Costs Less* (Moe, 1994: 111). Clinton and Gore had launched the National Performance Review, in which Osborne's and Gaebler's (1992) conception of 'reinventing government' was adopted. The 'steering, not rowing' notion of Osborne and Gaebler led to the imperative to governments: Do the things you are good at. For you that means: Govern! And leave the operational side to others.

In The Netherlands comparable trends occurred. In national public administration a new axiom was embraced: 'the separation of policy and implementation'. It led to the reduction of the ministries to 'nuclear departments' responsible for 'agencies' that from there are 'steered at a distance'. Several implementation organizations that used to be directly subordinated to a certain ministry now perform a specific (financial, inspection or other) function for a number of ministries at a time, having gained in relative autonomy (see Kickert, 1998).

The latter phenomenon – the similarity to the British 'Next Steps' exercise may be noted – provides an example of the creation of new public–public steering relationships. The notion of hollowing out is appropriate here because the nucleus became smaller while the archipelago of agencies around it was extended. Relationships of chain-like hierarchy and control were replaced by contract relationships or, at least, acquired a mixed character. Nevertheless, many of the arrangements referred to by the term 'hollow state' in an American context were of a public–private nature. So-called third-party organizations created new layers between government and citizen or corporation. In countries with a (neo-)corporatist tradition like The Netherlands, traditionally there was an extended societal midfield between the state and the citizen, consisting of organizations of 'private initiative' stemming from various denominations, but fulfilling public tasks, while being to a large degree publicly funded (Dekker, 1998). In countries with a different tradition, such as the USA, hollowing out in some respects can imply the creation of a societal midfield with such a character. Kickert distinguishes three main ingredients of *public managerialism*: business-like management, client-orientedness and 'market-like' competition (1997: 732). As each of these three fit better or worse into different national systems, in the various countries they get a different degree of attention. Similarly the pace at which both the intended and unintended effects of the developments as pictured became visible varied from country to country.

Implementation research and shifting agendas

Gray and Jenkins (1995) trace the rise of public management in Britain as a threat to the study of public administration, starting as far back as the late 1960s and early 1970s (see discussion in Chapter 2). They observe that an orientation towards reform in the practice of public administration then was accompanied by academic efforts to place the study of it on a firmer theoretical footing; among other things, by the development of policy analysis and policy studies (Hogwood and Gunn, 1984; Hogwood, 1995). As indicated above, Whitehall remained sceptical about the adoption of policy analysis, while the beginning of the Thatcher era in 1979 meant a change in the political as well as academic agenda. Public management became the new theme (Flynn, 1993), while as 'new managerialism' it was also criticized (Pollitt, 1990). The intellectual sources used in academic work changed, too. Although in Britain the links between political science and public administration, on the one hand, and (organizational) sociology and social policy, on the other, had traditionally been stronger than, for instance, those with law, now (micro-)economic thinking (rational choice, principal–agent theory, and so on) became an important source. The principal embodiment of this is Dunleavy's influential *Democracy, Bureaucracy and Public Choice* (1991), offering a critique of mainstream public choice theory but showing how a more robust analysis of the private interests of public officials might be developed.

In the USA, similar developments took place. Under the heading of 'the new public management' (Hood and Jackson, 1991; Kettl, 2000) an approach was introduced both to the practice and to the study of American federal government that was substantially different from the more traditional public administration. In an assessment of the state of the field, Kettl, referring to the work of Thompson (1997: 3), sketches the elements that distinguished the new public management itself: 'It focused on management rather than social values; on efficiency rather than equity; on mid-level managers rather than elites; on generic approaches rather than tactics tailored to specifically *public* issues; on management rather than political science or sociology' (Kettl, 2000: 27). In a reinforcing relationship of causes and consequences, the penetration of the ideology of managerialism in Western democracies, hardly leaving any layer or policy domain untouched, was accompanied by changes in the way in which analysts of government and administration approached the object of their studies. After Waldo's *The Administrative State* (1948), some authors now speak of the 'increasingly organizational state' (Laumann and Knoke, 1987) or the 'entrepreneurial state' (for instance, Eisinger, 1988). British writers picked up this theme, writing of the 'contracting state' (Harden, 1992) or the 'managerial state' (for instance, Clarke and Newman, 1997).

We have shown in Chapters 3 and 4 how implementation studies mushroomed after the initial challenge thrown down by Pressman and Wildavsky. As O'Toole (2000a) observes, policy implementation moved from nowhere to a position of prominence in the 1970s and early 1980s. There was, as we have seen, a proliferation of studies that, in turn, brought

> an explosion in types of research designs, varieties of models, and – especially – proposals for adding a bewildering array of variables as part of the explanation for the implementation process and its products. The cornucopia of investigations catalyzed, in turn, a set of sectarian disputes: qualitative and small-*n* versus quantitative, large-*n* investigations; top-down versus bottom-up frameworks; policy-design versus policy-implementation emphasis, and so forth. Implementation was even seen by some worried students of traditional public administration as a theme posing a hegemonic threat to the field. (O'Toole, 2000a: 264)

Despite the emergence of new agendas it was exactly in the early 1980s that – as shown above – European scholars joined the implementation debate. Dunsire (1995) presumes that this was, relatively separated from the new agendas, a reaction to policy failures in the 1970s. However, there was a strong 'bottom-up emphasis' in much of this work. In a 'bottom-up' view, implementation becomes 'a kind of bargaining activity between the objectives of the keepers of organizational resources and the perceptions of need by street-level executants' (ibid.: 18). Although British studies of the implementation of public policies would continue to appear, after the bottom-up contributions, according to Dunsire, the 'theoretical urge apparently lessened'. He explains this as follows: 'Postulation of an "implementation gap" as the key to delivery failures may have suddenly seemed *de minimis* in face of the trumpeted claims of the New Right impugning the whole institutional structure of services' (ibid.: 19).

Furthermore, Dunsire points at the sociological rather than political science roots of the British bottom-up contributions. More generally, he suggests, the number of British scholars of public administration is relatively small, hence individuals, having made a contribution in one area of the discipline, may want to move on to something else.

Not only in Britain, however, was there, from the mid-1980s, a decline in the academic interest in theory and research on public policy implementation as a central scholarly theme and perhaps sub-discipline of political science and public administration. In the premier policy schools in the USA the scale of implementation research diminished (Lynn, 1996a). Implementation scholars like DeLeon (1999a) speak of the implementation literature as 'lacking in any consensual theory', consequently labelling implementation studies as an 'intellectual dead-end'. O'Toole (2000a) observes in retrospect that, indeed, the spate of scholarly research aimed explicitly at the implementation theme had abated.

The comments above are about a relative decline. Implementation studies come in many forms and within various disciplines; as now has been documented by Saetren (2005). The present chapter focuses on the relation between the practice and the study of public administration in historical perspective, and we will address the issue of the future of implementation studies in Chapter 9.

The age of neo-interventionism

Pragmatism: the 1990s

The Netherlands has been traditionally known for its struggle against the sea. That same sea enabled the Dutch to gain profits as a nation of merchants and traders. The 'Golden Age' of the seventeenth century produced not only the picturesque canal centre of Amsterdam, but also painters like Rembrandt and Vermeer (Schama, 1987; Israel, 1995). Later, painters like Van Gogh and Mondrian would add to the reputation of this small country on the North Sea. It would be in the 1990s that The Netherlands would attract attention for what has been called 'the polder model' and its related 'Dutch miracle' (see below).

Given the segmented character of Dutch society, divided into 'pillars' along lines of denomination, there has been a long-standing tradition of consensus-making. Because of the need for collective defence against the sea (see Daalder, 1966), because of the possibilities of trade (on the combination of the merchant and the cleric, see Ter Braak, 1931), or just because of the logic of class behaviour (Lijphart, 1975), the members of the Dutch elites – pillarized as they are – have long been accustomed to meet, deliberate and negotiate with each other (see also Hupe, 1993b). Usually the result of this give and take is a compromise acceptable to all the parties involved. In social and economic affairs this consensus-making has to a large extent been institutionalized. In the tripartite Social-Economic Council, founded in 1950, representatives of employers' organizations and employees' organizations regularly meet, together with independent experts appointed by the Crown. This Council, the highest organ of advice in governmental social and economic affairs, is the epitome of Dutch labour relations. As such, it is a symbol of the more general culture of consensus that is characteristic of Dutch society, the state and the relations between them (Hupe and Meijs, 2000).

Consultation, decentralization – in both its territorial and functional variants – and participation are key elements in the contemporary practice of Dutch public administration. Changes in the National Assistance Act, a cornerstone of the Dutch *Verzorgingsstaat*, imply major qualitative alterations in the relationships of the governmental and other actors involved in the delivery of this type of social services. In this context the metaphor of *overturned relationships* between national and local government is used, while one of us speaks about *implementation as partnership* on all levels of the delivery system of national assistance (Hupe, 1996). Particularly in the last decade direct participatory ways of public decision-making – complementary to indirect-procedural ways such as voting as practised in the formal system of representative democracy – have spread into other policy fields as well as that of social and economic policy. Under headings like 'interactive policy-making' the direct involvement of citizens, in one way or another, has become more or less standard practice (for overviews, see Pröpper and Steenbeek, 1999; Edelenbos and Monnikhof, 2001).[2]

Against this background, in 1982, an agreement was made regarding the offer of moderate wage demands of the organized employees, in exchange for employment offered by the employers' organizations, both enabling government to reconstruct government expenditures. The positive results of this agreement, in terms of cuts in public finance, economic growth and recovery of job growth, form the essence of what has been called 'the Dutch miracle' (Visser and Hemerijck, 1997). From 1982 Christian Democrat Ruud Lubbers has led three successive coalition cabinets. In the first two the Christian Democrats governed together with the Liberal Party, while the latter in the third cabinet in 1990 were succeeded by the Social Democrats. Wim Kok, then Minister of Finance, paid particular attention to the task of 'getting government spending sound'. He managed to do so without losing touch with his – social democratic – electorate. From 1994 to 2002, he chaired a coalition unprecedented in Dutch parliamentary history: a partnership between the Social Democratic and the two Liberal parties. In this so-called 'purple' cabinet (a mix of red and blue) the traditional opposition between 'labour' and 'capital' seemed to have been eliminated.

In Britain, the emergence of a more pragmatic approach after the replacement of Thatcher by Major was described by Dunsire as follows: '[T]he erosion of the public–private distinction, and towards purchasing rather than supplying, towards enabling "voluntary" and community provision rather than delivering services, toward harnessing self-policing associations rather than enforcing regulations ... and so on' (1995: 34). In Dunsire's view, there is a kind of inevitability in the shifts in social mood underlying these trends: from hierarchism to individualism, from both of these towards egalitarianism. Using the 'grid/group' cultural theory-framework (Thompson et al., 1990; Schwarz and Thompson, 1990),

Dunsire sketches an actual way of life marked by 'a critical rationality, by general loss of faith in politics, by loss of trust in "authorities", by the enhanced sensitivities behind the silly face of "political correctness", and by "Green" forms of global awareness' (1995: 33). These cultural shifts imply a need for 'more complex, subtle conceptions of control' in which management 'has to be conceptually divorced from its residual associations with hierarchical authority' (Bellamy and Taylor, 1992: 39). In that respect, Dunsire sees the trends he observes not so much as the outcome of Thatcherite policies but of these deeper, one could say sociological and almost universal, socio-cultural changes. He observes a shift in attention away from linear processes 'from policy to bureaucratic action', towards the 'methods and outcomes of purposive social control eschewing the primary use of either coercive regulation or an extensive public sector'. Hence he argues that governments, regardless of their political 'colour', will be

> likely to search more for indirect administration-saving ways of discharging their inalienable duty to guard against external threat and internal disruption, and of achieving their electorally legitimated policy programmes; the outcome may be described as 'governance' rather than 'government'. (Dunsire, 1995: 34)

In the 1990s, progressives took office as government leaders in various Western countries; either chairing a one-party government like Blair in the UK and Clinton in the USA, or as Prime Minister of a coalition cabinet, like Schröder in Germany, Jospin in France and Verhofstadt in Belgium. The former two in particular took an interest in the Dutch *'polder model'*. They saw it as an example of the 'third way' they were aiming for in their respective countries (Giddens, 1998).

The approach of the Blair government in Britain was to embrace the administrative changes of the Thatcher/Major era inasmuch as they were believed to deliver good public services, but to reject the dogmatic commitment to privatization that had characterized much of the approach of their predecessors. Two typical developments were the response to the 'private finance initiative' and the replacement of compulsory competitive tendering by best value.

In the former case, Labour had been expected to reject the Conservative policy of encouraging private investment in public services, particularly the scheme under which new hospitals were developed on that basis. In practice, the government merely reshaped the scheme under a new name of 'public–private partnerships', arguing that what is important is to get new resources into the public sector in a context in which there are constraints upon public borrowing (stemming from macro-economic policy).

In the latter case, the 'best value' policy for local government is described as follows:

> Best value will be a duty to deliver services to clear standards – covering both cost and quality – by the most effective, economic and efficient means available. In carrying out this duty local authorities will be accountable to local people and have a responsibility to central government in its role as representative of the broader national interest. Local authorities will set those standards – covering both cost and quality – for all

the services for which they are responsible. But in those areas such as education and social services where the Government has key responsibilities and commitments, the Government itself will set national standards. (Department of the Environment, Transport and the Regions, 1998, para 7.2)

The 1999 Local Government Act imposes this duty on all local authorities except parish councils. The process started in 2000. Local authorities are required to establish the following for all their services:

- specific objectives and performance measures;
- a programme of fundamental performance reviews; and
- local performance plans.

Their efforts to secure 'best value' are required to be very much in the public domain. In addition to general public scrutiny, the government itself strengthened the system of auditing and inspection. Hence there is a system of reporting back to central government, which has given itself powers to intervene if the evidence suggests what it regards as below-standard services.

Focused action from the centre: the 2000s

On 11 September, 2001, terrorist pilots drilled two airplanes filled with regular passengers into the Twin Towers of the World Trade Center in New York. In a parallel action the Pentagon in Washington was attacked, while a simultaneous third attack was avoided. These assaults shocked the entire world. Since that date other non-war zones on the globe have suffered major terrorist bomb attacks, causing many civilian casualties, as well. According to various commentators, the world since then has not been the same. The Administration of George W. Bush legitimated the American military invasion of Iraq, supported by several allies, as a direct way to deal with global terrorist threat. What now is called 'homeland security' has been put high on the agenda in the USA, with more than only institutional consequences. International cooperation between intelligence organizations has been enhanced. Almost everywhere in the Western world travellers, commuters, and others in the public domain daily experience the concrete measures for enlarging security that have been taken – and not only there.

Empirical evidence in the form of a comprehensive overview is not available. Nevertheless, the supposition seems justified that on policy domains more or less directly related with national security, government since 9/11 in many countries has adopted a straightforwardly 'top-down' role again. In some aspects this role of the modern state may be more hierarchical than it ever was, even in the age of interventionism. Observers locate the flourishing times of postmodernity between the fall of the Berlin Wall in 1989 and the attacks on the Twin Towers in 2001 (Hofland, 2005). With that assertion they refer to the period of 12 years in which the ideological 'victory' of democratic liberalism proclaimed by authors like Fukuyama (1992) seemed universal. At least, the hegemony of that ideology seemed unchallenged. In fact, this claim appeared to function as a self fulfilling, or rather self-denying, prophecy. The sudden terrorist assaults mentioned made an end to the assumptions underlying the claim, forcing governments to appropriate action aimed at national security. A difference, however, with the character of government action in earlier times is that here a selective and focused, rather than general, interventionism is at stake.

In the present era that can be called 'post-postmodern', the unlimited embrace of the ideology of 'the market', and the unqualified self-identification of governments to be run like business corporations *tout court*, indeed seem over. Rather, perhaps because having been confronted with the adverse consequences of that ideology, governments seem to have become aware of their special role in the public domain (again).

Gray portrays this ideological change as one from neo-liberalism to 'neo-conservatism'. He describes the neo-conservative discourse as, in the United States, linking the 'powerful utopian current in Enlightenment thinking ... with the Christian fundamentalist faith that evil can be defeated' (2007: 33). While Gray, among others, emphasizes the impact of this thinking upon foreign policy, its implication for domestic policy is the acceptance of the view that governments can be active change agents. This is seen particularly in the UK where he describes former Prime Minister Blair as 'An American Neo-Conservative in 10 Downing Street' (ibid.: 95). Gray comments then:

> Unlike neo-liberals, neo-conservatives do not aim to return to an imaginary era of minimum government. They perceive that the social effects of free markets are not all benign and look to government to promote the virtues the free market neglects. (ibid.: 95)

Gray goes on to give Blair's stance on law and order as an example, and stresses the strong moralism in Blair's approach to public policy. Both Blair and Brown, his successor, show a continuing eagerness to intervene to tell the public how they should behave and to use public policy to try to influence this. In this context it is worthwhile noting that in a country like The Netherlands the current cabinet coalition consists of the Christian Democratic Party, the Labour Party and the Christian Union, a party representing orthodox Protestants. This 'Christian social' government pursues a reform agenda explicitly focused on enhancing traditional family values, strict law enforcement, and similar issues. Although the political-administrative systems of The Netherlands and the UK clearly have different characteristics, the recent shifts in political-ideological discourse in both countries appear to show convergent tendencies.

The scope of this *neo-interventionist* government role varies. In some cases it not only entails national security aspects of domestic policies, but the very nature of foreign policy as such, while the character of the interventionism goes beyond national boundaries. On the other hand, governments may pursue a new kind of interventionist approach on policy domains less related to national security, than to a wish to combine modernizing the Welfare State with enhancing 'pre-welfare' values. In several countries, for instance, via institutional reforms of the social security system, government recently has adopted a more 'activist' approach in leading benefit applicants towards jobs. In countries varying qua *welfare state regime* as much as the USA and The Netherlands (Esping-Andersen, 1990), similar policy initiatives aimed at getting citizens 'from welfare to work' can be observed. These initiatives can be seen as focused efforts of governments to bring the dynamics of supply and demand up to date with contemporary labour market requisites, criteria for public expenditures, and views on what a modern Welfare State may ask from its citizens in terms of rights and duties (see, for instance, Riccucci, 2005).

Implementation research and governance

Goggin and his colleagues see implementation studies as consisting of three generations. The first generation described single cases; in the second generation, analytical frameworks were developed; while scholars of the third generation, like themselves, aim at explaining variation. They argued: 'Clearly, the challenge for the next generation of scholarship is to develop and test explanatory and predictive implementation theories of the middle range' (Goggin et al., 1990: 15). Writing in 1998, Lester and Goggin seemed to have remained optimistic when they spoke of a 'rediscovery of implementation studies', wanting 'to stimulate a renaissance of interest in policy implementation research' (1998: 2). Earlier, Lester and his colleagues observed that the '"critical" variables have not been identified' (Lester et al., 1987: 200).

Kettl (2000), in his assessment of the state of the field of public administration around the beginning of the third millennium, develops an argument relevant to the study of implementation. He stresses the importance of the political culture present in a specific political system as far as susceptibility to a specific ideology of reform is concerned. Speaking about the USA, Kettl focuses on the various political norms and policy expectations implied by four different political traditions: Hamiltonian, Jeffersonian, Wilsonian and Madisonian. The essence of these different political traditions can be summarized as follows. Wilson's politics/administration dichotomy is relatively well known; Hamilton sought a strong and effective executive branch; in the Madisonian tradition the principle of balance of power is central; while in the Jeffersonian one there is a strong commitment to a small government protecting individual autonomy. On the basis of this variety, Kettl constructs a typology of administrative ideas, using the Wilsonian (hierarchical) and Madisonian (balance of power) political traditions on one dimension, against the Hamiltonian (strong executive/top-down) and Jeffersonian (weak executive/bottom-up) traditions on the other (ibid.: 17).

Kettl acknowledges that the new public management frames three important issues for American public administration. With its focus on a strong top-down executive, this reform ideology fits the Hamiltonian tradition. At the same time, in its separation between management and policy functions it is more Wilsonian than Hamiltonian, Kettl observes. Next, what President Clinton aimed at with his National Performance Review Kettl sees, on the one hand, particularly as far as reducing government's basic jobs is concerned, as less sweeping, but, on the other, as more ambitious than the new public management. With regard to the latter, Kettl refers to the incorporation of outcome-based measures and customer service standards for all government programmes (ibid.: 27). Furthermore, although the National Performance Review has been heavily influenced by New Public Management thinking, Kettl stresses its particular character based on the specificity of American institutions and political traditions. Kettl draws some conclusions about American public administration. First, it follows the political norms and policy expectations embedded in a specific political culture. Reform ideologies such as 'Westminster new public management', as Kettl calls it (ibid.: 28), do not fit the patterns of American political traditions. Therefore they either are ignored or must be tailored to fit the American system. Second, the values and norms of the various political traditions inevitably conflict.

Kettl explores three questions, fundamental for the field of public administration, upon which the new public management has cast fresh light:

1   What should replace the field's reliance on hierarchy (ibid.: 28)? Gradually hierarchy's theoretical preeminence has slipped. Instead of having evaporated, hierarchy continues, however, 'to describe how most complex organizations organize themselves and how elected officials think about holding government bureaucracies accountable' (ibid.: 28–9). Kettl regards organizational theories of networks and political theories of governance as promising here, because they offer possibilities, both empirical and normative, to incorporate the continued importance of hierarchical authority into broader models of public administration.

2   What should be the field's approach to the policy/administration dichotomy (ibid.: 29)? Kettl observes that, while since the 1950s policy decisions and administrative action have been mainly seen as seamlessly connected, the new public management reformers, aiming at the promotion of efficiency, have resurrected this dichotomy.[3] In the new public management theory the 'principal' hires 'agents' to perform the government's work. Contracts concern expected results; flexibility is given with regard to how to achieve them. 'The practice, however rapidly it is spreading, raises all the knotty questions about political accountability and administrative effectiveness that traditionally have needled public administration theory' (ibid.: 29).

3   There has long been criticism of public administration for a lack of rigour in theory and research, Kettl observes. How can this discipline advance the state of theory, ensuring the systematic testing of its theoretical propositions? For Kettl, game theory and statistical analysis are particularly relevant here.

Kettl concludes that these three questions 'shape the core puzzles in American public administration' (ibid.: 30). The differentiated ways in which public administration and political culture are related can explain many of the conflicts among scholars with competing theories, for because of its relation to a specific political tradition, after all, 'every theoretical proposition is also implicitly a political argument' (ibid.: 30).

For the sub-discipline of public policy implementation theory and research O'Toole (2000a) undertook an exercise similar to that carried out by Kettl for the field of public administration as a whole. In his assessment of the state of implementation research, his point of departure is that the practical world is now just as much in need of valid knowledge about policy implementation as it has ever been. If scholarship has not simply solved the problem, what has happened? Where has all the policy implementation gone, or at least the scholarly signs of it (ibid.: 265)? O'Toole's answer at the time was that the evidence was mixed.[4]

When Kettl makes his observations about the state of public administration, it is obvious that he is looking at the subject in the context of the specific American political-administrative setting and culture. Nevertheless, his argument has wider implications. Among British authors a further development of the field can also be observed. The shift in British work away from public administration to public management in the 1980s has already been noted. In the 1990s, however, the small number of British scholars in this field readily returned to a pragmatic stance that recognized the wide range of approaches to their subject. Christopher Hood's *The Art of the State* (1998) provides both an expression of that stance and a useful exploration of relevant ideas. He argues that 'variation in ideas about how to organize public services is a central and recurrent theme in public management' (ibid.: 6). He suggests that grid/group cultural theory (Douglas, 1982; Thompson, et al., 1990) can be used to encapsulate these different ideas. Here 'grid' refers to alternatives that public organizations should be constrained or, by contrast, that managers should be 'free to manage' (Hood, 1998: 8). 'Group', on the other hand, refers to debates about who should provide services. Hence Hood arrives at four 'styles of public management':

- High 'grid'/low 'group' – 'the fatalist way' where rule-bound systems are developed and low levels of co-operation are expected.
- High 'grid'/high 'group' – 'the hierarchist way' involving socially cohesive rule-bound systems.
- Low 'grid'/low 'group' – 'the individualist way' involving a high emphasis on negotiation and bargaining.
- Low 'grid'/high 'group' – 'the egalitarian way' with high participation expected. (1998: 9)

Hood argues that these four approaches represent choices, each with built-in strengths and weaknesses. Then, in a way that is consonant with the logic of his argument but perhaps surprising in relation to what may be observed in the real world, he argues that any balance between them 'is likely to be problematic and precarious because each of the approaches involves an underlying logic which, if taken to its limits, will tend to destroy all the others' (ibid.: 209). Hence Hood seems to be acknowledging contemporary diversity yet doubting that it can be sustained, a curious position perhaps qualified a little by the parenthetical comment 'if taken to its limits'. As far as the consideration of implementation this offers an approach to the various models considered for its control.

In 1995, Hogwood observed that within British political science and public administration in general, the quantitative analysis of policy was underdeveloped. He admits that much of (then) contemporary implementation literature was concerned with 'refinement, refutation, and the construction of artificial debates' (Hogwood, 1995: 70). In the second half of the 1990s, British interest in implementation theory seemed to have declined seriously. One of the few reviews of the topic was published by one of us, asking whether it was 'yesterday's issue'. It noted that

> the 1980s and 1990s saw the emergence of an approach to the policy/implementation process in which the 'top' (and particularly the politicians) have sought to inculcate dramatic value shifts at the lower level through institutional changes particularly directed at changing incentive structures. It has been prepared to carry these through rapidly and without experiment at the outset, apparently not worrying much about the way in which these changes might actually impact upon practice, but has then moved in with a variety of devices to try to control the behaviour of the implementers'. (Hill, 1997: 383)

The article went on to assert the continuing importance of implementation studies so long as it was noted 'how slippery the concept of implementation is' and 'the strong normative elements in the implementation debate' were recognized. Hence, it ended:

> If we want to have a debate about accountability by all means let us have one – after all the issues about the need for new approaches to public accountability are of enormous importance – but let us not confuse attempts to analyse how policies are put into practice with that debate. If we want to do the latter let us take our methodological lead from the organizational sociologists who have argued that an analysis of sources of power and influence must avoid either privileging or demonizing particular sources of that power and does not therefore require the prescription of a correct starting point, at the top or bottom. (ibid.: 383)

In this perspective it is relevant to notice, for instance, that in the 1990s the UK Economic and Social Research Council financially enabled a series of seminars organized from management schools of the Universities of Aston and Cambridge on the very subject of public policy implementation. In the UK, the political concerns about 'what works' (Davies et al., 2000) and about so-called 'joined up' government (Newman, 2001) have kept this theme alive. This seems particularly so in the field of social policy, where issues regarding the implementation of health and social care for adults and children are very much on the agenda.

What, in any case, does seem to have increased since the self-proclaimed first 'third generation' study of Goggin et al. (1990) is the consciousness of the multidimensional character of the object of implementation theory and research. In a way, and perhaps reinforced by those authors' endorsement of the use of multiple measures and multiple methods, their programmatic stance has been working as an 'intimidating standard', as O'Toole acknowledges. Yet, in the end, O'Toole views the glass as half full: 'There is more than meets the eye.' 'A considerable quantity of provocative, well-conceived, and well-executed recent scholarship bears quite directly on salient issues of policy implementation, even if not explicitly and obviously framed in such terms' (2000a: 265). O'Toole's major message is that nowadays one can see more 'implementation research' when one looks *beyond* investigations with a self-proclaimed focus on implementation. He refers here to Meier (1999: 6–7):

> My biased survey of literature suggest[s] that a wide range of journals publish articles that inform the study of policy implementation – the mainstream sociology journals, most of the public administration journals, the professions journals (public health, social work, sometimes law or medicine), many of the economics journals, and on rare occasion a political science journal. Much of this literature is not intended to directly answer questions of policy implementation, but it addresses concerns that are central to policy implementation.

O'Toole, however, distinguishes four indirect contributions to implementation research coming from outside implementation studies but from within political science and public administration: formal and deductive approaches; institutional analysis and development; networks and network management; and the study of governance. The latter three themes are seen by Frederickson (1999) as having infused the subject of public administration more generally, while it may be noticed that the latter two themes are recognized as promising by Kettl, too, in his assessment of the field of public administration. Both networks and governance therefore justify closer attention here. Kettl observes that particularly since the Second World War much governance has involved 'heavy and increasing use of multi-organizational teams and partnerships with non-governmental tools' (2000: 23). In Kettl's view, network theory (see the discussion in Chapter 4 of this book, pp. 67–8) has provided a framework for 'understanding the growing interconnections among varied organizations that find themselves working together to implement public policy' (2000: 24). This framework has helped public administration 'escape the pathologies of theory deeply rooted in hierarchical authority' (ibid.: 24), bringing theory closer to administrative practice. This has led to new approaches to co-ordination. Besides, according to Kettl, network theory has helped to provide the foundation for linking the study of governance with an understanding of the workings of government. Referring to the work of Frederickson, Kettl sees this last contribution as the most important one, because network theory provides the connection 'to the big issues of democratic government. It is in governance theory that public administration wrestles with problems of representation, political control of bureaucracy and the democratic legitimacy of institutions and networks in the time of the fragmented and disarticulated state' (Frederickson, 1999: 19).

What is attractive about the contemporary use of the concept of governance is its broad scope. Moving away from a concentration on government as a locus, using this concept as a focus draws attention to relevant forms of action aimed at governing that were not looked at as such before. These actions are practised by government, but also by corporate and non-profit actors. Irrespective of contexts, in principle they all, in their own way, fulfil public tasks in the overarching public domain. Away from a merely hierarchical perspective on the exercise of authority, the concept of governance opens up a view of a more 'horizontalist' way of governing. What is particularly relevant here is that the concept provides a different, but continued, focus on implementation. At the same time, however, this broadness is problematical, for both research and practice. Instead of reducing the number of variables seen as relevant for the explanation of implementation behaviour, implementation processes, policy outputs or policy outcomes, it seems to increase that number. As O'Toole observes: '[T]he variety of arrangements embraced by the governance notion defies parsimonious theory building' (2000a: 279). So, under the governance heading the 'too many variables' problem (see p. 73 above) re-emerges. In the practice of public administration the container character of the governance concept may mislead policy-makers. In our view, however, it all depends on the meaning given to this term. Against the background of the five types of use we distinguished in Chapter 1, we think that the term governance, indeed, stands for something substantively new. We will provide arguments for this contention below.

Assessment

Although the objective is not causal explanation here, there is a need to interpret and understand what we have found so far. As in the entire chapter, moving to and fro between the study of public administration, in particular implementation, and the practice of public administration sheds light on relevant linkages. Distinguishing between three phases in the previous sections we looked at common patterns from a macro-perspective. Under general umbrellas like 'interventionism', however, at the micro-level of single actors much differentiation can be observed. This seems valid for the study as well as the practice of public administration.

Differentiation in the practice of public administration

On 13 May 2000, in Enschede, a middle-sized city in the eastern part of The Netherlands, a fireworks factory exploded. Twenty-two people were killed and 600 were wounded. Because the factory was located in the heart of the city, in a densely populated district, hundreds of houses were completely destroyed (*NRC Handelsblad,* 10 May 2001). This disaster shocked the entire country. How could this have happened? Moreover, which officials had tolerated the location of a fireworks factory in the centre of the city? The former National Ombudsman led a major investigation. His conclusion was that the management of the factory was primarily responsible for the disaster, but immediately in connection to that, all government officials along the administrative chain from the local authorities, via the Army, to the Ministry of Environmental Affairs were to blame. The former Ombudsman called for a 'cultural revolution' in government, implying that, on any administrative layer, rules need to be enforced and responsibilities taken. Although the Mayor remained in office, the two aldermen most responsible for the permits given to the director of the company resigned. As a consequence the Cabinet took a set of measures aimed at the stricter compliance with the regulations concerned, both by local government and private actors.

In our view, this case can be seen as an illustration of three phenomena. First, the characterization of a certain time frame under a single heading may indicate the prevalence or fashionable status of a specific notion, but cannot be equated with or predict the actual behaviour of public actors A and B in situation X or Y. Within a deeply vested administrative culture of pragmatic 'wheeling and dealing', and in a period characterized above as the age of the market and corporate government, disasters like the explosion in Enschede – there was a major fire in a crowded bar in Volendam, as well – in The Netherlands led to pleas for 'strong government', as well as to corresponding actual manifestations of it. This 'new normativism', manifested at the political level, seemed a reaction to what may be perceived as the ultimate consequences of a pragmatic public-administrative practice, mixed with corporate elements. Second, and paraphrasing Kingdon ([1984] 1995), it can be argued that once too many adverse consequences of the introduction of a new public-administrative ideology have become apparent in practice, the opening of a potential 'window' on the reception of a succeeding new ideology is set. Third, Beck's (1992) notion of the 'risk society' seems valid here. Although this is not the place for a long discussion of risk theory, the reactions indicated above seem to provide evidence for a governmental pre-occupation with 'management of risk'.[5]

While Britain, as we saw, was prominent and early in embracing a comprehensive market ideology in the 1980s, later one could observe the succession of that ideology by a more pragmatic 'It does not matter how, as long as it works' orientation. It is illustrated by the 'best value' approach to surveillance over local government outlined on pp. 93–4. However much, on a comparative scale, they may seem to be doctrines of administrative reform showing certain similarities, they are implemented with specific accents, at a varying pace, into political and cultural environments that may fundamentally differ. What seems to remain, however, becoming apparent in cases of fiascoes, crises and disasters, is the public need to find answers to two questions: 'What went wrong?' and: 'Who is responsible?' The consequence seems to be a context-bound but continuing attention to a 'hierarchical' mode of governance.

Differentiation in the study of public administration

In the three sections following the introduction of this chapter we used labels to characterize historical phases in the relation between the practice and study of public administration. Concerning the latter, too, behind these generic labels a certain differentiation can be assumed. When we particularly look at individual implementation researchers, to what extent does the given characterization in phases apply? Evaluating the 'evolution of implementation studies', Lester and Goggin (1998) position the various implementation scholars within a typology. Their dimensions are:

- whether a specific scholar is positive (or not) about the continuation of implementation studies; and
- whether he or she advocates (or not) the modification of the conceptual or methodological approaches used in those studies.

On the basis of this typology, Lester and Goggin distinguish the following types of scholars: 'reformers', 'testers', 'sceptics' and 'terminators'. Inspired by Lester and Goggin's effort, but aware of the limits of classification, we can explore developments in the field of implementation research within their societal context. The questions set out at the beginning of this chapter concerned the relevance of implementation theory and research and the possible changes in that relevance, given certain developments in state and society. Therefore it may be useful to distinguish between, on the one hand, the scientific and, on the other, the normative or political orientation that the various implementation scholars express in their work. On the scientific dimension they may be distinguished in terms of their particular epistemological stance, between, at one end of the continuum, a more positivist one and, at the other, a more interpretative/hermeneutic one. On the political or normative dimension authors vary in the extent to which they favour the procedural, indirect, form of democracy called representative democracy, or the alternative, participation-oriented, more material and direct forms of democracy, called deliberative or discursive democracy (Dryzek, 1990; Elster, 1998). When a study of the implementation of a specific policy is aiming to explain an 'implementation gap', its normative stance may be characterized as one in favour of representative democracy. Depending on the stated research objective and some related elements to be taken into account, the epistemological stance may be called positivist here.

Thus a variety of leading perspectives in implementation theory and research is distinguished in Table 5.1. Operationalization of the dimensions of this typology makes it possible to position any specific implementation study within it. Although this is not the place to carry out such a bibliometrical exercise, we can facilitate it by giving some illustrative examples. Studies like Pressman and Wildavsky's *Implementation* and much of the early work by Sabatier have, at least, one feature in common. They may be characterized as being written from a combination of amazement about what is happening with the good intentions

Table 5.1   Leading perspectives in implementation theory and research

	Epistemological stance	
Stance on democracy	Positivist	Interpretative
Representative democracy	'Reform'	'Description'
Deliberative democracy	'Criticism'	'Activism'

formulated in a public policy and a drive to contribute to improvement by producing knowledge of the facts: the 'reform' perspective. We see a similar preoccupation in the more recent work on mandates (see Chapter 7, p. 41). Contrastingly, an 'activist' challenging of 'top-down' policy-makers can be observed behind the statement that 'the policy–action relationship needs to be considered in a political context and as an interactive and negotiative process, taking place over time, between those seeking to put policy into effect and those upon whom action depends' (Barrett and Fudge, 1981a: 29; see the discussion of their work in Chapter 3, pp. 54–5). A similar stance can be noticed in Hanf and Scharpf's (1978) plea to look at the world – perceived as being inter-organizational – fundamentally in a 'horizontal' rather than hierarchical way (see the discussion in Chapter 4, pp. 67–8). It was noted in Chapter 3 that while Lipsky's seminal work on street-level bureaucracy has sometimes been taken for a demonstration of 'bureaucrat bashing', the book should be read as its opposite: a, finally political, charge against high-ranking policy-makers who from 'top-floor suites' impose financial cuts on lower-level functionaries and for the rest leave them alone in their 'crowded offices' (1980: xii). His book therefore can be seen as emblematic of the 'criticism' perspective. Later, the perspectives of 'criticism' and 'activism' seem to be continued in the work of some public policy scholars. As we showed in Chapter 2, rather than focusing upon high-ranking government officials, the focus in some of those publications is on citizens or public servants and their participation in processes of (self-) governing (compare Stivers, 1994). Other contemporary studies imply, for instance, a critical analysis of administrative language (see Yanow, 1993, 1996).

Many implementation studies still focus upon a single policy process, in a mainly descriptive way. Sometimes the authors are explicitly aiming to explain what is perceived as a policy or implementation 'failure', although both their epistemological and normative stances may vary. These descriptive-explanatory kinds of studies still form the most numerous category of studies (see O'Toole, 1986; Saetren, 2005); they can be called the mainstream of implementation theory and research and may be located right in the middle of the typology. Ahead of that stream there are contributions deliberately designed to accumulate knowledge, deducting hypotheses and performing empirical research in as systematic a way as possible. In a small number of cases, notably those in which Laurence O'Toole and Kenneth Meier have been involved (see p. 203), hypotheses are tested on large aggregates of data, with the use of formal models. The epistemological stance in those cases is clearly positivist (in any variant) here, while the normative stance – almost by definition, because of the theory-driven aim of testing – remains unarticulated and just implied. It is, however, rather explicit in the stress in much public management literature on the need to contribute to ways of 'managing' implementation better.

The policy-implementation paradigm and beyond

The typology presented here does not say anything about the relative importance of the various types, neither in terms of, for instance, explanatory value – a scientific dimension; nor in terms of use in the public domain – a societal dimension. However, in this chapter it has been suggested that links can be made between the study and practice of public policy implementation. Our assumption is that such patterns can only be found if the developments in both worlds are observed in relation to each other. Therefore, we go back again to try to identify patterns, but now on a level between, on the one hand, the general characterization in historical phases we gave, and, on the other, the differentiation we observed at the level of concrete situations in the practice of public administration or singular implementation researchers. For that purpose Kuhn's conception of a 'paradigm' (1970), in amended form, may be helpful.

Kuhn argues that if, in a certain domain of science, the practice of theory and research for a certain period is guided by a legitimate and more or less coherent set of problems and methods, this practice can be called 'normal science', while the set can be labelled as a specific 'paradigm'. Scientific progress is made when that particular set of problems and methods is changed and one paradigm is succeeded by another; then a paradigm shift takes place. A paradigm functions as a kind of 'glue' between the members of a community of researchers – and here we would add practitioners – in a certain field, who share a set of values, conceptions and views on issues central to that field.

When raising the question whether there is or has been something like an 'implementation paradigm', we specifically refer to the more or less coherent and in a certain period legitimate set of problems and solutions connected with turning public policies into actions, as perceived by both practitioners and analysts of implementation. A paradigm shift, then, would mean that the legitimacy and coherence of such a specific set at a specific time seem to have diminished in favour of other sets of problems and solutions. In order to be able to make such observations with an eye on the future, it may be appropriate to go back to the developments sketched above, and focus more closely on the ways in which sets of problems and solutions related with turning public policies into actions, successively have been leading the study of public administration. Doing so, it goes without saying that we may overlook aspects of the kind of differentiation we addressed in the two previous subsections. The gain, however, is that we thus may be better able to position the rise and decline of scholarly attention to public policy implementation.

Looking at the development of the study of public administration, Dunsire states: 'Having been "public administration" in the 1970s, and become "public policy and management" in the 1980s, the name of the discipline may well become "governance" in the 1990s' (1995: 34). Analyzing theory–practice links in the evolution of public management and public administration, Gray and Jenkins relativize the 'numerous claims of a paradigm shift [that] have been made' (1995: 76). In their view, the rise of new public management implied less a revolution in paradigm, supplanting traditional public administration, than a 'competing vision' remaining in many ways 'separate and distinct' (ibid.: 92). In our view, however, it seems as if in the practice and study of administration in a certain period the dominant way in which problems as well as solutions are framed is specific, while, over time, this dominant frame is 'succeeded' by another one. In fact, within the distinction in the three phases presented above, we can identify five successive 'paradigms' (see Table 5.2).

Table 5.2   Paradigmatic shifts in the practice and study of public
administration

Period	Characterization	Paradigm
The age of interventionism (1930s) 1950s, 1960s 1970s	Social-democratic agenda Rising expectations Disappointing results	The problem-solving paradigm The policy-implementation paradigm
The age of the market and corporate government 1980s	Neo-liberal agenda Private = public	The New Public Management paradigm
The age of neo-interventionism 1990s	Neo-conservative agenda Public is not private	The embedded market paradigm
2000s	Action matters	The governance paradigm

When one looks more in particular at the development of the study and practice of public policy implementation one can see it coming onto the agenda in the 1970s, in the context of the extension of Western welfare states, which had grown rapidly after the Second World War. As sketched above, government, in almost all Western countries, initiated sometimes very ambitious policy programmes. At the same time, particularly within the academic disciplines of political science and public administration, new public policy schools were founded. Politicians, civil servants, and academics shared a widespread belief that government should and could provide solutions for poverty and other major problems in society. Economic growth was enhanced by the Keynesian doctrine that government should keep purchasing power up, creating a substantial effective demand for goods and services. Both cause and effect were rising expectations of the public: the acceptance of its claims by politicians and the fact that these claims were turned into policy programmes, enlarged rather than diminished the desire for more. Rein speaks of a 'problem-solving image'. He calls this image a myth: inadequate as a model of reality, but with real consequences (1983: 215–6). One of the major consequences seems the rise of what was labelled 'policy analysis' (Dunn, 1981). As directly inherent to the 'policy orientation' (Lasswell, 1951), one could speak here of *the problem-solving paradigm*.

Growing from post-war economic prosperity, with its roots in the anti-crisis actions of government in the 1930s, enhanced by wartime government performance, problem-solving oriented policy analysis reached its peak in the 1970s. After 1973, when Pressman and Wildavsky discovered and explained the possibility of a gap between the intentions and outcomes of a policy, a major new part of the public administration research agenda was filled by the study of implementation. Therefore, one can, indeed, identify more specifically a *policy-implementation paradigm*.[6] Essential to it is the concept of the policy process; implementation is approached as following, in time and substantively, what has been laid down in a specific programme as the result of a previous 'stage', in particular policy formation. It is the often experienced disappointment stemming from studies based on this top-down view on the relation between intentions and achievements that, later, would lead to the characterization of many of such studies as 'misery research'.

At the beginning of the 1980s – the Thatcher–Reagan era – this paradigm, which had been so closely connected to large-scale policy programmes of an interventionist central government, was replaced. Or, rather, the prevailing problem/solution mind-set lost its ideological dominance. This happened both in the practice and in the study of policy implementation. Implementation was defined away; it was management that mattered instead. More precisely, with the contractualism embodied in what can be called the *New Public Management (NPM) paradigm*, the ins and outs of implementation were left to the managing 'agent', with whom the 'principal' makes a contract specifying expected outputs. In that paradigm, implementation was being contracted away; and with that, the responsibility for possible failures related to it. It may, however, be said that another aspect of the implementation issue emerged with this: the implementation of effective regulatory policy. Although the vertical orientation inherent in the policy–implementation distinction remained intact, the stiff 'chain' became a 'rope'. It is in this period that implementation studies no longer dominated the research agendas of political science and public administration. Nevertheless, interesting contributions appeared, particularly ones written from a critical or activist perspective, in the first half of the 1980s. In any case there was an inevitable 'time lag' inasmuch as academics continued to publish work inspired by the concerns of the earlier era. Moreover, the introduction of New Public Management was a slow process, opposed by many. Gradually, and relatively separated, new themes, like the importance of networks, arose, away from the main part of the stream, while at the same time broadening it.

It is important not to characterize this development as one from hierarchy via markets to networks, as Lowndes and Skelcher say: 'A crude periodization of modes of governance can also carry with it the myth of progress – bureaucracy is all bad, markets as a necessary evil and networks as the "new Jerusalem"' (1998: 331). At the same time it seems that for each of these a specific flourishing period can be pointed at. A 'rise' may be followed by a 'fall', not in the sense that the 'old' mode of governance loses its relevance in the practice of public administration – as was shown above – but that ideologically its prevalence is withering away. In The Netherlands, for instance, in the 1990s, the intended but also unintended consequences of the privatization of several former government organizations became visible (Algemene Rekenkamer, 1987, 1998). The backlash from these privatizations pursued in the 1980s led in the next decade to the foundation of various institutions of oversight (Hupe and Klaassen, 2001). With that, issues of accountability came on the agenda again. Also, or perhaps even more, when relationships between principals and agents take a different form than that of the politics/administration dichotomy, holding to account and being accountable remain at stake. Hence the institutionalization of this accountability in the newly created market- and semi-market settings gained attention. In several countries governments became aware that simply leaving matters to 'the market' is not enough. As institutions, markets are being created, while their proper functioning needs guarding, and all these are public tasks. To the extent comparable phenomena can be observed on a more general scale, one could speak here of *the embedded market paradigm*.

Phenomena such as the latter point to the fact that governments around the turn of the millennium became aware of the need to distinguish between what they were able to do and what they could not; between what society legitimately could expect from them and what it could not; between what they confidently could leave to 'the market' and where governments have a special responsibility of their own. As we saw in the preceding section, the combination of pragmatism, on the one hand, and a selective interventionism, on the other, appeared. What these two have in common – after all, the pairing looks a bit paradoxical – is a focus on action. And that is what can be assigned as essential in the shift from 'government' to 'governance': the explicit attention to action. This attention is given by governments to what they are doing themselves, as well as expressed in governments' expectations from other actors in the public domain. Attention to action also seems the substantively new element in the ways several contemporary researchers approach the study of public administration, looking behind the policy-on-paper, for instance, at factors determining policy change or government performance.

The *locus* of traditional politics in and around 'government' in the centre of the nation state, according to some authors, to a certain extent has become emptier. Bovens et al. (1995), for instance, speak of the 'relocation of politics' into several directions, like supra-national institutions. The *focus* of 'the political', on the contrary, gained relevance (see Hupe, 1994). Thus one can identify a *governance paradigm*, emerging in the course of the 1990s. Next to the attention to action as mentioned above, its difference from the previous paradigms is, second, the greater awareness of context. On the one hand, this implies that (central) governments find themselves not always expected to do everything on their own; on the other hand, however, the same governments know that in particular situations they are the *only* ones expected to act legitimately. In the study of public administration this awareness of context is expressed, for instance, in the development of general analytic frameworks aimed at the identification and positioning of a variety of factors (Heinrich and Lynn (eds) 2000; Lynn et al., 2001). Third, there are more and other values relevant than just the ones connected with the market, particularly those related to the specific public character of governing and government, such as security, justice, equity, equal treatment of equal cases, and so on. Fourth, there is a case for a rehabilitation of the hierarchical model of governing – although not a sufficient condition, since appropriate application in the practice of public administration necessarily depends on the fit with the context involved. Finally, as started in the preceding embedded market paradigm, issues of accountability gain attention again, although now no longer exclusively in the vertical dimension of 'the bottom' versus 'the top'. Public functionaries function within hierarchical relationships between 'politics and administration', or between 'core department' and 'contractor', but are held – horizontally – accountable by their peers and citizens, as well (for instance Hupe and Hill, 2007). In the study of public administration the governance paradigm enables, among others, a more than solely normative approach to matters of public accountability. In a way, one could say that, after the introduction of the stages model of the policy process, as well as the proclaimed institutional split particularly between the stages of policy formation and policy implementation under the New Public Management paradigm, with the governance paradigm, attention to the connections between parts within the 'whole' are put on the agenda.

Under the governance paradigm, implementation is still there, but as under the NPM paradigm, in a hidden form. Other than in the policy-implementation paradigm, implementation is not seen as following formulation-and-decision in a vertical chain-like relationship. Nor is it hidden behind contracts, as under the New Public Management paradigm. In the governance paradigm, inasmuch as the focus is on the new more 'horizontal' mode of governance in the form of network management, the latter can be seen as an externalized process of policy formation in which government acts together with a variety of public and private actors. The nuts and bolts of implementation – in a narrow sense – are defined further away, located in one of the 'latest' parts of a policy-making process that has been made longer in the 'early' parts. The vertical *chain* and *rope* here have become a lightly *woven thread*, loosely coupling societal actors of various sorts. It is because of this variety that implementation and the managing of it will vary from case to case.

In the succession of the different paradigms, the traditional anchor-point for implementation, located in the making of public policies as formulated and decided upon by organs of representative democracy, seems to have become less visible. With that, scholarly attention has moved to other agendas. At the same time, in particular the governance paradigm, as argued to be presently prevalent, with its attention to action and other characteristics may provide unforeseen possibilities for the study of implementation. It is what may be called *the discovery of government-in-action*, and especially the research on the relations between government and performance following from it, that makes the notion of governance in a pertinent way relevant here. In Chapter 9, we will elaborate on what this might mean for the future of implementation studies.

Conclusion

All the categories of implementation studies, as typified in Table 5.1 above, seem to be ongoing, still producing contributions to the knowledge on public policy implementation. Nevertheless, in the successive periods what may be seen as mainstream and what is not have changed. The rise of new issues to scholarly attention has broadened the agenda substantially. When we link national backgrounds with the history of leading perspectives in implementation theory and research presented above, it can be observed that the policy-implementation paradigm and its connected 'reform' perspective originated in the USA, while it is also that country that currently evidences what can be called most frequently the 'testing' perspective. Undoubtedly the time factor plays a role here. Given the sheer number of mainstream implementation publications, it is clear that, if anywhere, a practice of 'normal science' in this field could have developed, it would be in the USA.

At the same time it seems to be in the UK where a fertile soil was present for the establishing of the New Public Management paradigm. Under pressure from market ideology, the Whitehall tradition could be persuaded to accept the pragmatic, and intellectually relatively shallow, management discourse, where it had been unwilling to accept the public policy orientation. Since the late 1980s, after several outspoken contributions particularly written from an 'activist' perspective, it looks as if the British have become less visible in the field of implementation studies, while at the same time they are prominently present in the development of the scholarly theme of New Public Management. Apart from certain key exceptions like Exworthy and Powell (2004) and Peck and 6 (2006), the very pragmatic focus of much of this work involves the use of the basic ideas of implementation studies without much attention to the way it is theorized.

In The Netherlands, attention has been paid to both 'reform' and 'activist' perspectives, which are perhaps less seen as alternatives. Given the Dutch tradition of consensualism, it may not be a coincidence that it is particularly the theme of networks, network management and governance, on which a substantial and steadily growing contribution from Dutch academics to the international debates has been important (see Chapter 4, pp. 67–71).

Looking at each of the leading perspectives in implementation theory and research, it can be expected that the mainstream of studies in which the implementation of a specific public policy is described and analyzed will continue. The critical and activist stream will, in a different way, persist in the form of the attention given by some postmodern(ist) implementation scholars to citizens' and participatory perspectives. The fact that most postmodernists seem to have other interests than implementation research can now be explained. For them, the phenomenon of 'implementation' in the narrow sense has become obsolete, something belonging to a past era. Besides, postmodernists, as was argued in Chapter 2, are uninterested in causal effects, while central to the study of implementation are questions about why something did happen or did not happen.

In the practice of public administration the 'new normativism' observed in what has been called the age of neo-interventionism may involve a return to earlier perspectives on implementation. Under the influence of crises and disasters, for instance, the shadow sides of privatization (the NPM paradigm) or the adverse consequences of an ultimately pursued pragmatism (the network mode under the governance paradigm) may become visible. This may lead to appeals for oversight and other forms of appropriate institutional design. Possible links with institutional theory may provide fruitful perspectives for contextualized research here, both in a descriptive and a prescriptive sense (see, for instance, Hoppe et al., 1987). Bringing the mainstream of implementation studies, overall, to a higher level of scientific sophistication does not happen automatically. Therefore some methodological issues of a general kind need further attention. We will deal with them in Chapter 7. First, in the next chapter we shall explore the consequences for implementation theory of thinking in terms of governance.

Notes

1 Specific research on the hollow state was reported in a symposium of the *Journal of Public Administration and Theory* (April 1996). Scholarly inquiry there concerned case studies of mental health services (Milward et al., 1993; Lynn, 1996b); human services collaboratives (Bardach and Lesser, 1996); revolving loan programmes for wastewater treatment infrastructure (O'Toole, 1996); child care regulation (Gormley, 1996); public use of information technology (Milward and Snyder, 1996); and substance abuse services (Smith and Smyth, 1996).

2 Even in defence policy – traditionally seen as a policy field suited only for a hierarchical way of governing – sometimes direct citizens' participation is sought (for a case description see Hupe, 2000).

3 What in this book is called the *implementation follows formulation and decision theorem* (as explained in Chapter 1) certainly has been – and still is – a central element in the usual image of public policy-making seen as a cycle or stage model. A logical and a normative justification should be distinguished here. As far as policy formulation and decision-making were seen as taking place 'at the top' of the public-administrative system, this view at the end of the 1970s and beginning of the 1980s was challenged by 'bottom-up' implementation theorists. These theorists showed, although rather implicitly, that the positioning of formulation and decision 'at the top', that is to say, in the centre of national government, involves a normative or political view; not one that is logically necessary. The 'bottom-uppers' (particularly Hjern) contrasted this

normative view with an alternative one. Their picture of empirical reality, in which the connection of implementation action with policy decisions in fact appeared to be much looser than expected, formed the basis for their implicit view that this *should be* so. What, later in the 1980s, the new public management theorists did also implicitly concerned a specific normative-prescriptive view; implementation proceeds better if separated from policy formation and managed by contracts (see also Chapter 3).

4 As examples of efforts aiming at synthesis, O'Toole (2000a: 268) mentioned Mazmanian and Sabatier (1983); Bressers and Ringeling (1989); Goggin et al. (1990); Stoker (1991); Matland (1995); and Ryan (1996).

5 In the UK, for instance, HM Treasury published in 2004 *Risk Management Assessment Framework: A Tool for Departments*, followed by *Managing Risks to the Public Appraisal Guideline* in 2005.

6 It is not the 'implementation paradigm', because the object – what is implemented – always presupposes a subject: what has to be implemented; usually a policy goal. This is not a normative, but a logical matter.

6

IMPLEMENTATION THEORY AND
THE STUDY OF GOVERNANCE

Introduction

The present era can be designated as the age of neo-interventionism. We used that label in Chapter 5, arguing that governments in the Western parts of the world have become more selective in the way they are proceeding. This then happens after a period in which government retrenchment was proclaimed as the leading norm. Contemporary focused action also appears to contrast with the less selective interventional stance taken by governments that characterized the period of the expanding welfare states from the Second World War till the 1980s. In that previous chapter we even went one step further. Looking at the level of shared sets of problem-and-solution definitions, we identified what we labelled a current *governance paradigm*. As its major feature we pointed to the attention to action. In the practice of public administration, public officials do not just rely on the intentions stated by agents and other actors in the public domain, but tend to get a view on what the latter are actually doing and what is 'working'. Researchers of public administration, too, are inclined to search behind the policy-on-paper – certainly when using an empirical research design aimed at causal explanation. The matter is then, however, that they see themselves confronted with an overwhelming array of factors that could be expected to contribute, one way or another, to the explanation of what is observed as being happening. The aim to explain variation implies a need to structure the vast range of candidate explanatory variables. A few contemporary authors, like O'Toole and Meier (1999), have developed a formal model for that purpose, with which they address a limited selection of variables. Not many authors so far have engaged in the formation of what, in the sense of the methodology of the social sciences, can be called middle-range theories. An exception may be the Advocacy Coalition Framework initiated by Sabatier and Jenkins-Smith (1993) and since then developed further (for a recent exposition of it, see Sabatier and Weible, 2007). Although perhaps not immediately a fully-fledged theory comparable to, for instance, Durkheim's sociological theory of anomie, the mentioned approach of explaining policy outputs and outcomes, applied as it has been already, has reached a certain level of sophistication. Interestingly enough, despite its name, this approach is closer to a theory than to a 'framework' in the meaning that will be given to this term in the present chapter.

In this chapter we address the theoretical consequences that can be drawn from the conception of governance for the study of implementation. If 'implementation' concerns an important aspect of turning intentions legitimately decided upon into achievements, how can it be positioned in relation to other aspects of government-in-action? Given the prevalence of what has been called the governance paradigm, this question seems pertinent to the contemporary study of public policy implementation. In Chapter 1, we distinguished five ways in which the term 'governance' currently is being used. First, we observed the use of the term as a label for a certain – read: the contemporary – phase in the evolution of Western government. Second, the term may refer to a specific form of 'steering', that is, via networks. Third, 'governance' is used as an umbrella term for government action in general, under which (mostly three) variants are distinguished. Fourth, the term is used as a label to conceptualize the multi-dimensional character of what Kooiman (2003) has called 'governing as governance'. Finally, the term may function as a norm for government behaviour. In that chapter we announced that we would use the term as a conceptual basis for an analytical framework for studying 'government-in-action', in the variety of aspects related to it. Doing so, we particularly approach the term governance according to the fourth, analytical, type of use. In Chapter 8, we will speak of modes of governance, the third type of definition, as well.

In Chapter 5, we identified a number of characteristics in which the governance paradigm differs from previous ones, including the policy-implementation paradigm as prevalent particularly in the 1970s. These characteristics entail attention to action; awareness of context; a reassessment of traditional public values; a rehabilitation of the hierarchical mode of governing; and a renewed attention to issues of accountability. As argued, these features as implications of looking in terms of 'governance' can be observed both in the practice and study of public administration. In the present chapter we explore these implications further, asking what they would mean for the study of implementation. It seems obvious that one of the consequences must be a re-assessment of the so-called stages model of the policy process: How useful is it still? We address this question in the following section. Next we look at the alternatives available. In the fourth section an exposition is provided of what we have labelled the Multiple Governance Framework. In developing this meta-theoretical analytical framework we have been inspired by the Institutional Analysis and Development Framework (IAD) as first presented in 1982 by Larry Kiser and Elinor Ostrom (1982). Connecting elements from the latter explicitly with governance analysis, we introduced the original version of our own framework in the eighth chapter of the first edition of this book. After that we gave a full treatment in Hupe and Hill (2006), while one of us elaborated some aspects in a book, published in Dutch, on the political foundations of public policy (Hupe, 2007). The presentation of our insights in section four draws on these earlier publications. In the fifth section of this chapter we finally address implementation from the perspective of the developed analytical framework. The chapter ends with some concluding remarks.

───────────── The stages model of the policy process ─────────────

Institutional origins of the stages notion

Anderson (1975: 19) views the policy process as a 'sequential pattern of action involving a number of functional categories of activity that can be analytically distinguished ... problem identification and agenda formation, formulation, adoption, implementation, and evaluation'. Others have provided a very similar image of the way public policy is made. As we indicated in Chapter 1, the essence of that image is that the policy process can be decomposed into a number of successive phases or stages. Although the terms may vary, usually these stages are designated as agenda setting, policy formation – consisting of policy formulation and decision-making – implementation and evaluation. Introducing the notion of the 'policy orientation' Harold Lasswell (1951) was one of the first to divide the process of public policy-making into a number of successive phases or stages. He uses the latter term to indicate that these steps relate to each other in a logical, but particularly, chronological order. The labels he gives to each stage are abstract: intelligence, promotion, prescription, invocation, application, termination and appraisal (Lasswell, 1956). With this distinction Lasswell (1970: 28) offers 'a conceptual map'.

Lasswell, with Simon, Lindblom and Wildavsky, can be justifiably seen as one of the 'founding fathers' of what since their first publications has been called 'the policy sciences' (Parsons, 1995). Nevertheless one may argue that it was Woodrow Wilson (1887) who conceptually laid the basis for a 'stagist' view on government when theorizing about the politics/administration dichotomy. The latter also indicates that a chronological order in stages usually implies a hierarchy. In a parallel direction, although from a different point of departure, Max

Weber (1947) constructed his 'ideal type' of bureaucracy. Both Wilson and Weber with their classical texts not only laid the foundations for what would become scholarly themes in the study of public administration, their insights lay at the basis of principles that since then have been institutionalized in the rule of law and democracy. While in the politics/administration dichotomy the primacy of politics has been normatively anchored, in the conception of a policy process as a succession of identifiable 'stages', a hierarchy is also implied. Policy formation is assumed to precede policy implementation, and the former is supposed to determine the latter. When the objectives of a policy have been legitimately decided upon, their implementation is expected to follow accordingly. A hierarchy can be identified here, that can be described as the primacy of policy-on-paper. As such, the stages notion, apart from anything else, is normatively firmly rooted in the institutions of Western democracies.

Functions

In fact, the stages model seems to fulfil several functions. One may distinguish between a societal, practical, analytical, and programmatic function. First, the normatively embedded character of this so-called model implies societal functions beyond the principles institutionalized in the rule of law and democracy. Looking at public policy in terms of stages appears to be normatively attractive, overall. According to Howlett and Ramesh (2003: 13), each phase refers to a specific element of problem-solving. Thus agenda-setting stands for problem-recognition; policy formulation and decision-making for proposal and choice of a solution; policy implementation for putting the chosen solution into effect; and policy evaluation for monitoring results. Van de Graaf and Hoppe (1996: 79) speak about 'policy-making as problem-processing'. They make a distinction between three transformations taking place in that processing: (1) from values and facts to relevant information and action-oriented knowledge; (2) from information and knowledge to political-administrative action; and (3) from that action to solved problems. Speaking of 'the rationality project' Stone (2002) addresses the stages model as a constitutive element of that 'project'. As its characteristics Stone identifies rational decision-making as the model of reasoning, and the market as the model of society inherent to the project of rationality. A third feature is a 'production model' as the model of policy-making. According to Stone, the latter refers to 'a fairly orderly sequence of stages, almost as if on an assembly line' (ibid.: 10).

All these metaphorical constructions used in relation to the public policy process – problem-solving, problem-processing, production line, as well as the notion of phases itself – indicate not only the normative attractiveness of looking at that process as neatly structured, but also the functionality of doing so. Given the need to act, political-administrative actors have a desire to reduce complexity. The stages notion may fulfil such a function, for instance, enabling political authorities in the centre to shift the blame in case of a perceived 'implementation gap'. Journalists, too, seem to like the surveyability that the division in policy stages provides. If the implementation of policy A in Bedford turns out to be failing, should Members of Parliament in London then not hold the minister concerned accountable for the apparent fact that this policy, as formulated by his department, is obviously not effective?

The second function is a more practical one. Even when addressed as a cycle, the ordering implied by the chrono-logic of the stages is that of a hierarchy. As such the stages model matches the action perspective of the policy-maker – minister, civil servant, or public manager – 'at the top'. The intentions as formulated and decided upon next have to be implemented accordingly. The orientation being a prescriptive one, the prescription may take the form of a checklist (cf. Spicker 2006: 181). Used in many academic textbooks on public policy – Nakamura (1987) calls it the 'textbook approach' – each stage provides the chapter concerned with a clear assignation for the treatment of a range of connected subjects.

The third and fourth functions are fulfilled in the context of academia. The stages model supplies a way to order the study of public policy. After all, political authorities on the one hand, and civil servants on the other, as well as policy advisers and street-level bureaucrats, do not do the same kind of things. The fact that the stages notion is used both in the practice and the study of public administration is helpful; one could speak here of an analytical function. The labour division in the practice of public administration being reflected in the stages model, the latter enables the research of such differentiated phenomena in an academic specialization. DeLeon (1999) points to the fact that the focused attention enhanced by the notion of separate policy stages has led to a number of classic studies. One could think, in particular, of Kingdon (1984) on agenda setting; Lindblom (1959) on policy formation; Pressman and Wildavsky (1973) on implementation; Lipsky (1980) on street-level bureaucracy; and Fischer (1995) on evaluation. In a way, each of these path-breaking studies set the agenda for what would develop as scholarly themes of their own. Therefore, finally also a programmatic function of the stages model can be observed.

Criticisms

The range of functions the stages model fulfils leaves aside the fact that in the meantime academic criticisms on the model in an articulated way have been formulated, as well. John (1998: 36), for instance, states: 'The stages idea confuses more than it illuminates. There are no neat divisions between different types of activities. There is too much change and messiness in public decision-making for the simplification to capture enough reality.' Howlett and Ramesh (2003: 14) observe, first, that, different than implied by the stages model, often there is 'no linear progression' of policy-making. Second, they find it unclear at which level and with what unit of analysis the stages model should be used. Third, in their view, the model lacks any notion of causation.

Referring to some 'devastating criticisms' like the ones given by Nakamura (1987) and by himself (Sabatier 1991; Sabatier and Jenkins-Smith, 1993), Sabatier comes to the 'inescapable' conclusion that 'the stages heuristic has outlived its usefulness and needs to be replaced with better theoretical frameworks' (2007: 7). To underline his stance Sabatier summarizes the expressed criticisms – speaking of a stages 'heuristic'. The essence of that summary comes down to the following: (1) the stages heuristic is not a causal theory; (2) the assumed successive order is often descriptively inadequate; (3) it has a top-down bias and focuses on major pieces of legislation. Thus it neglects 'the interaction of the implementation and evaluation of numerous pieces of legislation within a given policy domain'; and (4) focusing on 'a policy cycle' makes little sense in a situation characterized by 'multiple, interacting cycles involving numerous policy proposals and statutes at multiple levels of government'.

A model?

The range of functions the stages model appears to fulfil, paired with the array of criticisms of its academic usefulness, makes the question relevant what it is and what not, and what may be expected from it and what not. A swift replacement by the word 'heuristic', as Sabatier and Jenkins-Smith (1993) propagate, leaves aside the issue about what makes a 'model' a model. Elinor Ostrom (2007) stresses the necessity of distinguishing between levels of specificity of academic work that are often confused. In particular, she identifies models, theories, and frameworks. Models

> make precise assumptions about a limited set of parameters and variables. Logic, mathematics, game theory, experimentation and simulation, and other means are used to explore systematically the consequences of these assumptions in a limited set of outcomes. (ibid.: 26)

Theories

> enable the analyst to specify which elements of the framework are particularly relevant to certain kinds of questions and to make general working assumptions about these elements. Thus, theories focus on a framework and make specific assumptions that are necessary for an analyst to diagnose a phenomenon, explain its processes, and predict outcomes. Several theories are usually compatible with any framework. (ibid.: 25–6)

A general framework, finally,

> helps to identify the elements and relationships among these elements that one needs to consider for institutional analysis. Frameworks organize diagnostic and prescriptive inquiry. They provide the most general list of variables that should be used to analyze all types of institutional arrangements. Frameworks provide a meta-theoretical language that can be used to compare theories. ... Thus, the elements contained in a framework help analysts generate the questions that need to be addressed when they first conduct an analysis. (ibid.: 25)

It is obvious that these three forms of theoretical work vary first and foremost on the dimension of scale of generality. Frameworks are the most comprehensive and robust, while models are the least. The latter entail specific sets of expected relationships between a limited range of selected variables, while the former empirically offer a lesser degree of specificity. Theories, in the middle of the ranking order, address a certain phenomenon in empirical reality that seems to have a more or less universal character. One could say, a general framework is meant to enable theory formation and specified model building. It should be noted, however, that this logical order says nothing about the level of occurrence of each type in academic practice.

What, then, is the stages model? It looks as if, among the three types of theoretical work Ostrom identifies, it is a framework, rather than a 'model'. As such it is relatively 'empty', enabling various theoretical approaches to be positioned within the framework (for slightly different characterizations see John 1998: 14–5; Schlager 2007). Parsons (1995: 81) underlines the need to have a conceptual tool that can be used for 'mapping'. Elsewhere we addressed the question of which criteria could be seen as relevant for an analytical framework to be useful as a 'general map' (Hupe and Hill 2006: 20). The first criterion is *comprehensiveness*. The framework must have the capacity to encompass conceptually the 'multiple multiplicity' character of public policy processes. Many actors are involved, of all sorts, often on a variety of administrative layers, while these various actors interact in multiple ways. The framework must enable their identification. The second criterion is *empirical openness*. The framework needs to be empirically as open as possible. Given its overarching character (cf. the first criterion) it must facilitate systematic and normatively unbiased, empirical research. The third criterion is *enhancing middle-range theory formation*. The framework must invite the development of 'localized' theories about specific phenomena. It can be noted that a framework as defined here has a *meta*-theoretical character. It may suppose a kind of logic, but is not a theory itself. To explain variation, more is needed.

Having concluded that the stages model is neither a model, nor a theory, we now can put it alongside these criteria: Can it then be called a framework? One could argue that the stages 'heuristic' aims at comprehensiveness, the first criterion. At least it claims to conceptualize an entire policy process. At the same time the dimensions it specifies are singular. For instance, the localization of the stage of the implementation of a public policy is presupposed, rather than specified. One could say the stages heuristic invites theory formation. The fully fledged character of the concerned approaches as a *theory* can be discussed. Nevertheless, DeLeon's reference to the fact that the stages heuristic facilitated some classic studies justifies a positive judgement regarding the third criterion. Meeting the criterion of empirical openness, however, seems to be difficult for the stages heuristic. After all, fundamentally it implies a 'top-down' or 'managerialist' view of the policy process (Parsons 1995: 81). The matter here is not the link with normative principles of the rule of law, democracy and perhaps also the welfare state. The point is that, for instance, looking at 'policy implementation' entirely as normatively subordinate to 'policy formation' may prevent an open observation of what is happening and therefore thwart its systematic explanation. Finally, it may lead to less than well-grounded advice to practitioners, so that, after all, neither the scientific nor the normative goals are achieved.

According to these criteria for an analytical framework, we can conclude that the stages heuristic meets to a certain extent the criteria of comprehensiveness and enhancing theory formation; the first and third criteria. It has particular difficulty, however, in meeting the second criterion, for it appears to be normatively biased. It seems no coincidence then that it is exactly in this realm where the major contribution of the stages heuristic lies, as we saw when we gave an overview of the functions it fulfils. A paradox can be observed here; what makes the stages heuristic in terms of social science less useful, its normative bias, makes it more attractive in society. Therefore, it is undesirable to write off the 'stage model' of the policy process completely – particularly if it is expressed in a dynamic variant sometimes referred to as the 'policy cycle'. First and foremost, the reasons not to do so lie in the practice of public administration: the societal and practical functions we distinguished. In the latter world the perceived phased character of the policy process can supply actors with insight into their own positions in that process, and, related to that, may provide clues about how to act. Additional to, but distinguished from, this cognitive function of the stages heuristic is the normative function that gives sense, direction and legitimation to the things actors at various positions in the policy process are expected to do. Both these cognitive and normative functions can be considered as specifications of, respectively, the practical and societal functions distinguished above.

Theoretical reasons not to discard the stages heuristic entirely also lie in its programmatic function. Each of the separate stages has been turned into scholarly themes of their own; academics continue to undertake studies under the heading of 'implementation', 'evaluation', and so on. Most major restrictions in the functionality of the stages heuristic concern its analytical function. The issue here is not so much that it would not provide researchers with a tool 'to grasp how the entire system works in verifiable … theory' (DeLeon, 1999b: 28). Not being a model, it certainly does not have to provide a theory. Rather, the matter is that the heuristic is incomplete in what it *does* prove to be: a general analytical framework. For overall, the stages heuristic can be characterized as a framework for the analysis of policy processes, of which not all relevant dimensions have been articulated, while its all-penetrating normative orientation makes it less suited for systematic enquiry. This situation makes the question relevant whether there are available alternatives.

Alternative analytical frameworks

Although the stages heuristic seems a widely used general framework for the study of the policy process, some alternatives have been developed. In this section we will look at the ones developed by Lynn; Parsons; Ostrom; and Lynn, Heinrich and Hill. It is clear that these authors come from contrasting scholarly backgrounds: respectively, the study of public management (Lynn, Heinrich and Hill), public policy (Parsons), and public choice (Ostrom). Nevertheless, they all aim at providing, indeed, a 'general framework' with which preliminary questions for research can be asked and answered.

Lynn (1981: 146–9; 1987) uses the concept of 'nested games' to assign the various parts of the policy process. There is the 'high game' in which it is decided whether or not a policy will be made. Then in the 'middle game' the direction of the policy is determined. The 'low game' is about the practical side of the policy-making; implementation is central here.

Parsons (1995: xvii) distinguishes 'three broad and overlapping levels or dimensions of analysis'. Each of those 'may be seen through a variety of different frameworks and approaches' (ibid.: 82). The way in which issues and problems are defined and policy agendas are set Parsons calls 'meso-analysis'. As a level of analysis cutting through the various phases of the policy process, it is 'meso' because it:

> explores approaches which link the input side of the policy-making process with the policy/decision-making and output process focusing on the relationship between the 'pre-decisional' dimensions of policy-making and its decisional and post-decisional contexts. (Parsons, 1995: 82)

The analysis of 'how decisions are taken and policies are made and how analysis is used within the decision-making process' Parsons calls 'decision analysis' (ibid.: 82). Then 'delivery analysis' refers to 'how policies are administered, managed, implemented, evaluated and terminated' (ibid.: 82).

Third, there is the 'institutional analysis and development' (IAD) framework developed by Elinor Ostrom and her colleagues, presented as such for the first time in 1982 by her and Larry Kiser. Stemming from micro-institutional analysis, Kiser and Ostrom (1982: 184) specify three related but distinct levels of analysis. The operational level explains the world of action, the collective choice level, the world of 'authoritative decision-making'. The constitutional level explains 'the design of collective choice mechanisms' (ibid.: 184). It may be noted that these are listed in the original formulation in an order that reverses the conventional order of the stages model.

Individuals at the operational level 'either take direct action or adopt a strategy for future actions, depending on expected contingencies'. They are often 'authorized to take a wide variety of actions at this level without prior agreement with other individuals' (ibid.: 207–8).

Collective decisions are made 'by officials (including citizens acting as officials) to determine, enforce, continue, or alter actions authorized within institutional arrangements'. These collective decisions are plans for future action. 'Unlike individual strategies, collective decisions are enforceable against nonconforming individuals … The authority to impose sanctions is a key attribute of the collective choice level of decision-making' (ibid.: 208).

On the third level, 'Constitutional decisions are collective choices about rules governing future collective decisions to authorize actions. Constitutional choices, in other words, are decisions about decision rules' (ibid.: 208). In the framework institutional arrangements are 'linking each level of decision making to the next level. Constitutional decisions establish institutional arrangements and their enforcement for collective choice. Collective decisions, in turn, establish institutional arrangements and their enforcement for individual action' (ibid.: 209). In this framework it is only at the operational level where an action in the physical world flows directly from a decision.

In an updated discussion of the framework Ostrom (2007: 22) elaborates some 'key difficulties' in the study of institutions. They involve the multiple meanings of the term institution, the invisibility of institutions, the multiplicity of inputs coming from various disciplines and the corresponding need to develop a specific 'language', and the configuration character of relationships. An additional matter Ostrom mentions is the multiplicity of levels of analysis. Particularly important here is the analytical treatment of the nested structure of the framework (ibid.: 22–5).

Finally, Lynn, Heinrich and Hill (2001) provide 'a logic for governance research'. At stake is an 'aggregated framework' aimed at 'directing attention to the dynamic relations within and between the institutional, managerial, and operational levels of governance' (ibid.: 36; see also Heinrich and Lynn, 2000). Lynn and his colleagues argue that 'the logic of governance involves a hierarchy of relationships' (2000b: 14). They differentiate 'stake' relationships: (1) between citizen preferences and legislative choice; (2) between legislative preferences and the 'formal structures and processes of public agencies'; (3) between formal authority and 'the structure and management of organizations, programs, and administrative activities'; (4) between 'organization, management and administration and the core technologies and primary work of public agencies'; (5) between the latter and outputs or results; (6) between the latter and stakeholder assessments; and (7) between these assessments and 'reactions and, back to the top of the list, political preferences and interests' (ibid.).

Positioning their work, the authors state:

This logic of governance is neither a paradigm nor a unified 'theory of governance'. It does not depict how governance 'works'. Instead, it is a schematic or heuristic framework that suggests how the elements of governance – the values and interests of citizens, legislative enactments and oversight, executive and organizational structures and roles, and performance assessment – might be linked through a dynamic and interactive process. Within an institutional frame of reference, it is a particular way of identifying relationships that potentially influence policy, program, and organizational performance. Identifying their actual influence requires theory, models and data. (Lynn et al. 2001: 36–7)

In Table 6.1 we set out the principal components of the analytical frameworks presented here.

Table 6.1   Alternative general analytical frameworks for the study of public administration

Nested games	Institutional analysis and development	Multiple stages	Logic of governance
Lynn (1981, 1987)	*Kiser and Ostrom (1982), Ostrom (2007)*	*Parsons (1995)*	*Heinrich and Lynn (2000), Lynn, Heinrich and Hill (2001)*
High game	Constitutional level	Meso-analysis	Institutional level
Middle game	Collective choice level	Decision analysis	Managerial level
Low game	Operational level	Delivery analysis	Technical level

One cannot say that the frameworks shown here were deliberately developed to function as alternatives exactly for the stages heuristic. At least they were meant for the study of an object broadly conceived as 'public administration'. Besides, however, they have in common that they all aim at comprehensiveness and empirical openness, while having a meta-theoretical character. And therefore they meet the requirements we formulated for analytical frameworks. This makes them potential functional equivalents to the stages heuristic, as far as the academic functions of the latter are concerned.

We think there is still room for an additional framework because we assume that more consequences of looking at government-in-action can be addressed. As an explicit alternative for the stages heuristic, our framework has been developed driven by the aim of all four, but particularly inspired conceptually by Ostrom's. In our view, with that aim in mind, some amending of that framework is necessary. Specifically, there is a need to specify the links with the concept of 'governance'.

The Multiple Governance Framework

Dimensions of governance: the *Trias Gubernandi*

In the tradition of micro-economic analysis and 'new institutional economics' Elinor Ostrom is interested in 'how institutions affect the incentives confronting individuals and their resultant behavior' (2007: 21). The initial article written with Larry Kiser presented the 'institutional analysis and development framework' (IAD), with two major components (Kiser and Ostrom 1982). One was the distinction between 'three tiers of decision making' and the relations between them; the other, an exposition of the elements to be used for the analysis of outcomes in 'action arenas' and their evaluation at any of these three tiers. The term 'action arena' refers to

> a complex conceptual unit containing one set of variables called an action situation and a second set of variables called an actor. One needs both components – the situation and the actors in the situation – to diagnose, explain and predict actions and results. (Ostrom 2007: 28–9)

In order to identify and measure institutions and understand how they work, it is necessary to look at the ways the rules of such an institution work. Thus a researcher may see how rules-in-use affect an action situation. Kiser and Ostrom specify various sorts of rules, like entry- and exit rules, position rules, etc., which add up to specific 'rule configurations'.

Because of its composed character, the framework as 'a multi-tier conceptual map' indeed offers, literally, a meta-theoretical 'framework' for ordering various sorts of institutional analysis (Ostrom 2007: 41). Particularly relevant here is the first component mentioned above. Kiser and Ostrom refer to the three 'tiers of decision making', that is: constitutional choice, collective choice, and operational decisions, as 'the three worlds of action'. In our view this variety of action can be seen 'everywhere', in the sense that the distinction refers to different sets of activities, but leaves open where and by whom these activities are being performed. More particularly, the conceptual differentiation Kiser and Ostrom's framework provides can be reflected upon with an eye on the study of governance. Then for that purpose a leading, preliminary question can be formulated. Lasswell (1938) defined 'who gets what, when, how' as the essence of politics (!). In a certain parallel we propose the following meta-question to precede governance research: *Who acts where, doing what, on which scale and how?*

Each part of this question refers to an element in the structure of a policy process if the latter is viewed as positioned in a multi-dimensional setting of government-in-action. Successively these elements concern actors, administrative layers, sets of activities, action situations and action scales, and political-administrative craftsmanship. Each of these central concepts is elaborated here. The order in which this happens is a practical one and refers to the formulation of the overall question above; it is not a 'stagist' order.

Who? Actors. Ostrom's definitions of an actor ('a single individual or a group functioning as a corporate actor') and of action ('those human behaviors to which the acting individual attaches a subjective and instrumental meaning') cannot be improved (2007: 30). Taking the concept of governance seriously means that the answer to the question who is the 'governing actor?' is empirically open. The actors whose actions are researched can be persons or organizations; government officials or a corporation to whom a task has been mandated. Within government, the distinction between elected representatives and appointed officials can be made; between a Cabinet minister or a civil servant acting as a policy-maker; as well as between departmental public servants in the capital and those working 'at the street-level'. Citizens, too, in varying roles can be seen as actors in relation to governance. Addressing the question of the researched actor as an empirical one will show a variety of sorts and numbers. Besides, the legitimacy of the actors actually involved in a particular policy process may differ from what may be expected on normative grounds.

Where? Administrative layers. Going 'downwards' in a system of vertical public administration a policy process encounters a range of actors and loci as action situations. Within that empirical range a specific assembly of such actors and actor situations has been normatively cut out as one or more layers. The term 'administrative layer' refers to a specific kind of action locations: the formal, legitimate political-administrative institutions, including representative organs, with certain territorial competences. While the term 'locus' concerns action situations in political–societal relations designated in the threefold aggregated distinction that will be elaborated below, it refers to a series of spots on a line of vertical public administration from which 'real' actors participate in a particular policy process.[1] Related to each other in a nested configuration like Russian dolls, both the number of real persons actually involved in a given policy process, and the variety of action situations in which they act, usually is larger than implied by the specific formal administrative layer. When we examine the latter we are (only) looking at legitimate constitutional settings within a specific political-administrative system, while the study of the policy process needs a broader perspective on relevant variables.

What? Action levels. Taking our lead from Kiser and Ostrom's (1982) 'three worlds of action' outlined above we see the policy process as governance consisting of three broad sets of activities that we call constitutive, directional and operational governance. The notion of constitutive governance derives from Kiser and Ostrom's notion of constitutional choice which they define as the framing of rules that 'affect operational activities and their effects in determining who is eligible' together with rules 'to be used in crafting the set of collective-choice rules that in turn affect the set of operational rules' (Ostrom 2007: 44). This somewhat ambiguous formulation, defined elsewhere as 'decisions about decision rules' seems to embrace both fundamental decisions about the content of policy and about the organizational arrangements for its delivery. This distinction is important. For example, a major policy innovation in the field of health care delivery will contain both rules on who is to be entitled to new health benefits, together with rules about how those benefits are to be delivered. In that respect it may be a bit misleading to speak of 'constitutional choice' directing the reader's attention to the latter when that has little significance without the former. Hence we prefer the term 'constitutive'.

The direction in directional governance, our alternative to Kiser and Ostrom's 'collective choice', stands for the formulation of and decision-making about collectively desired outcomes. Facilitating the conditions for the realization of these situations belongs to this part of governance. Rather than the term directive that we originally used, we now prefer the adjective directional. For the essence of the collective choice character of this set of activities is to show the direction towards reaching the stated objectives, while the way in which this happens – the *mode* of governance: more or less 'directive' – is empirically then still open. Operational governance concerns the actual managing of that realization process.

Respectively these three action levels refer to structure-oriented, content-oriented, and process-oriented sets of activities. What Kooiman (2003) addresses as 'governing as governance', or what we have labelled above as government-in-action here becomes apparent. The three sets of activities distinguished, both in their specifics and their relations constitute 'governance'. The fact that these sets capture the action-orientation as its most characteristic feature made one of us speak of the *trias gubernandi*. The 'trinity of governing' entails the combination of creating settings, giving direction, and getting things done (Hupe 2007: Chapter 2). The position of each towards the other sets is a logical one. As such, each of these sets of activities that governing consists of, in principle can be practised by any actor in a policy process.

Ostrom's illustration of a shift of action levels is worthwhile quoting here:

> [W]hen a 'boss' says to an 'employee', 'How about changing the way we do X?' and the two discuss options and jointly agree upon a better way, they have shifted from taking actions within previously established rules to making decisions about the rules structuring future actions. (2007: 33)

In the terminology of the Multiple Governance Framework presented in this chapter, what is at stake here is a shift from the level of operational governance to the level of directional governance. Speaking of 'a policy (or collective-choice) tier' (ibid.: 27) and even of 'policy-making (or governance)' (idem.: 46) it looks as if Ostrom, although only casually, unintentionally anticipates the kind of explicit policy-process-as-governance conception proposed here. At one place she calls policy subsystems 'multiple linked action arenas at all three levels of analysis' (ibid.: 43). What Ostrom then states about the nested character of her framework also goes – of course with an amended terminology – for ours. Ostrom thus specifies the way institutional rules (a central concept in the substance of her framework) cumulatively affect the actions taken and outcomes obtained in any setting. Although the centrality of the concept of 'rules' is specific, the working of the nesting mechanism could not be better pictured, and is very similar to the consequences of the nested character of the Multiple Governance Framework. Schlager (2007: 315) interprets this as follows: '[T]he rules-in-use that structure the operational level originate from the other two levels.' In the same paragraph she concludes: 'Although the analyst can choose to keep the analysis focused on a single level, the other two levels are always implicitly included.'

On which scale? Action situations. The three sets of activities generally distinguished above as action levels have a specific form dependent on the locus observed. When we speak of 'locus' our definition is comparable to (although perhaps less refined than) the one Ostrom gives of her concept 'action situation': 'An analytic concept that enables an analyst to isolate the immediate structure affecting a process of interest to the analyst for the purpose of explaining regularities in human actions and results, and potentially to reform them' (Ostrom, 2007: 29).

Empirically, both the number of actors and that of the potential action situations in which they act – as Elinor Ostrom has pointed out – can be thought of as infinite. Since the latter category does not coincide with the former, can a usable taxonomy be devised? Here, too, a threefold distinction can be made. Irrespective of the kind of formal administrative layer looked at, a researcher may observe specific activities in action situations on a scale that can vary from action of and between individuals (in practice called 'the street-level'), via action of and between organizations, to action on the system-scale.[2] This varying degree of aggregation can be labelled as, respectively, the locus of individuals, organizations, and composed systems.

How? Political-administrative craftsmanship. Other than might have been expected, the how-question does not regard means–ends relationships. Different from an instrumentalist and/or prescriptive view, this question in the Multiple Governance Framework concerns what can be described as the quality of human agency. Also in the same position and with similar tasks, actor A can do the job in a different way to actor B.

Positioning the framework

We call this 'the Multiple Governance Framework (MGF)'. Its multi-dimensional and nested character makes it possible to specify research questions and identify contextual relations. Besides, empirical observation and the normative judgement about what has been observed can be distinguished. Whether, for instance, in a given policy process at the layer of local government just 'implementation' or rather 'policy co-formation' is practised, is, to begin with, an empirical question. The nature of the observed activities should be compared with the measures involved, respectively for situation-bound rule application, and general rule setting. Any judgement about whether the specific empirically observed action is desirable, is a normative matter. Similarly, there are various acts of 'operational governance' – consisting of managing trajectories, managing inter-organizational relations, and managing external and internal contacts. They can be regarded as sublevels of action and are not confined to one specific layer of government. Thus, the connections between actors, acts and action spots are of an empirical instead of an *a priori* nature. Rather than assuming them on normative grounds, they are to be investigated empirically.

The Multiple Governance Framework as presented here is partly intellectually inspired by the IAD framework. At the same time, however, there are some major differences that amount to more than terminological amendments and justify the development of a separate framework. First, the framework links the study of the policy process explicitly with the concept of governance. Essential to this is the shared focus on action rather than (only) on institutions in the traditional-legalistic sense of the word; the combination of a 'vertical' and 'horizontal' orientation; and the stress on specifying levels of analysis and on distinguishing empirical from normative matters. Second, a specific characteristic of the framework outlined here is the localization of the various governance activities, in the variety of action situations within a range of political-societal relations. The general 'employee' of Elinor Ostrom becomes, for instance, a street-level bureaucrat, maybe a fire officer, while his or her 'boss' maybe the head of the local Fire Brigade. Third, the Multiple Governance Framework draws the micro-economically rooted assumptions of the IAD framework into mainstream social science, making links with the classical scholarly themes of public administration. Thus a framework has been devised which is particularly suitable for the study of the policy process. Fourth, Ostrom's formulation has a strong institutional emphasis while, as we pointed out above to explain our adaptation of the concept of 'constitutional choice', we see 'content' issues in respect of policy innovations as of great importance in structuring subsequent decisions.

Studying implementation as governance research

The use of the Multiple Governance Framework

In the stages heuristic the position of implementation seemed clear; it concerned a relatively 'late' stage, in a vertical dimension – even if the policy process is conceived as a cycle. It is obvious that the position of implementation is different when viewed as part of a multi-dimensional interpretation of the phenomena referred to by the concept of governance. In this section we will explore the consequences for studying implementation when the latter is conceptualized within the matrix showed in Table 6.2. Given the character of that framework, we do so on a meta-theoretical level.

In the framework the singularity of the notion of stages has been specified in a number of dimensions. To address these, a composite question – actually implying five meta-questions – is asked. We differentiated between actors, action levels, action situations and action scales, and administrative layers, as the central concepts related to these questions. In addition, we proposed the concept of political-administrative craftsmanship, as related to the how-question – being aware

Table 6.2   The Multiple Governance Framework

action level / action scale	Trias Constitutive governance	Gubernandi Directional governance	Operational governance
SYSTEM ORGANIZATION	Institutional design Designing contextual relations	General rule setting Mission formulation	Managing trajectories Managing relations
INDIVIDUAL	Internalization of values and norms	Situation bound rule application	Managing contacts

Source: adaptation of Hupe and Hill (2006: 23).

of the fact that this concept would need separate treatment, beyond the scope of this book. One can observe at least three differences between using the Multiple Governance Framework (MGF) and the stages heuristic for the study of implementation. First, analytical *differentiation*. Inherent to the notion of stages is the supposition of an intrinsic mix of the who, the what, and the where. When Pressman and Wildavsky (1973) talked about the relationship between 'Washington' and 'Oakland' (see the subtitle of their book), they started from the expectation that policy formation takes place in the capital, and that the implementation of that policy is a task for authorities elsewhere in the country. When the term 'implementation' is used without any further qualifications (for example, 'the decision has been made, now the rest is implementation') the actors and activities, as well as the formal and actual authority to engage in such activities, are not specified. The framework presented, in contrast, enables this specification to occur.

Second, at the same time there is an eye for *connections*. With its multidimensionality the MGF stresses the nested character of the range of factors determining the acts of governing actors. This means that, like Russian dolls, the more aggregated scale of the whole system comprises the less aggregated ones of separate organizations and individual actors, while, the other way around, the latter undergo the influence of the more aggregated scales. In a similar way, the level of constitutive governance offers cadres within which directional and operational action can occur. At the same time, in ways that may empirically vary, the operational level is influenced by the other two action levels. When, for instance, an individual bureaucrat working 'at the street-level' grants an assistance benefit, (s)he takes an operational decision. However, in a situation where 'the handbook' does not foresee the circumstances of the client at hand, this decision may imply one on the directional level – taken by the same 'implementing' actor.

The third difference with the stages heuristic regards its scope to enhance *theory formation*. The MGF explicitly is identified as having a meta-theoretical character, while it makes a variety of dimensions of governance visible. As such, it enables one to trace causal relationships that might have had little attention so far. When explaining variation (variance) in outputs or outcomes is seen as the level of scientific ambition aimed at, and the dependent variables are operationalized in terms of any form of public service performance (Boyne et al., 2006), the framework may be helpful in specifying research questions and identifying relationships between explanatory variables theoretically deemed relevant.

These three differences between studying implementation as a stage or within a framework of multiple governance may change the nature of what traditionally has been conceived of as 'implementation studies'.

Implementation as a focus and a locus

In the practice of public administration one sometimes may hear: 'The decision has been made; the rest is implementation.' When the results of a policy appear to be disappointing, often 'the implementation' is blamed. What one sees here are two different ways in which the same term is being used. On the one hand, the term refers to a range of activities; on the other, to the world of street-level bureaucracies or agencies, the so-called 'implementing organizations'. The latter meaning concerns implementation as a locus, the former as a focus. When these different meanings are considered in the context of the dimensions of the Multiple Governance Framework as set out in this chapter, the first of the two meanings refers to what has been called operational governance. It is the part of governing aimed at the realization of given goals; the right column in Table 6.2. The second meaning, rather than being an action level, concerns an action scale. More in particular, the scales of organizations and individuals – the middle and bottom rows in Table 6.2 – often function at the sub-layer usually addressed as 'the street-level'.

In mainstream implementation studies, the focus traditionally has been on the links between results observed 'at the bottom' and intentions formulated 'at the top'. In studies with the respective labels, factors on either side were stressed, as we saw in Chapter 3. In Chapter 4, we showed that in the 'synthesizing' approaches the sources for identifying relevant factors were no longer confined to either 'the top' or 'the bottom'. In fact, the number of such variables grew to unmanageable proportions (O'Toole 1986; Meier, 1999). For researchers it seems possible to use the MGF for a more systematic exploration of what they want to know, having identified which knowledge about the aspects concerned has been accumulated already and which not. It also may be that the orientation in such research will shift from a vertical one, questioning the relation between intentions and achievements, towards a more horizontal one, aimed at explaining variation in actual behaviour and its impacts on performance. In the latter instance, it is possible that the explanatory variables will be more sought in and around 'the street-level' – in fact a layer or, rather, sub-layer – than at the level of national government. Interestingly enough, this would not have to lead to a loss of explanatory power. On the contrary, the nested character of the framework implies a co-weighing of factors from more than one action level. It seems exactly in the determining of the relative weight of explanatory variables that much could be gained. Then we are talking about developing models, specifying expected relations between limited sets of variables, but even more about the formation of (middle-range) theories. The presented framework enhances the possibility that such endeavours are undertaken from different theoretical and even disciplinary angles. It seems desirable that the Multiple Governance Framework should contribute to making the study of implementation thus more theory-driven. In Chapter 9, we will address this issue further, looking at the future of implementation studies. After the following concluding section we first explore, in the Chapters 7 and 8, matters of implementation research on a scientifically more operational basis.

–––––––––––––––––––––––––––––––––– **Conclusion** ––––––––––––––––––––––––––––––––––

In this chapter we have addressed the theoretical consequences that can be drawn from the conception of governance for the study of implementation. We did so after our conclusion in the preceding chapter that the policy-implementation paradigm has been succeeded by other paradigms, while currently the governance paradigm seems prevalent. The central question was how implementation can be positioned in relation to other aspects of governance as government-in-action. After all, implementation concerns at least an important aspect of turning intentions legitimately decided upon into achievements. The point is that looking in terms of governance, in any case in the way the term is conceived in this book, enlarges rather than reduces the number of variables deemed relevant in the study of implementation. So even more now, Matland's dictum is relevant that the latter needs structure (see p. 73)

The stages model was shown to be not a model; instead it is a general analytical framework, with shortcomings. As a heuristic, the stages notion fulfils functions, certainly societal and practical ones. In research, however, its functions prove to be limited. This is the case, for instance, because it has hardly any explanatory power. Besides, the degree to which the stages heuristic may provide the required 'structure' for the study of implementation falls short – certainly when the latter is conceived of as part of governance.

There are alternative analytical frameworks, all with a validity and functionality of their own. The 'logic of governance' framework of Lynn and his colleagues seems one of the most developed ones, as does Ostrom's framework. Particularly elements from the latter inspired the authors to develop an additional framework especially designed for governance research as well as combining attention for management, content and institutions. Capturing the specific nature of governing as action, the latter combination is addressed as the *trias gubernandi*.

Although it can be assumed that the study of implementation will develop further (see Chapter 9), the direction of that development is empirically open. The flourishing times of the policy-implementation paradigm having been in the past, the availability of general frameworks like the ones pictured justify the expectation that the manifestations of that study will be more pluriform. Studying contemporary implementation, above all, can be conceived as governance research.

Notes

1 For the distinction between locus and focus, see Chapter 1.
2 In our conceptualization the term *street-level* refers to an actual '(sub-)layer' within a formal administrative layer, rather than to a 'level'. However, it is hard to give a term a specific definition when this term is used with a different meaning in daily practice. In a similar way, this applies to the use of the notion of 'stages'.

7

RESEARCHING IMPLEMENTATION

Contents

Introduction

In this chapter we examine issues of research on implementation. We do so while building on what we have said about the importance of embedding implementation analysis in a flexible understanding of the policy process, as set out particularly in Chapter 6. Our aim is to outline considerations we regard as relevant, drawing upon theory and upon our examination of the empirical literature. In the first edition of this book we reported on a systematic study of the latter. Although we do not repeat that report here, the range of themes elaborated in Chapter 4 as recurring in the implementation literature clearly had a relation with the seven clusters of variables identified in the systematic scan of journals carried out for our first edition. Since that scan we have sought to identify new key studies.

While in Chapter 4 we addressed several issues arising from existing implementation theory, in the present chapter we give attention to the same kind of issues, but from a different angle, that is of doing implementation research. The central question is: Given the state of the art of implementation studies (cf. Chapters 3 and 4) and the perspective of governance (particularly Chapters 5 and 6), how can the actual theoretical issues be dealt with while doing implementation research?

In talking of a body of theory and of the practice of research a reference point for many is the model of 'normal science' in which hypotheses derived from more or less generally accepted theories are tested. This activity leads on to the establishment of a series of propositions, which can be retested and modified over time. Only very exceptionally do new theories emerge that cut across the mainstream work and lead to a paradigm shift in the established body of knowledge (Kuhn, 1970). We recognize that some political and social scientists deny that their discipline can be described in these terms, and indeed that some are unhappy about the use of the word 'science' in connection with their activity. Some authors on implementation, as well, have challenged that kind of approach to the topic – with testable propositions and probably causal assumptions. Our stance is not one of absolutist interpretivism, but it is not the opposite either, as was made clear in the discussion of this issue in Chapter 1. Instead, we acknowledge the importance of the interpretative challenge, inasmuch as we certainly do not equate a positivist standpoint with a rejection of qualitative methods, while recognizing that some situations will be best analyzed in interpretative terms. Hence, our stance can be labelled one of a moderate positivism.

In general, we place our work within the conventional literature of political science and public administration which treats it as feasible to frame work, in at least broad terms, within the 'normal science' model. Such an approach fulfils the expectation of the wider public for the social sciences that findings will be specified in terms of propositions supported by evidence. This is particularly important in relation to a topic like implementation, where there is an expectation that the discipline will make a contribution to questions about 'what is feasible' or 'what will work'. The suggestions in this chapter on doing implementation research are rooted in the perspective outlined here.

In this chapter, we follow the range of issues elaborated in Chapter 4. We start with some reflections on the difficulties in defining exactly what is meant by studies of implementation, building on our discussion of the overlaps with other disciplines or sub-disciplines in Chapter 2. That leads to two crucial issues: how to identify dependent variables for research, and how to deal with the often intertwined policy formation/implementation relationship. A key aspect of the argument we developed in Chapter 6 was that the best approach to the latter problem requires a less biased, more open conceptualization than that of the so-called 'stages model' of the policy process. Accordingly, as far as research is concerned, careful attention needs to be paid to the salience of politico-administrative layers in the policy process and their complex relationships in respect of categories of policy-making activities. That subject is therefore given attention in the next section. After that, attention is turned to horizontal, as opposed to vertical, organizational relationships, but recognizing that these may be intertwined. The next section is concerned with issues of the management of activities within single organizations (or samples of them). It is divided into subsections: one looks at issues regarding the characteristics of agencies while the other explores issues of the growing body of research on the management of street-level bureaucrats. There follow two closely related sections on issues about building in variables that deal with the context of implementation activities: the impact of responses of those affected by a policy and wider macro-environmental factors.

Last, but by no means least, comes a long section on an issue that runs through the whole field of implementation research: the respective places of quantitative and qualitative studies.

Defining studies of implementation

Moving targets

In a wide range of disciplinary and sub-disciplinary areas, researchers have been, and still are, producing findings relevant to the understanding of the policy implementation process (see Saetren, 2005). In Chapter 2 we addressed the various ways in which implementation issues are also explored in other areas of political science, organizational sociology or studies of law. Within political science and public administration the long-standing concern about the basic relationship between politics and administration continues to draw researchers' attention.

Similarly, in an era in which classical economic theory became much more important for political rhetoric, the analysis of politics, government and administration took on board all kinds of economic approaches. The particular implication of this for the study of implementation was that the top-down perspective, as well as propositions about the politics/administration relationship, were reframed in terms of propositions about relationships between 'principals' and 'agents'. Bureaucratic interests were expressed in terms of the self-interests embodied in rational choice theory (see Dunleavy, 1991, for a critical review and development of the original theory). Propositions derived from game theory were also developed in efforts to model implementation processes. In Chapters 3 and 4, some observations were made about the problems of applying the formalistic propositions derived from these sources to the implementation process. Here we merely note that some contemporary empirical studies take these sorts of propositions, rather than more complex implementation theory, as their starting points.

However, it is elsewhere in the study of implementation that it is more difficult to disentangle the contributions of explicit 'implementation studies' from those made by work with other theoretical perspectives. Since a great deal of the analysis of complexity within the implementation process stresses inter- and intra-organizational relationships, it is inevitable that important contributions to the understanding of these processes come from writers whose theoretical underpinning stems from organization theory, or more precisely from organizational sociology. The more detailed analysis of these relationships concerns issues about actual behaviour at 'the street-level' where the links between research inspired by Lipsky and research rooted in the sociology of work are very close. Moreover these two veins of research mingle closely with a socio-legal concern with issues about discretion and rule application. This is seen most particularly in studies of police behaviour, but there are related concerns for the study of service and benefit delivery and for the study of regulation. They also come together in much research described as concerned with public management.

If relevant research for our topic is conducted under a variety of theoretical and disciplinary rubrics, it will inevitably be difficult to define a clear range of publications in which relevant outputs may be found. The task of delimiting a relevant literature is compounded by other factors, too. First, in addition to the direct disciplinary literature – in political science, sociology, etc. – there is a considerable amount of work on implementation issues that is published in books and journals defined in terms of their substantive area of concern rather than in terms of a disciplinary one. Such areas are, for instance, social policy, housing policy, health policy, environmental policy, criminology and policing, and planning. Second, since much implementation research is carried out for specific customers with explicit practical concerns, a substantial 'grey' literature of reports and pamphlets has been generated. This literature may contain much that can advance our understanding of implementation, but it is hard to locate. When located, there may be a need to translate its specific concerns into 'evidence' that can be related to more general hypotheses. Third, the factors that determine what is published and where it is published may be unrelated to whether findings advance our understanding of implementation or not. It has, for example, been alleged that much early implementation research essentially highlighted disasters and implementation failures and provided a distorted impression of implementation difficulties. At the same time it is probable that studies of failures are more likely to be published. More recently, changing political concerns and administrative fashions may have affected awareness of implementation issues (as was shown in Chapter 5). Additionally, academic agendas, language and labels change over time, and the decisions of journal editors and publishers reflect those changes. New studies with new insights may be given more attention than studies that replicate earlier ones while old ideas may be dressed up in new concepts.

Given ends

Unlike some other authors experienced in the field (cf. for instance, the debate in *Policy Currents* in the 1990s), we take a pragmatic stance towards the nature of implementation studies – as we will elaborate in Chapter 9. While our approach to the delineation of the field of research avoids any protectionist concern with the boundaries of the sub-discipline, we think it is nevertheless important to seek clarity about what it is that implementation studies aim to explain. In the chapters exploring the development of implementation theory, a strong emphasis was noted, in much early work, upon 'implementation deficits' as expressed by the famous subtitle of Pressman and Wildavsky's founding classic. There has thus been a danger that implementation studies work a taken-for-granted assumption that aspirations will not be achieved, that policies will not live up to the rhetoric of those who formulate them and that 'disasters' will occur. In the same vein there has been a tendency to work with the notion of 'perfect administration' (see note on Hood, pp. 50–1) so that the inevitable adjustments, compromises and shortfalls in the real world are used to challenge the aspirations of the policy formers or to condemn the efforts of the implementers. Throughout this book we have recognized the importance of the normative questions that these notions throw up, acknowledging that accountability and control issues are important. However, they do raise severe problems for the design of implementation research which may often be avoided by framing questions about dependent variables in terms which do not have implicitly normative assumptions about 'success' or 'failure' built into them. This is a point that has been made cogently by Lester and Goggin:

> One of the most intractable problems in implementation research has been how to measure the concept of successful implementation. In our view, policy implementation is a *process*, a series of subnational decisions and actions directed toward putting a prior authoritative federal decision into effect. The essential characteristic of the implementation process, then, is the timely and satisfactory performance of certain necessary tasks related to carrying out the intent of the law. This means rejecting a dichotomous conceptualization of implementation as simply success or failure. (1998: 5)

DeLeon echoes that point, noting that:

> 'things' do get implemented and carried out on a regular basis ... The main problem with implementation is that the discrepancy between 'something' and 'that idealized thing' is often a matter of rose-colored expectations ... It might be long and arduous and uncertain but implementation is a bureaucratic fact of everyday life. (1999a: 322)

Winter (1999) more prosaically emphasizes that the process emphasized by Lester and Goggin needs to be explained by its outputs.

This emphasis on 'process' and 'outputs' leads us to return to a point made in Chapter 1 about the relationship between 'implementation' research and 'evaluation' research. Implementation studies are clearly concerned with similar questions to evaluation studies, but in many respects their objectives can be specified more narrowly. Let us take a comparatively simple example. Vehicles entering a specified zone of Central London have to pay a congestion charge. There is controversy about the objectives of this scheme. Can it simply be seen as a scheme to reduce traffic congestion, or does it go further than that to contribute to improvement in the ambient air quality or indeed to the overall reduction in the use of fossil fuels? There is also a cynical interpretation of the scheme that it was introduced to increase the resources available to the new Mayor of London for his spending objectives. It was even seen as a bit of 'class war' by the self-same Mayor. Nevertheless the implementation of the scheme can be studied without engaging with any of these arguments: simply asking whether the system of charging drivers works efficiently. Do the photographic machines effectively identify vehicles and ensure their drivers are charged, or are there high error rates and high levels of evasion? In this sense – while evidence on implementation difficulties will have an important role to play in the evaluation of this scheme – implementation studies may be carried out without getting into wider controversy about policy goals. Of course, researchers do not do their work in a value-free vacuum. Acknowledging the principles of the rule of law and democracy and adhering to them in the practice of researching, however, is something different than adopting a partisan instead of a clinical way of observing empirical reality. We develop this topic in our discussion of dependent variables in the next section.

Explaining what needs explanation

Outcomes or outputs

Problems with dependent variables in implementation studies arise because of a confusion between issues of ends (goals), issues of the relationship between means and ends (whether means chosen are appropriate) and issues of success in adopting means. Typical policy goals are such things as reduction of crime levels, or air pollution, or unemployment, or teenage pregnancy, or smoking. Policies to achieve these may then be: increasing numbers of police on the beat, curbing the activities of specific pollution emitters, creating places on a youth training programme, making contraception more available, increasing health education. In each of these cases there are two separate questions about effectiveness, one being 'Are the specified activities established?'; the other, 'Do they have any effect on the problem?'

Nevertheless, many implementation studies are not concerned with this distinction. Hence policy goals or policy outcomes are chosen as the dependent variables. It is understandable that this choice is made on the grounds that the objective is to judge policies in terms of what they really achieve. There are four problems following from that.

- The first is that outcomes may be influenced by factors that have nothing to do with the policy intervention. Unemployment may fall because the world economy moves out of recession, pollution may be reduced because economic activities reduce, and so on. In principle, research models can try to factor in these 'environmental' variables.
- The second problem is that a judgement about outcome may be a judgement about the appropriateness of the policy, not about its implementation. The policy may be an inappropriate response to the problem. More police may have no impact on crime, curbing some emissions may increase others, training may not reduce unemployment, the availability of contraceptives may not change risk-taking behaviours by teenagers, health education may have no impact on smoking, and so on. The extreme case here concerns so-called 'symbolic policy' (Edelman, 1971),

produced rather more to convince the public that the government is concerned about an issue than to actually deal with it. When symbolic policy fails, this should not be seen as implementation failure, if there simply has been no realistic consideration of the relationship between means and end.

- The third problem is particularly difficult in the common situation where the supposition is that system changes will lead to better outcomes. Hence, in the United Kingdom at the time of writing there is a great emphasis upon the achievement of more co-ordinated working between different professions in social services. Organizational changes are being tried that are seen as leading to that end. Then a sort of hierarchy of potential dependent variables may be seen. It may be asked: Does the organizational change occur, or does that change lead to more effective collaboration between the relevant professionals? But the ultimate outcome question is surely about the impact of the policy change upon the members of the public served by the new arrangements.
- That leads us to a fourth problem: Can unambiguous and agreed outcome variables be established? In social policy interventions desired outcomes may be disputed. The customers of services may have expectations of services that are not shared by those who deliver them. Exceptionally services may be designed to control behaviour rather than to deliver what people want. The choice of an outcome variable may require the researcher to recognize competing policy goals, and indeed perhaps even make a choice 'Whose side am I on?'.

It must be recognized, as in Matland's analysis of kinds of implementation (see pp. 73–5), that a lack of consensus on policy goals may be an influence on implementation. In the London congestion charge case discussed above, the United States Embassy refuses to pay congestion charges on the grounds that foreign embassies are exempt from tax, a direct invocation of the point noted above about the revenue-raising goal. We might indeed, even within an approach that confines attention to outputs, suggest that there are here two – not necessarily compatible – outputs: reduced traffic flow in the congestion charge zone and revenue for the London government.

Process and outputs

In more complex policy areas multiple and incompatible outputs are identifiable. In the extensive research activity on the implementation of welfare policy change in the United States, it is possible to find both one very narrowly defined explicit outputs used for the dependent variable – the numbers of people cut off the welfare rolls, for example, in Keiser et al. (2004) – but also the use of a number of measures of employment achievement and family welfare enhancement (see Cho et al., 2005). These are obviously potentially incompatible. There are grounds for argument here about whether the latter are really outputs or perhaps outcomes or goals. However, we do not think it helpful – at the margins – to get into an argument about the exact definition of outputs in cases like these. What seems to us important is to try to ensure that implementation studies:

- can be carried out without at the same time any necessary identification with the goals of policies;
- steer away from the rather pointless systematic study of symbolic policies (as identified above) where no attempt has been made to specify expected outputs.

The first of those propositions relates to a substantial area of discomfort for implementation researchers. In the first edition of this book we used, as an example of how an implementation study might be set up, the case of efforts by British central government to increase the use of adoption in cases of original family failure. In presenting this in a seminar we found social workers who were very unhappy with this example, because they strongly disagreed with efforts to rush this process. Where we simply saw a government-specified output as a useful example of an independent variable, they focused instead on what they saw as a questionable child welfare 'goal'. We may similarly note in this chapter that we will mention some studies of American welfare reform that seem to us to embody excellent implementation research practice. We would surely be wrong to assume that all the researchers working on these studies were happy about the cuts to welfare that they analyzed. In fact, in both these cases, top-down goals can be turned on their heads. Good implementation research may enhance top-down goal achievement, but it may also be used to help those opposed to that goal. In other words: systematic exploration of what affected the implementation of a new policy on adoption or cuts in welfare can inform those who criticize a policy, as well as those who want to enforce it.

To sum up this section, we agree with Winter that researchers should 'look for behavioural *output* variables to characterize the *performance* of implementers' to explain variation in performance, thereby avoiding contestable questions about goal-achievement (see discussion in Chapter 4, p. 45). It is the choice of the latter as dependent variables that contributes to pessimism about implementation.

Isolating implementation

The policy formation/implementation relationship

The concepts used in this book were defined in Chapter 1. We do not want to go back over the same ground but do need to emphasize some implications of those definitions for our presentation here. In that chapter a distinction was made between, on the one hand, formulation and decision-making as, together, policy formation; and, on the other hand, implementation. Clearly therefore it is the latter that has to be given attention in the design of research. This may be difficult, however, in situations where there is a particularly strong 'iterative' process between implementation and formation – this is when implementation is essentially an experimental or evolutionary process where strong feed-back is actively expected (what Wildavsky and Majone call 'implementation as evolution', see Chapter 3, p. 45). In such a situation any attempt to look at implementation *per se* must involve the study of a 'moving target'. Here a descriptive approach may be all the researcher can attempt. In such a case it even may be more appropriate to decline to study implementation because of an extreme lack of clarity about 'what is being implemented'.

A policy may be no more than a political response because there is a need to be seen to be doing something, although there may be grave doubts about the effect of that 'doing' upon the perceived problem. It was noted earlier that some of those who seek to give advice to 'top' policy-makers urge them to work with a clear cause/effect model, but the political need for a response may make this a vain hope (see, for example, the approach adopted by Hogwood and Gunn, see pp. 49–51). We find instead a variety of initiatives, many of which may be described as 'symbolic' (see the discussion above). The study of the implementation of such policies provides evidence that pours scorn upon the rational model of the policy process as entailing formulation, decision-making, and implementation as identifiable 'stages' (see, for example, Yanow, 1993). Yet it is reasonable to ask: Is there any point in systematic implementation studies in these circumstances? And is it reasonable to use the particular problems associated with responses to 'wicked problems' as evidence to condemn the study of implementation in general? In other words, those who study implementation should beware of being lured into the systematic study of policies formulated without any serious attention to their actual implementation.

There is a need to beware of a particular 'dead end' here that seems attractive to the researcher eager to show that 'the emperor has no clothes'. The latter is the case when what is involved is showing that something that no one seriously expected to happen has not happened. It may also be necessary for researchers to say in some situations, for example, when negotiating a commissioned project, that the implementation of a particular policy is unresearchable. There are some difficult issues here about sorting out the implications of policy rhetoric. We in no way wish to condemn the study of policy rhetoric, and think there are plenty of grounds for regarding some of our contemporary 'emperors' as short of clothes, but do want to distinguish that study from implementation research.

In Chapter 1, we examined the case for the study of implementation in terms of the notion that it can be identified and analyzed as a separate part of the policy process. Some of the difficulties about doing this were identified. The examination of the key theoretical contributions in Chapter 4 explored the controversy about this matter. Then, in Chapter 6, an approach was suggested that enables the use of a flexible version of the stages model. What, therefore, can be said now by way of practical advice to researchers wrestling with the problem? There is a rather obvious point that what a policy is trying to do will affect its ease of implementation. The key issues about the policy here will be its complexity, and the extent to which it can be specified in unambiguous terms. As already noted, a rather similar point will need to be made about symbolic policies. The whole topic relates back to the issues about the dependent variable discussed in the last section, inasmuch as it is vital to try to sort out what a policy intervention is trying to achieve before attempting to examine its implementation. It may be that narrative and interpretative research designs are most appropriate in situations where policy formation and implementation are very closely interlocked.

It was shown in Chapter 3 that one of the concerns of the early implementation theorists was to give advice to policy formers on the contents and shape a policy should take to ensure its successful implementation (see, for example, the work of Hogwood and Gunn, discussed on p. 49–51). The ingredients of this literature are best expressed by Van Meter and Van Horn's (1975) specification of the importance of policy standards and objectives. The latter 'elaborate on the overall goals of the policy decision ... to provide concrete and more specific standards for assessing performance' (ibid.: 464). These authors also identify the importance of the resources and incentives made available, a variable emphasized by Goggin and his colleagues as top-down 'inducements and constraints'.

If independent variables are to be specified under this heading, it is necessary to develop criteria that will enable policies to be distinguished from each other in terms of the extent to which they are clearly specified, resourced and supported. During the 1980s and 1990s a very distinctive vein of studies of this kind was developed – which may be described as 'mandate' studies (Fix and Kenyon, 1990). A good example of these is a study by Meier and McFarlane (1995) in which a number of policy initiatives are compared. They all appear to have the same objective, but in practice one statute sets policy goals much more clearly than any of the others. P.J. May (1993, 1994, 1995; May and Burby, 1996) has carried out a number of studies which explore 'mandates' supplied by one layer of government to another. The substantive policy was flood and erosion control and he explored the impact of state laws on the behaviour of local governments in both the United States and Australia. Of particular interest is a comparison of the extent to which, in different situations, mandates that are either coercive or seeking co-operation produce significant responses. However, salient among May's findings is evidence that choices between these options may need to take into account the problem to be solved and the predisposition of the agencies being mandated.

Any propositions about the effectiveness of mandates are likely to depend upon the extent to which the layer of government doing the mandating is seen as a legitimate policy-maker for those being mandated. In that sense, implementation studies in federal systems may be as Cho et al. put it, 'at the confluence of two literatures that deal with policy implementation and intergovernmental relations' (2005: 31).

One of the more complex issues in relation to policy formation concerns the extent to which feedback occurs (an important feature in Goggin et al.'s model, see Chapter 4, pp. 64–5) and policy adjustments are made over time. This is a theme that tends to provide difficulties for quantitative studies. The underlying questions about the nature of the 'game' being played between layers tend to require a more qualitative approach. This is seen, for example, in Castellani's (1992) study of the closure of mental health care institutions in New York State or Clark's (1997) study of the negotiations between the Australian federal government and the states over changes to the assessment of need for geriatric care. In the latter we find questions being raised such as 'why should we help them solve their problem?'.

Identifying reformulations

Where policy formation is an iterative process, it may be possible to recognize key points at which key reformulations occur; a common example of this is adjustment of funding. In these circumstances, research designs that recognize phases and use time-series data may be able to handle these phenomena satisfactorily.

For the understanding of implementation it will probably as important to be studying *how* policy re-formulation occurs as to be identifying *that* it occurs. Here are two examples of the use of this approach using qualitative methods.

Glennerster, Matsaganis and Owens (1994) studied the early history of a British health policy initiative designed to enable primary health care doctors to secure hospital services for their own patients by entering into contracts without reference to health authorities. These 'general practitioner fundholders' were allocated budgets based upon the size of their lists and past referral practices. The initial setting of those budgets was very much a matter of 'trial and error'. Similarly the establishment of rules to regulate this activity – to prevent possible abuses of autonomy and to cope with unexpected problems – was an evolutionary process, involving collaboration between the health authorities, the national Department of Health and the 'fundholders' themselves.

Glennerster and his colleagues describe this as 'Lewis and Clark planning' (adapting an idea from Schultze, 1968). They say:

> The American explorers, Lewis and Clark, were merely told to find a route to the Pacific. They did so by finding the watershed, following the rivers to the sea using their wits as they went.

> The implementation of fundholding can be seen as a Lewis and Clark adventure – but in this instance there was telephonic contact between the field explorers and the equivalent of Washington and regular flights back to discuss progress with other explorers. (1994: 30)

This is an analogy illustrative of the way the implementation of a policy initiative may involve exploratory activity. Research on such an initiative has to mirror and record that exploration.

The second example comes from a study of education policy. Here the issue was the development, under the 1988 Education Act, of a 'national curriculum' in England and Wales, setting parameters for school teaching. In this case the legislation did little more than prescribe broad subjects to be included (mathematics, English, science, etc.). Organizations and procedures were set up to determine more detailed content and to enforce compliance. Then even within the implementation process there was – not surprisingly given the complexity of the issues – considerable latitude to enable individual schools and teachers to select topics to emphasize, approaches to teaching and so on. Bowe, Ball and Gold (1992) use a concept from sociology and linguistics, 'texts' (Atkinson, 1985), to explain this process. They argue:

> Texts carry with them possibilities and constraints, contradictions and spaces. The reality of policy in practice depends upon the compromises and accommodations to

these in particular settings ... our conception of policy has to be set against the idea that policy is something that is simply done to people. (1992: 15)

For Bowe and his colleagues, then, 'policy texts' are a variety of official documents, together with speeches and other commentaries designed to make sense of these. Taken as a whole, these are 'not necessarily internally consistent and clear', 'fraught with the possibility of misunderstanding' and never exhaustive (ibid.: 21). They go on to make the point that 'policy is not done and finished at the legislative moment' but embellish this by saying 'it evolves in and through the texts that represent it, texts have to be read in relation to the time and particular site of their production. They also have to be read with and against one another – intertextuality is important' (ibid.: 21).

Thus Bowe, Ball and Gold argue:

> Policies ... are textual interventions but they also carry with them material constraints and possibilities. The responses to these texts have 'real' consequences. These consequences are experienced in ... the arena of practice to which policy refers ... policy is not simply received and implemented within this arena, rather it is subject to interpretation and then recreated. (1992: 21–2)

This qualitative study thus involved the examination of the development, elaboration and interpretation of these texts using, like Glennerster and his colleagues, systematic and carefully documented case studies.

The language used by Bowe, Ball and Gold draws upon postmodernist discourse. We see in the work of Yanow a postmodernist concern to examine issues of 'the communication of policy meanings' (1993: 41). She argues that attention must be given to ambiguous and multiple meanings in policy and modes of interpretation of those in implementation. These are of course then the subject of qualitative examination, in case study contexts.

Overall, it is in relation to situations like this that researchers need to have regard to the way in which the 'operational' activities may be combined in practice with 'directional' and perhaps even 'constitutive' ones (as analyzed in the last chapter). The next section continues that theme more explicitly.

Dealing with layers

Ongoing policy formation

We argued earlier that it is possible to speak of *levels* to indicate the distinct parts in the policy cycle as logical-analytical constructions, while using the term *layers* to refer to separate (sub- or co-) governments exercising legitimate authority with relative autonomy and probably controlled by democratic representative organs. Thus it may happen that an American state, as a formal 'layer' in the political-administrative system, fulfils a task on the 'level' of *implementation* regarding policy A, but on the 'level' of *policy formation* as far as policy B is concerned.

Issues about the impact of vertical links in the chain from policy formation to the street-level have been on the agenda of implementation studies ever since Pressman and Wildavsky's effort to model this set of links mathematically (1973). In Chapters 3 and 4, we explored the work of various theorists who have struggled with this issue. Among them Goggin and his colleagues (1990) are most relevant to this chapter as they worked out their analysis using a number of empirical studies. All of these concerned federal government/state relationships in the United States. What that book brings out very clearly is the methodological complexity inherent in 'multi-level' implementation research. A major factor contributing to that complexity is the fact that often intervening levels, as layers in the political-administrative system, have a legitimate claim to engage in policy formulation and decision-making: Where does 'policy formation' end and 'implementation' begin? It is in recognition of this that Goggin et al. refer to federal 'messages' to states rather than federal policies.

Similarly, studies of the implementation of European Union policies indicate very distinct processes of re-formulations within individual nation states. What is called 'implementation' in those studies in fact may be seen as 'policy formation'. Lampinen and Uusikylä (1998) note widespread variation in the implementation of EU directives. They hypothesize that political institutions, political corporatism, public support for EU membership and political culture will influence implementation. They find that only two of those variables seem to be important: political institutions (high stability) and political culture (high levels of trust). Knill and Lenschow (1998) compare the implementation of EU environment policy directives in Britain and Germany. They hypothesize that different administrative traditions will affect implementation, with nation states showing a tendency to reject regulations embodied in a form that is alien to those traditions. Knill and Lenschow find in fact that reality is more complex; changing political and administrative agendas also have an impact.

From a literature review and their own research, Falkner et al. (2007) suggest that there are 'three worlds of compliance' varying from issue to issue and state to state. They distinguish 'a world of law observance' in which efforts are made to implement directives faithfully; a 'world of domestic politics' where in the face of internal political pressures 'domestic concerns dominate over the fragile aspiration to comply' (ibid.: 405), and a 'world of transposition neglect' characterized by a neglect of EU goals stemming from what they call a 'posture of national arrogance' (ibid.). In some respects, only the first of those might be called implementation. In the second case there may be policy formation, with EU goals only one influence among many. In the third case, implementation discourse is rather meaningless.

While some policies are formed and implemented within one domain of judicial authority (for example, an American state, using state agencies for implementation), in other policy processes a variety of political-administrative layers can be found, on several of which the (co-) formation of the policy involved takes place. Thus, one could, alternatively, introduce the concept of *multi-layered policy (co-) formation* here.

One solution to difficulties about levels and layers in the empirical study of policy implementation is to limit attention to the relationship between two levels in a policy-making process, preferably together connected to one single political-administrative layer. In a certain case both the formation of a specific policy and the implementation of it might take place within the domain of judicial authority of, for instance, an American state. In other cases, what is seen as 'implementation' of a policy may involve separate layers. Many of the studies from the United States are in practice either about federal/state relationships or about state/local government ones. In such cases 'gaps' between two bodies may be misleadingly seen as 'deficits' when the 'lower' tier has clear rights to adapt or even disregard policies emanating from the 'upper'. In fact, both layers then have *policy formation* prerogatives. In several US and Australian studies concerning federal/state relations, there is little doubt that the language of implementation deficit is relevant if states are failing to carry out clearly *mandated* federal policies. At the same time, in a policy area already shown above to involve multiple and to some extent competing goals, Keiser and Soss (1998) observe of a US federal law on child support, that:

> Our analysis indicates that levels of bureaucratic disentitlement are shaped by partisan control of state governments, by the values of the state bureaucracy, by the funding decisions of elected officials, and by the levels of demand placed on the bureaucracy. (ibid.: 1152)

Similarly, Scholz, Twombly and Headrick (1991) highlight local political influences upon responses to a federal measure within one particular US State, and Cimitile et al. (1997) explore the limited local impact of unfunded federal mandates.

The alternative to treating policy-making layers in this way is provided by Pressman and Wildavsky's analysis of the handling of a policy issue in an inter-institutional context, in which layers of this kind are seen as making distortion of the original policy goals more probable. We prefer to recognize that there is likely to be what may be described as interpretative space within a complex inter-institutional framework, allowing 'agencies' to exercise discretion. This leads us to suggest that it is inappropriate to use a concept like 'implementation deficit' in contexts like these.

These points may be put together by suggesting that there may be distinguishable goals applicable to parts of a total system, of, for example, central government, local government, schools, etc. Questions about the success of any one part of that system in imposing its *goals* upon other parts need to be separated from questions about the capacity of the stakeholders in any single part to secure the *implementation* of those goals.

Cline (2000) picks up this issue in a rather different way. He contrasts two theoretical contributions, which were examined in Chapter 4, that from Goggin and his associates and that from Stoker. Exaggerating their emphases a little, in our view, Cline sees the former as exploring vertical public administration as setting communication problems between agencies, while the latter woukd see it as setting collaboration problems. In the first case, the issue is about how to get the 'messages' right; in the second, it is about the management of a bargaining process. It may be noted that this has similarities to Cho et al.'s distinction between policy implementation and inter-governmental relations mentioned earlier. While both communication and collaboration are likely to be involved, the distinction Cline makes is pertinent to the issues about claims to legitimate participation in the policy formation process. Inasmuch then as implementation studies focus upon these collaboration problems, they are likely to need to draw upon game theory. Then in methodological terms hypotheses may be developed about the way those games are likely to proceed. We see such an effort in the work of Torenvlied (see Chapter 4, p. 72–3) where he models the strength of the policy messages, on the one hand, and the motivation of the implementation agencies, on the other.

Local variations

Implicit in what has been said here is then the view that relationships between layers of government in which the *layers* problem is entirely absent – that is, there is no effort by the lower *layer* to influence policy *formation* – may be quite rare. Central/local relationships in the UK are often characterized in these terms. In this case there is certainly no absence of local government aspirations to influence policy formulation (and indeed it is a feature of the bottom-up contribution to the analysis of implementation made by Barrett and Fudge, 1981, that such aspirations are regarded as legitimate). Nevertheless the formal legal structure casts local government as confined to the implementation of policy made in Parliament.

A study in which one of the authors participated explored local implementation in England very much in the terms of a relationship between layers of government (Vick et al., 2006). The study was concerned with the implementation of a government policy under which individuals in need of social care could be given direct payments of cash to purchase services for themselves instead of being provided with services commissioned by local authorities. While some local authorities had been pioneers of this approach, the study dealt with a period in which central government had become a strong advocate of direct payments and was increasing pressure on local governments to implement the policy and local authorities varied significantly in their enthusiasm for the policy. There was thus a relatively straightforward 'dependent variable' published in official statistics which could be used for each authority: numbers of payments over a period corrected to take into account variations in overall population size.

One published study looks at this topic using quantitative material available from nationally reported statistics (Fernández et al., 2007). That study suggests that policy implementation is shaped by both local circumstances and 'local policy preferences', but the data available do little to throw light upon what that means exactly. The study we report here aimed to go further with a similar dependent variable but with independent variables secured from (1) a postal survey of key responsible officials in local authorities; and (2) a telephone survey asking more detailed questions of respondents from a sample of authorities. The former was readily quantifiable; the latter was not.

The questions used in the postal survey aimed to secure judgement on the factors affecting implementation. Hence influences from the source of the policy (central government), from within the local authority (at various *sub-layers*) and from the wider environment were considered. There were statistically significant differences between authorities in terms of performance data in respect of:

- the extent of leadership on this issue within the local authority;
- local political support;
- the establishment of an effective direct payments support scheme;
- the training and support for front-line staff in respect of work on this policy;
- whether a 'direct payments development fund award' had been received;
- the existence of a positive attitude to direct payments among staff;
- the use of a ring-fenced budget for direct payments.

These variables were derived from scaled ratings made by local officials. All except the fourth concerned solely the local reception of the policy. In contrast, the measures of experience of pressures from central government did not, on the whole, discriminate between authorities.

The limitations of the approach can be seen to lie in the highlighting of obviously inter-correlated factors (leadership and political support, for example) and from the fact that the data source for the independent variables is people themselves involved in implementing the scheme. Nevertheless the approach enabled the respective contributions of the two *layers* of government to be assessed, suggesting that – while central government set the basic parameters – variations in local government organization, orientation and disposition were crucial to variations in output.

Specifying inter-organizational relationships

Analyzing network management

The last section has been about aspects of vertical inter-organizational collaboration; we shift here to consider horizontal collaboration, something that is also very central to modern approaches to governance. The problem is that collaborative relationships at the same time may involve both vertical and horizontal collaboration (this is explored in Koppenjan and Klijn, 2004, although that book is as much concerned with making recommendations about management of networks as with suggesting how to research that process). Exworthy and Powell's (2004) research, however, examines horizontal collaboration in the context of vertical relationships, suggesting that strong hierarchical controls can undermine the former. A great deal of the 'misery' emphasis in writing on implementation has been in relation to problems where horizontal collaboration is very important (see Challis et al., 1988; Hardy et al., 1992).

Nevertheless that 'problem' focus often leads on to a discussion of ways of overcoming such problems (see Mattesich and Monsey, 1992; Hudson et al., 1999). This is also an area where sociological studies of organizations, falling on the margins of the concerns of this book, have been very important. Emphasis tends to be upon circumstances in which 'domain consensus' (Thompson, 1967) and 'resource dependency' (Benson, 1975) can be developed. A variety of ideas that are clearly susceptible to operationalization for research has been developed here – about collaborative capacity and purpose, about trust and about ways in which collaborative roles can be engendered at street-level. Powell and his colleagues conceptualize these in terms of the importance of three streams: policy streams concerning 'the extent to which local goals are shared (2001: 44); process streams concerning the 'mechanisms or instruments to achieve the goals' (ibid.: 44); and resource streams, money of course. In this way we see issues arising about the links between vertical and horizontal aspects of the implementation process.

Measuring networking

There are many articles in which activities where there is a need for inter-agency working are examined. However, quantitative causal analysis in these situations is rare. One exception is Provan and Milward's study (1991) in which they collected data on the attitudes of street-level staff to help to explain collaboration in networks. Their study looked at services for mentally ill adults, using involvement in a collaborative network as its dependent variable and collected attitude data to measure the commitment of the staff of individual organizations to that network.

Prima facie it should be possible to factor in data on some of the following into a quantitative study:

- the salience of a collaborative relationship with others where the behaviour of one (lead) agency is under scrutiny;
- the quality of collaborative relationships within an implementation system depending upon a network;
- attitudes to collaboration, and the extent of trust of other organizations;
- the extent to which collaborative roles are developed (the classic formulation of this was Friend, Power and Yewlett's notion of the importance of the presence of 'reticulists') (1974).

Work by Meier and O'Toole (for instance, O'Toole and Meier, 1999; Meier and O'Toole, 2001, 2003) is injecting a more comprehensive quantitative approach into the exploration of this important subject. Their 2003 article explores data from Texas school districts relating, with a sophisticated statistical methodology, network management to educational performance while taking into account the wide range of 'environmental' factors (see the discussion below) that are likely to be important.

Again, in relation to this topic there is a very clear incidence of overlap between the academic disciplines since relationships between organizations have been given considerable attention in the sociological 'branch' of neo-institutional theory.

When we shift our attention to qualitative studies, we find many discussions of inter-organizational collaboration in, for example, case studies of military base redevelopment, milk marketing, the designation of toxic waste dumps, food programmes for children, water basin clean-up, erosion control, preservation of rare species and several general articles on environment policy (these examples are cited, without references from the review of the literature we reported in our first edition). In the light of British concerns with inter-agency collaboration in areas like health and social care, this topic has been given substantial attention in a range of studies (Pettigrew et al., 1992; Wistow et al., 1994; Flynn et al., 1996; Hudson et al., 1997; Powell et al., 2001). On the whole, these studies do not draw upon implementation theory (for a discussion of the relevant literature, see Hudson, 1987, and Hudson et al., 1999). However, a key theme in much of this British work has been the importance of relationships between street-level workers for collaborative initiatives imposed or encouraged from 'above'.

Differentiating agency responses

This section will explore implementation agency responses in terms of:

- overall characteristics and disposition of agencies;
- issues about the behaviour of front-line (or street-level) staff.

Sub-sections within this section deal separately with these two issues.

Agency characteristics and disposition

Overall organizational rigidity and resistance to new initiatives are highlighted in some studies, such as, for example, the study by Ringeling and Koppenjan of problems with the development of a new Dutch passport (Koppenjan, 1991). It also appears in studies of the relative ineffectiveness of new US Presidential initiatives (see, for example, Durant, 1993; Krause, 1996). In the light of the heavy emphasis upon intra-organizational characteristics in the theoretical literature, it might be expected that many studies would be found that operationalized these. The absence of this is perhaps an indicator of the extent to which in social science a division of labour has occurred. Much of this work has been done by organizational sociologists who developed the propositions emerging from Max Weber's theory into various forms of contingency theory and neo-institutional theory (see Hickson et al., 1971; Di Maggio and Powell, 1983; Scott, 1995; see also Chapter 2 of this book, pp. 34–7).

Studies that can compare the responses of a number of similar agencies – states, counties or cities – clearly offer scope for an exploration of the influence of agency characteristics and disposition in a systematic way. A good example of such a study is one by Harbin et al. (1992) of services for handicapped children which developed what is called an 'assessment of influential characteristics scale' to analyze agency characteristics. This has four key subdivisions:

1   Climate (history of services and levels of support from decision-makers and advocacy groups).
2   Resources (financial, qualified personnel, existence of specialized facilities).
3   Policies (current inter-agency agreement and existing legislation).
4   System (experience with interagency services).

The question of agency disposition is addressed in some studies in terms not of implementation theory, but in relation to the notion of 'representative bureaucracy' (see Chapter 2, p. 28). This means they ask what the impact is of the ethnicity, gender or social class of implementers upon their decisions. A study of equal educational opportunities explores this issue in a sophisticated way, showing that:

> Political forces ... were able to influence policy outputs to benefit minority students. This political influence is indirect. Black school board members influence the selection of black administrators who in turn influence the hiring of black teachers. Black teachers then mitigate the impact of bureaucratic decision rules and provide black students with better access to educational opportunities. (Meier et al., 1991: 173–4)

Similarly, a study of loan allocations for rural housing shows the impact of variations in the number of staff from minority groups, between different offices, upon loans to people from that group (Selden, 1997). That really takes us on to the other sub-theme of influences upon the behaviour of street-level staff, on which there has been an extensive amount of research relating to this theme. We therefore return to it below.

Before leaving the topic of institutional disposition, a connection with another literature needs to be noted. This is the study of the relationship between the social, political and economic characteristics of *local* governments and public policy outputs (key examples of work on this theme are Boaden, 1971; Newton and Sharpe, 1977; Danziger, 1978; Valente and Manchester, 1984; Hirsch, 1995). Where local government is in the role of implementer of policy formed elsewhere, this literature is surely relevant. We examine research that is explicitly about implementation in which political control is an important independent variable in our discussion of quantitative studies later in the chapter.

Influences on the behaviour of street-level staff

At least since the seminal book by Michael Lipsky (1980) (see pp. 51–3) it has been recognized that any attempt to explain implementation must look within agencies at the factors that affect the behaviour of staff working at the 'street-level' – in fact, a *sub-layer*. Empirical research on implementation contains at least the following variants on this theme:

- single agency case-studies where behaviour is examined qualitatively;
- studies of the attitudes of bureaucrats that are used to deduce their impact upon actual behaviour (in this case, attitude is the dependent variable);
- studies comparing agencies to make quantitative analysis of individual bureaucrat behaviour possible;
- studies that take an already recognized implementation 'gap' and seek to explain this by an examination of the bureaucratic task and the bureaucrat/client interaction.
- studies with a public management perspective that particularly focus upon control over street-level bureaucrats.

There are many studies in the first category. One particularly interesting study in this category is a Californian one of the way in which policy reforms requiring 'welfare' recipients to increase their labour market participation were implemented. This involved observational techniques and showed that workers were primarily concerned to carry out normal eligibility interviews. In the course of these they might give information about policies that would be applied if clients secured work. Most responses about work were prompted by questions from clients, and this was only in a small minority of cases. There was very little evidence of efforts to direct people towards training opportunities (Meyers et al., 1998; see also similar findings in Jewell and Glaser, 2006).

It may be noted that again we encounter a boundary with other areas of research activity, in this case particularly hard to delineate, sociological studies of the determinants of behaviour by workers in organizations of all kinds. Lipsky's theoretical work drew heavily upon studies of this sort, particularly studies of police behaviour. The latter has developed into a substantial research industry (for reviews see Holdaway, 1983; Grimshaw and Jefferson, 1987; Reiner, 1992).

Street-level theory may be elaborated by going beyond single-agency case studies to comparative ones which explore the different organizational and political contexts in which public officials work. Jewell's study of caseworkers in social assistance in the United States, Germany and Sweden in *Agents of the Welfare State* (2007) does just that, making interesting links between the exploration of street-level bureaucracy and comparative welfare state theory.

An example of the second category is Chan's study of Chinese environment policy, attributing a 'gap' to the attitudes of officials who recognize alternative local economic considerations (Chan et al., 1995). Rather further from actual policy is a study in which the theories of justice held by street-level bureaucrats are explored (Kelly, 1994).

It is the third category that involves, in methodological terms, the most adventurous approach to this issue. In a study of Medicaid spending, Weissert shows that office managers' 'activism' in the community influences the generosity of local spending decisions (1994). Maupin (1993) includes some data on street-level attitudes in an exploration of the activities of parole offices. An interesting contribution in this field is a study of child protection in Scotland. There street-level behaviour that might be deemed to involve disregard of policy is shown to derive from assumptions of social workers about appropriate action. This is the case in a situation in which their immediate managers share those values and thus tacitly condone this action (Murray, 2006).

Clearly also, as noted above, there are studies to be found of this kind within the literature on the sociology of organizations too. Although labelled differently, Blau's study of a public employment service (1955), a classic study in the latter genre, was very much about public policy implementation. A study by Chaney and Saltzstein (1998) shows that female representation in police forces is positively correlated with active responses to domestic violence. This brings us back to the 'representative bureaucracy' theme identified above. Riccucci and Meyers' (2004) study of the impact of both gender and ethnicity on welfare administration starts with a review of the burgeoning literature on this theme. They make an important distinction between 'active' and 'passive' representation. The literature on passive representation explores the social or demographic characteristics of bureaucracies while the crucial question is: 'Are passive and active representation linked? That is to say, do ascribed characteristics of an individual ... relate to or predict policy preferences, as well as actions to achieve certain policy *outcomes*?' (ibid.: 585). The research then reported indicates stronger evidence on preferences than on outcomes. There is thus an interesting contrast here between this and an article by Pitts exploring the impact of ethnic identity upon teachers' performance (2005).

Several articles in the fourth category take a known implementation gap as the starting point and seek to explain it, without really working with a dependent variable. Examples are two studies of the ineffectiveness of a new provision in the US AFDC ('welfare') law that expected beneficiaries to be penalized if their children did not attend school regularly. Ethridge and Percy (1993) show that the policy was premised upon a 'rational actor' theory in which quite complex linkages were expected. They set this out in terms of steps in a logical chain: parents want to maximize AFDC payments, parents are able to monitor the school attendance behaviour of their children and interpret messages about this, parents are able to control the behaviour of their children, and the threat of sanctions will lead parents to take action. Ethridge and Percy go on to question these assumptions and illustrate their problematic character using evidence about practice on the ground or derived from litigation about the law. Stoker and Wilson (1998) focus more precisely upon flaws in the verification process for this policy, using evidence from interviews of staff. They explore the weaknesses of the two alternatives essential for verification: depending upon the transfer of administrative information or getting clients to produce the evidence that they had complied with the requirements of the legislation. Evidence is used from interviews of staff.

In the fifth category, Riccucci's work is important, brought together in a book *How Management Matters* (2005). Contrary to the more ambivalent stance taken in Lipsky's original work (see the discussion in Chapter 3), Riccucci writes from a top-down perspective in seeking to explore managerial success in controlling street-level bureaucrats. Nevertheless this study provides a very good model for research on this theme. Riccucci identifies the factors that might be expected to lead to diversity of practice: the personal characteristics highlighted by the representative bureaucracy work, the personal experience and attitudes of workers and work norms and cultures. She relates those factors to the extent to which policy goals were advanced by effective approaches to the practice of public management at the meso- and micro-levels. Some comparable research in a European context is done by May and Winter on employment policy reforms in Denmark. Their work is aimed at 'unpacking ... the political and managerial influences on caseworkers' policy emphases' (May and Winter, 2007 – quote is from the abstract).

Identifying stakes

It is important to recognize that the process of implementation is influenced by the responses of those affected by the policy to be implemented. This is seen most evidently in studies of regulatory policy, particularly where those regulated are powerful (large companies, for example). There is a literature here that sees co-production as a fundamental aspect of public policy-making, involving negotiation and bargaining (Whitaker, 1980; Parks et al., 1981; Kiser, 1984; Hanf, 1993). Even the responses of weaker actors – the clients of welfare programmes – may feed back into policy implementation.

Studies of this topic are, of course, embedded in a wider literature that emphasizes the impact of powerful actors upon policy-making – stressing phenomena such as regulatory capture and the influence of corporate power (see *inter alia* Lukes, 1974; Lindblom, 1977). It should perhaps be taken as self-evident that actors that can influence the policy formation sub-process may also influence the implementation sub-process.

What this implies is a need for research in which implementation 'games' (Bardach, 1977) are analyzed, with attention to the resources possessed by the various actors. Hence such studies could bear resemblances to the one outlined by Knoepfel and his colleagues. On the basis of extensive experience of research on environmental policy (Knoepfel, 1986, 1997; Knoepfel and Weidner, 1982), Knoepfel at al. (2007) underline the need to identify roles played by those who directly benefit from policies, those who directly lose (are 'targeted) by policies and a range of third parties who may be either gainers or losers. The conceptual scheme used in that study is set out in Figure 7.1.

Turning to issues about individuals as influences providing a feedback to policy, attention obviously needs to be given again to some of the studies that focus upon the behaviour of street-level bureaucrats. The latter category in particular regards studies of efforts to build regulatory controls into American 'welfare' policy (Ethridge and Percy, 1993; Stoker and Wilson, 1998; Meyers et al., 1998). Hupe (1993a) has explored the way in which discretionary behaviour in welfare administration may involve co-production (see also Knegt, 1986).

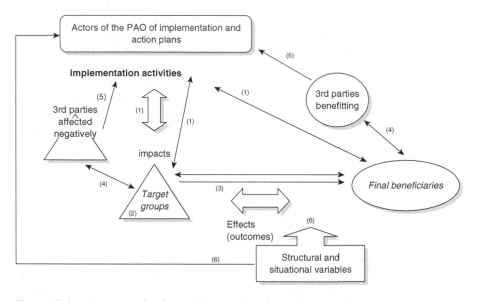

Figure 7.1   Actors and substantive results of implementation
Source: Knoepfel et al. (2007: 213).

Reference has been made above to the importance of police studies for exploration of street-level behaviour. The interaction between police officers and presumed law breakers has been shown as important for 'disposal' decisions (Fielding and Fielding, 1991; Campbell, 2001). Murray's study of child protection practice in Scotland, quoted above, suggested that managers' attitudes may be important for street-level practice, also argued that welfare clients – even as in the case of her study 'involuntary clients' – can shape policy outputs (Murray, 2006: 221–4).

There is an interesting theoretical and methodological issue here about the extent to which this theme – of the response of those affected – should simply be seen as a variant on the inter-organizational collaboration theme discussed in the previous section. Where modern governance involves inter-organizational collaboration in which private organizations may be as involved as public ones, the distinction between the two sections can be challenged. The conceptualization of this target group involvement has been examined under different headings, each referring to a different aspect. The concept of co-production, as used for example by Parks et al. (1981), Kiser (1984) and Hanf (1993), refers to the joint contribution delivered by partners in a system. Depending upon institutional culture and style of regulation, the interaction between government officials and business corporations may take some form of negotiation (for examples in the field of environmental regulation, see Hanf, 1993). The concept of co-production is also used in relation to the participation of citizens, for instance, in the form of client councils around municipal social services departments (Hupe, 1993a). Some authors use the concept to refer to citizens' participation in general (Tops, 1999).

But then, of course, there are all kinds of conceptual equivalents available, such as 'citizenship' (Van Gunsteren, 1998); 'local democracy' (Daemen and Schaap, eds, 2000); 'discursive democracy' (Dryzek, 1990); 'deliberative democracy' (Elster, 1998); and also 'participatory policy making' (Edelenbos, 2000). This takes us again back to some key concerns in the last two chapters – about the nature of governance and its consequences for the way in which the impact of participation is factored into implementation studies.

In a country like The Netherlands the phenomenon of 'interactive policy-making' can be observed as a contemporary expression of a long-standing tradition of consultation and consensus-making (Hendriks and Toonen, 1998). This tradition, so characteristic in Dutch water management, rural and local planning and social economic affairs (Visser and Hemerijck, 1997), has now spread to other parts of the public domain. Citizens are sometimes invited to have a say in, for instance, the formulation of a plan for enhancing traffic safety, the sale of social housing, or the location of a centre for asylum seekers. In its broadest definition co-production refers to a specific phenomenon in the practice of policy-making in which a national, local, or other government involves citizens, non-profit-making organizations, business companies, and/or other governments in contributing to the making of a specific policy. Inasmuch as co-production particularly concerns the extension of the 'early' parts of the policy process, the implication for implementation may be a limited one.

There is a need to distinguish between situations in which collaboration is central to the policy activity and those where essentially there is an attempt to influence, regulate or benefit some outside party. In this sense co-production of social services – involving private or voluntary organizations as service delivery agencies under contract – does largely belong to our 'horizontal relationships' category. On the other hand, co-production, meaning a negotiative relationship in which a powerful polluter's compliance with regulation depends to some extent upon its consent, does not. In these cases the borderline between seeing those affected as active players or just the policy 'environment', as discussed in the next section, may be a narrow one. In education policy studies (such as the work of Meier and O'Toole, 2003 or Pitts, 2005), in the context of much evidence from research that the social characteristics of the 'input' (children) are a very strong influence on the output, then two options may be pursued. One is treating this input as an 'environmental' given (as discussed in the next section); the other option implies exploring the constraints upon co-production of outputs.

Recognizing macro-parameters

Inasmuch as implementation studies are concerned with policy outcomes, there are some difficult questions about the policy environment that have to be dealt with. These are about the extent that policies can effectively address issues which may be influenced by phenomena over which governments can have little or no influence – changes in the moral climate of a nation, demographic change, global economic forces, etc. As suggested earlier these factors are important where implementation studies seek to explain outcomes, and some of the issues and methodologies for dealing with them were explored there.

There is an issue here about change over time – an aspect that has been noted as affecting all implementation studies. The development of techniques to incorporate changes into regression studies, with appropriate lags, has been significant in the recent development of quantitative implementation studies. Hence we find studies incorporating variation in migration pressures into the study of the implementation of French immigration policy (Hollifield, 1990) and changes to agricultural markets into a study of the evolution of agricultural policy (Meier et al., 1995).

Careful consideration of wider factors that cannot be brought under the control of those who formulate and implement policy is very important for a satisfactory implementation study. The success or failure of implementation studies depends upon this. The pessimistic view of both policy interventions and their implementation is that their real effects are often determined by factors outside government control. This point was made above in relation to the issue of the choice of outcomes for dependent variables.

The critique of implementation studies as taking an unnecessarily pessimistic view of policy processes rests to some extent upon the fact that researchers have had difficulty in taking into account variables outside the policy process. To continue with the employment policy example, it may in fact be the case that a change in the economic environment would have made unemployment much worse, and placement activities much more difficult had it not been for the policy innovation under review. In that case it may be unreasonable to interpret the fact that implementation had become more difficult as 'implementation deficit' implying ineffectiveness or culpability on the part of the implementers.

It is therefore important for implementation researchers to work with methodologies that pay very careful attention to methods to take into account and 'control for' environmental variables. It is also important to take a broad rather than a narrow view of those variables. In that sense the label *'macro-parameters'* used in relation to this topic may be a little misleading. Within the limitations of real-world research, methodology factors in the previous category – the impact of responses of those affected – may need to be treated as if they were 'macro-environmental factors'. For example, it may be very difficult to identify in any specific way, let alone any quantifiable way, the resistance of powerful industries to pollution control policy. Nevertheless it may be possible to build into a research design some 'controls' for the relative strength of industrial interests in different districts.

Quantitative versus qualitative studies

Throughout the discussion so far references have been made to both quantitative and qualitative studies. In this section we look at some of the arguments about these alternatives. We confine our attention to the particular issues about studying

	Organizations	
	Single	Multiple
Events		
Single	1	3
Multiple	2	4

Figure 7.2   Categories of implementation studies

implementation, not getting into either the wider issues about social science methodology or the issues about how to analyze statistical or qualitative findings. Our stance is a pragmatic one and entails the following:

(a) It seems appropriate to answer questions about 'what happened' using quantitative methods wherever multiple quantifiable observations can be available.
(b) In the last analysis, the argument between protagonists of quantitative and qualitative methods is a sterile one, since there is a case to be made that use of either (or both) depends upon the situation and on the data available.

We will go on from those two propositions to explore their particular applicability to implementation research.

At the core of this issue are two distinctions that can initially be put side by side within a simple matrix. The study of implementation may involve multiple or single implementing organizations and it may involve multiple or single events. Hence we may set out these two as in Figure 7.2.

1. Single organizations, single events

It does not require much imagination to see that if one has a single actor, say, a government implementing a policy that in its essence involves a single 'event', say, the reorganization of a ministry or the privatization of a utility, then researchers have little scope for the carrying out of a study in which quantitative methods can be used to try to explain 'what happened'. There are nevertheless some relevant questions to be raised here about the scope for comparison through comparative studies. One of the authors is involved in a comparative study of long-term policy in which data on expenditure and on the use of residential care across a sample of countries are related to differences in family systems. However, essentially the comparison is of different *policy-making* environments rather than differences in implementation.

A related issue is the study of the impact of policies where the initial formation activities are outside the nation state. We earlier mentioned the growing volume of studies of the implementation of European Union policies that indicate very distinct processes of re-formulations within individual nation states. Such studies are likely to need to be broadly qualitative in nature because of the difficulties in securing a policy definition that holds constant across nation states. Otherwise it is unlikely that studies in category 1 can involve quantitative analysis. In all the other categories, quantification may be feasible; what this will involve varies from case to case.

2. Single organizations, multiple events

In category 2, one focuses on a single organization making multiple decisions. The first point to make is another obvious one: it all depends upon what multiple' means. We may use two contrasting examples here. One is a centralized social security agency responsible for decisions on individual benefits; the other example, a central regulatory agency making decisions about allowable levels of pollution from large enterprises. Two considerations influence the feasibility of quantification. The first one is simply the methodology textbook issue that, with a limited number of observations, one has limited scope for statistical analysis of the impact of the relevant independent variables. The second consideration is particularly pertinent to implementation studies; that is that when one observes a limited number of 'events', there are likely to be close connections between them. The numbers of separate actors within the organizations will probably be small and the decisions involved may be visible to those upon whom the policy impacts. In other words: feedback and organizational learning issues tend to be very salient. Hence, while in the social security case a large sample of separate decisions may be relatively easily assembled, in the pollution control case, the combination of a smaller sample with issues of interconnections between decisions may imply that a qualitative study is more appropriate.

Where, as in the social security example used above, there are large numbers of quite separate decisions implementing a single policy within a single organization, two rather different opportunities for quantitative research open up. The first is the study of the way decisions may change over time. Agency characteristics may alter over a period, or new external influences upon the agency may emerge (here political changes are particularly pertinent), and this may be charted through the use of appropriate statistical models, taking into account time lag effects (see Durant, 1984, 1985; Durant and Legge, 1993).

In Chapter 2, it was recognized that one of the literatures from which implementation studies emerged was that concerned with the relationship between politics and administration. Changes to the respective roles of executive, legislature and bureaucracy fall really within the purview of agenda setting and policy formulation studies. However, some studies have involved the use of quantitative studies using time-series data, which explore the way in which political impacts may occur, and therefore raise questions about implementation. For example, a study of US regulatory agencies uses statistical time-series data to show that 'political appointments – a shared power of the president and Congress – is the most important instrument of political control; changing budgets, legislation, congressional signals, and administrative reorganizations are less important' (Wood and Waterman, 1991: 801).

The second opportunity for quantitative research on the work of a single agency arises when there are many separate implementation decisions. Multiple decision-making is likely to mean the need for multiple decision-makers, and perhaps even the division of a single agency into separate sections or local offices. Such is the case within UK social security administration, making large numbers of decisions. Hence Walker, Huby and their colleagues were able to carry out studies of some of the influences upon discretionary decisions in social security (Walker and Lawton, 1988; Huby and Dix, 1992). In American research on welfare administration, particularly welfare cuts, work falling into this category has been possible (for example, Meyers et al., 1998; Ewalt and Jennings, 2004; Keiser et al., 2004; Riccucci, 2005). Some of this literature may also be seen as belonging to the fourth category, inasmuch as differences between states have been pertinent.

3. Multiple organizations, single events

Category 3 involves single events but multiple implementing organizations, for example the privatization of a local government service. Here the two qualifications mentioned in relation to category 2 are again of course relevant. The second of those points about inter-connections is particularly relevant, but in this case it may be very important to explore questions about these. This is central to the research discussed above which explores 'mandating' between layers of government (May 1993, 1994, 1995; May and Burby, 1996). Here it is the variation in the adoption of a policy overall – as, for example, in relation to much environmental policy – that is the focus of attention.

One of the advantages of the existence of more than one separate implementing agency is that the factors that influence implementation are more likely to be in the public arena, and data assembly may be easier. Two aspects of this sort of situation, important for the implementation research agenda and yielding important data for attention but making operationalization very difficult, were explored earlier in this chapter. One of these is a situation in which the legitimacy of the policy former may be challenged; the other is a case where action involves multi-agency collaboration.

4. Multiple organizations, multiple events

On reaching category 4 there is little more to be said. Clearly in this case – where multiple organizations make multiple unrelated decisions – the scope for quantitative study is considerable and cross-agency differences may be compared with within-agency differences. Much of the work of local authorities, police agencies, health authorities, etc. comes within this category.

Meier has used conventional multivariate techniques effectively to analyze implementation processes. He has joined with others to argue for the development of new techniques designed to highlight specific features of the behaviour of particular implementation actors (Keiser and Meier, 1996; Gill and Meier, 2000).

One particular contribution has been the advocacy and exploration of the use of 'substantively weighted analytical techniques' (SWAT; see in particular Meier and Gill, 2000). These techniques:

> involve weighting data to reveal how certain organizations, programs or policies differ in their impact upon their target populations. It [*sic – there seems some doubt whether this should be described as a single technique or a group of techniques –* MH/PH] may be thought of as a form of regression diagnostics with a different twist. Rather than avoiding the unusual and seeking the safety of techniques that are highly resistant to outlying cases, SWAT encourages the analyst to seek out the unusual cases and understand the valuable information they contain. (Meier and Gill, 2000: 2)

Obviously at this stage we could go on to explore the various multivariate analysis techniques available for use in implementation studies. Clearly, the strengths and weaknesses of these need attention on the part of researchers. However, this is not a textbook on research methods and we are not experts in that field, so we will leave that issue here.

Mixed research designs

This discussion so far has attempted to delineate the scope for quantitative studies and to explore some of the logical limits to their use. As two European authors we are impressed by how much bolder Americans have been in the use of quantitative methods for the study of implementation than have most of our own compatriots. There is scope for an increase in their use in European studies. Equally, there is a case for thoroughly designed qualitative studies even in situations in which there is no lack of numbers of organizations or events. Crucially that case rests upon three considerations:

1   the value of the exploration of the way actors have understood and/or interpreted processes;
2   the fact that it may be important to work qualitatively in order to formulate appropriate quantifiable hypotheses;
3   difficulties in operationalizing and/or quantifying key phenomena. The mixing of quantitative and qualitative approaches allows analyses that may go further and be more flexible than elaborate multi-variate analysis techniques.

One of the authors was involved in a study of changes in care home provision in the UK between 1991 and 2001. Until 1997, a Conservative central government was pressing local government to privatize provision. Statistical analysis explored the hypothesis that Conservative-controlled authorities were keener privatizers than others (Banks et al., 2006: 26–7). The mean average decline in the numbers of local authority-owned homes between 1991 and 2001 was related to evidence on local political control. Results showed a higher rate of decline of local authority-owned homes in those boroughs that were

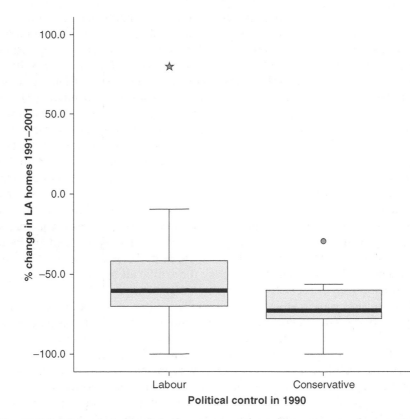

Figure 7.3   Box plot showing the range and median average of percentage change in local authority homes by local authority political control

Conservative controlled than was the case in those that were Labour controlled. The difference between the mean averages for Conservative and Labour areas was statistically significant. The distribution of the percentage changes in residents for both groups is illustrated in Figure 7.3. Each box contains 50 per cent of the percentages and the protruding lines represent the full range from the lowest to the highest percentage. The black lines represent the median average. Outliers (extreme cases) are shown by the circles and stars.

Political difference was, as far as that study was concerned, the only significant predictor of difference in behaviour. Yet scrutiny of the data suggests a large but unexplained number of what may be called 'deviant' authorities: Conservative-controlled ones that seemed less committed to privatization than most Labour-controlled ones and vice versa. In such situations there is surely a case to be made for examining the sources of this deviance by means of qualitative studies. This may throw light upon factors that are difficult or impossible to identify statistically, for example, in this case, the attitudes and commitments of officials, as opposed to politicians, or patterns of organization that are easy or difficult to change.

Such studies may also offer more evidence about how a particular statistical association may be explained. Choi (1999) studied a British central government initiative designed to increase the privatization of local government services: legislation requiring local authorities to put out certain local services for tender by private companies. Choi observed that there was great variation between authorities in the extent to which services went either to private companies or to internal Direct Service Organizations (DSOs) and set out to explain that variation. The crucial variable for Choi's study – as in the study quoted above – was one measuring the 'disposition' of the implementing agencies: political control of the authority. Choi went on in case studies to explore how political disposition had an impact, in the light of the fact that central government had taken considerable steps to prevent an authority 'disposed' to ignore the policy from doing so. The legislation required a visible tendering process. It expected that in any competition between DSOs and privatized organizations there should be, to use terms from the related jargon, a 'level-playing field'. Choi's case studies examined the 'strategies' used by local authorities to influence the 'slope' of that 'playing field'. These revealed both strategies by Labour authorities to make tendering more difficult for private companies and the reverse from Conservative-controlled authorities.

As this last discussion implies, the issue of choice between quantification and more qualitative approaches does not only depend upon the relationship between numbers of events and numbers of organizations suggested in Figure 7.2. It must also be influenced by the extent to which it is feasible to quantify variables. The advocates of quantification often have to be very imaginative in their search for appropriate ways of measuring phenomena. They may have to make assumptions about appropriate surrogate measures for things they want to measure. Cho et al. (2005), for example, use the age of the department director, his or her educational level and years of experience to contribute to an index of 'expertise, experience and entrepreneurship'. Or researchers may have to treat the attitudes and judgements of actors as measures, in situations in which there are grounds for questioning the objectivity of those actors. For instance, we quoted above a study in which one of the authors was involved in which actors were asked what they thought particularly contributed to implementation (Vick et al., 2006). Hence, as themselves leaders in local implementation, they could well be predisposed to think that leadership mattered (note a similar approach by May and Winter, 2007, using caseworkers' perceptions for key performance variables). An interesting alternative, avoiding that problem, is Torenvlied's use of expert assessors of implementation situations (1996a and b, 2000). Here other problems may arise both about the availability, expertise and objectivity of such people.

It is obvious, however, that researchers in qualitative studies face equivalent difficulties, centring on some of the classic problems about their methodologies (we will not digress here and dive into that 'deep water'). Concluding this section we emphasize the view expressed above that it is futile to argue the respective cases for quantitative and qualitative models. This seems so not only because we are talking about what is in the end a matter of 'horses for courses', but also because we believe that good work can combine both.

Conclusion

The aim of this chapter has been to explore the kind of difficulties researchers of implementation are facing. We started with the issue of defining implementation studies, not merely in terms of the mixture of disciplines that contribute to knowledge on this subject, but also in terms of the relationship between studying implementation and studying evaluation and of distinguishing policy formation and implementation. This led on to an examination of research issues that may be said to centre around the core of the topic. These include how implementation researchers may deal with the multiplicity of layers in policy processes; how to specify inter-organizational relationships; how to differentiate ways in which implementation within single organizations is managed; how to identify the impact of the responses by those affected by a policy; and relevant factors in the wider context within which implementation occurs. The chapter ended with a long section on issues about quantitative and qualitative methods in implementation research.

While in the present chapter we have aimed to make helpful suggestions on the practice of issues about implementation research, the chapter does in fact reflect a substantial dilemma, concerning research in general. On the one hand, there is a pragmatic case for precision – about variables and about methods. On the other hand, the reality is that we have here a diffuse subject concerned with policies and administrative arrangements that differ widely and with a complex relationship to various different academic disciplines. Hence we find ourselves advocating precision where precision is possible, but not at the expense of an appreciation of the complexity of the real world. This is particularly important for the handling of the complex formation/implementation relationship and for choices of research methods.

8

IMPLEMENTATION IN CONTEXT

Contents

Introduction

Practitioners in public administration are working under an action imperative. They constantly need to answer questions for themselves about how to act. The study of implementation is about those acts. At the same time, 'practice' appears in so many forms that it is difficult for academics to give advice to practitioners other than either in a one actor-related consultancy situation or in a general way. It is possible, however, to explore the various dimensions of the situations in which governance is being practised. The first aim of this chapter is to make such an exploration. Given the variety of situations in which public actors practise governance, on which aspects do these situations differ? Some authors have reflected, although perhaps under different headings, on the action dimensions of governance. That fact provides a second aim. We want to look at the insights those authors have developed, in implementation studies and beyond, and at the kind of advice they have to offer to practitioners in public administration.

The variety of situations in the practice of public administration is endless. Exactly because of that we give in the second section of this chapter a stylized construction of that practice. Next we focus on the knowledge/action relation: both as such and on the level of recommendations from implementation studies (third section). Then the literature is explored about what we consider to be the two most salient categories of dimensions of variety: policy settings (fourth section) and institutional environments (fifth section). In the sixth section we address some contributions to the conceptualization of the various ways actors may practise governance, centred on a number of typologies. After the presentation of those, we conclude the chapter by stressing the 'normal' character of mixed forms.

Implementation in practice

Sometimes the results of a policy are judged as disappointing, or even worse (Bovens and 't Hart, 1996). Particularly in judgements expressed in daily conversations, analytical distinctions between outcomes and outputs, between content and process are not always made. Rather, such judgements have a highly 'political' character; they say something about the way the world is observed, interpreted and evaluated. A standard reaction to policy results perceived as disappointing is to blame the implementers of that policy. The degree to which such blame is justified, however, is an empirical question. In what kinds of circumstances do policy implementers as well as policy formers do their work? And what is the relationship between the work of both? In order to assess the nature of the practice in which practitioners fulfil their tasks, it is necessary to make some descriptive observations of their practice. On the basis of empirical evidence particularly gained by experience on both the academic and practice side of public administration, we will try to sketch a picture of 'policy in process' that may be recognizable for practitioners.

The world of implementation

At the very end of the line between policy intentions and policy outputs, street-level bureaucrats interact with citizens. Facing all sorts of dilemmas in those daily contacts, these public servants practise coping strategies, as Lipsky (1980) and others have pointed out. Although the relationships between bureaucrats and citizens are certainly not symmetrical, there is a mutual dependency and negotiation may even take place. Much of what police officers, teachers, social workers and other public functionaries are doing has not been laid down in formal documents. In circumstances that have never been foreseen, and confronted with norms that are often vague, these public servants have to act. In such situations they see themselves as required to interpret the public policy involved in a creative but justifiable way. Being implementers, they may, in fact, sometimes practise 'formulation and decision-making' additional to the policy formally at hand, as has been noted earlier in this book.

It is obvious that empirical reality varies greatly here. One of the dimensions along which implementation practices vary is the type of implementation organization involved. Not only is a general hospital as an organization different from a fire station, but the way in which each of those types of organization is structured may vary as well. And while social workers clearly differ from medical practitioners, there are likely to be ways in which, even within each of these groups, professional styles may vary. What all of these professionals in public service have in common is that they are working in direct contact with individual citizens on behalf of the 'general interest'. Because of the *public* character of their work, they are confronted with the rules and regulations of the government policies that, in one way or another, they are expected to implement.

Hence, the literature about street-level bureaucracy and about professionalism reminds us of the diversity of implementation in practice. Is it the case then that we can draw a distinction between these actors and those within administration who have much more routine tasks? Actually this is not easy to do; after all, there are elements of discretion in *any* task. While it is particularly evident that professionals may be aware of a gap between 'policy' and 'practice', this perception of distance is widespread. This may be expressed in terms like: 'Those people there seem to know everything better; while we are doing the dirty work here.' In this way perhaps the relationship between policy implementation and policy intentions has a material side; by their 'inhabitants' the two seem to be experienced as separate worlds.

The world of policy intentions

At the other end of the line between outputs and intentions, policy formers, at the ministries in that very same 'Whitehall' or 'Washington', do not always fully understand why the rules and regulations they laid down in laws and other official documents are sometimes not entirely executed in the way they intended. In the event of disappointing results these policy formers, like the lay observers referred to above, tend to blame the implementers. The former are inclined to see the objectives of the policy involved as clearly stated and the means as provided; the rest is implementation. However, the connection between these different elements in the world of implementation as pictured above may not always be seen as a straight line going from problem to solution. Official policy documents, as formulated and decided upon in the national capital, may be seen by implementers as less clear and directive than the policy formers in the ministries might think they are.

Often the formulations in such a policy document are the result of compromises, of various natures. A policy document is as much the product of bureau-political struggle as a rational answer to a political or social problem (Allison, 1971). As such, it can be ambiguous in its messages to implementers. It may be the case that a specific policy instrument, for instance, a subsidy, was chosen not because it was seen as the means fitting the ends, but because the struggle of governmental politics was 'won' by a ministry that used subsidies as central in its standard repertoire (see Howlett, 1991; Howlett and Ramesh, 2003: Chapter 4). In addition to that, a policy document is seldom the fruit of the pure intellectual cogitation of one single actor sitting behind his or her desk. Simon (1945) indicated the cognitive limitations that inhibit 'rational' decision-making in administrative behaviour, while Lindblom (1959) showed that these limitations may be compensated to a certain extent by the social interaction in which policies are made. Such interaction takes place in the formation of a policy. The compromises resulting from there may add to the ones stemming from the ideological and party-political struggle in the agenda-setting process, the previous 'stage' of the policy cycle. It seems no wonder, then, that implementers sometimes have difficulty in knowing not only how to implement a policy adequately but also what is to be implemented.

Inter-organizational relations

Between the formulation of the intentions of a policy, for instance, to guarantee a minimum level of existence, and the delivery of related policy outputs, such as assistance benefits, in fact a process of transformation takes place (Van der Veen, 1990). This process is embedded within a range of vertical and horizontal relations between organizations involved in the making of the specific policy. In the world of implementation, horizontal relations concern the connections between the organization primarily responsible for the implementation and related organizations. For example, the delivery of National Assistance benefits in The Netherlands to citizens entitled to them is a task for local government. The Municipal Social Services Department has a central position in a local network in which, for instance, the Labour Office, Social Work and the Tax Office are other actors involved.

Also in the world of policy intentions, there are horizontal linkages: between political parties and other societal organizations, such as those of employers and employees; between departments; between the units of one such department, and so on. Vertically, there is the general system of inter-governmental relations within which public policies in a country are formed and implemented. In addition, there is a 'trajectory' specific to a policy. This 'policy trajectory' entails the range of organizations involved in the policy process at stake. In the case of Dutch National Assistance the formal administrative layers of the Ministry of Social Affairs and Employment and of the municipalities are particularly involved, but alongside those also, for instance, client organizations participate as stakeholders.

Two worlds, different reactions

In a stylized form, the picture above sketches the variety of actors and factors that play a role in the implementation of public policy. Earlier in this book we described the notion of 'the implementation gap' as analytically somewhat difficult. In research the notion has hardly any explanatory value. Nevertheless, it seems as if in practice the perception of different 'worlds' has a relevance for action. When the results of a policy are seen as disappointing, actors involved in that specific policy process may commonly blame the 'other world'. Various consequential actions follow.

On the street-level, actors held accountable for the delivery of policy outputs may react to perceived shortcomings by streamlining standard operating procedures, enhancing professionalism, strengthening leadership and perhaps restructuring their organization. The public servants who directly interact with citizens are familiar with the need to cope with shortcomings in as justifiable a way as possible. For them, almost by definition, resources are scarce, while nevertheless the conceptions of their occupation, practised in public service, urge them to make the best of it. Doing so, they see themselves as professionals.

When policy formers initially responsible for a specific policy process are confronted with disappointing results, their standard reaction will be a different one: they will be inclined to take additional measures. Those actors accountable for the managing of the policy process involved will aim at a more strict control of the implementation of that policy by making more (internal) rules and regulations. Stated briefly, the outcome of disappointing policy results will be more policy. As In't Veld observes: 'The general reaction of government to successful policy and not-successful policy is identical: successful policy breeds a taste for more of the same, while not-successful policy asks for corrections in the form of new policy, naturally made by that same government' (1984: 19). In't Veld speaks here of the *accumulation of policy*. Paradoxically, the empirical consequence of more rules for implementers may be that their actual action space, referred to as 'discretion', unintendedly may be enhanced rather than diminished. The more rules the handbook contains, the more inclined an implementer will be to fulfil the task at hand according to his or her own judgement and/or by consulting a colleague. In this *paradox of increasing policy discretion* the standard reaction of piling rules on top of rules has effects opposite to what rule makers intend (Hupe, 1993a).

Because of the different 'logic' working in the two worlds as pictured, real-world perceptions of a 'gap' may be expected to continue. Yet recently in countries like the United Kingdom and The Netherlands the awareness of the relevance of implementation among policy formers seems to have increased. The possibility cannot be excluded that there is a relation here with the occurrence of results of some policies that were obviously perceived as disappointing but at the same time could not be waived away as entirely caused by bad implementation. After all, sometimes economic and cultural developments may have changed the function of a policy in society. (More divorces, for instance, produce more single mothers, which leads to more claims for social assistance.) And besides, it may be the exact content of a policy, as formulated in the world of policy intentions, that can make it difficult to implement. In the countries mentioned it looks as if this *discovery of implementation* has led to a greater inclination towards a self-critical look by policy formers at the very substance of the laws and policies they formulate. In The Netherlands some years ago 'implementation checks' and 'implementation assessments' were introduced in the policy formation part of the policy process. Checklists thus force policy formers to give explicit attention to implementation aspects of a policy proposal *before* the final political decision-making at Cabinet level takes place.

The picture of the two worlds as given above, each with its specific logic, has revealed such a variety of factors and dimensions that in the practice and management of implementation two completely identical situations can hardly be expected. This is even more evident when the variance between institutional environments in different countries is taken into account. In Chapter 2, we looked at the issue of democratic leadership over administration, raised by Woodrow Wilson and others. There we also discussed institutional theory. In Chapter 5, we made some comparative statements about the USA, the UK and The Netherlands. Further in this chapter we will take a next step in the exploration of this theme and look at the differences in national administrative arrangements and political-administrative cultures that form the context within which implementation is being managed (fifth section). In the section preceding that one, we will elaborate on the differences in the nature of the policies to be implemented (fourth section). Before doing so, however, it first seems relevant to develop a more articulate view on the relation between practice and theory; or, in other words, action and knowledge.

The quest for appropriate action

Action imperative

When we aim to specify the contexts in which implementation takes place, two fundamental dimensions need to be kept in mind. First, there is the distinction between what is *general* and what is *specific*. Reform ideologies like the ones described in Chapter 5 have an almost universal character, but their application is context-bound. The moment and pace of introduction of such reform ideologies as 'meta-policies' (Dror, 1986; Hupe, 1990), and the variants and institutional settings, will differ. There will also be differences in the political perseverance with which they are pursued. These factors will all influence the 'local' success of those 'global' reform ideologies. Second, the distinction between *what is* and what *should be* is relevant. Social trends, like the global phenomenon of cultural individualism, have objective, material consequences and on a general level are hard to control (Ester et al., eds, 1993). A similar observation can be made for economic trends, like the merging of multinational mass media corporations into large worldwide conglomerates. At the same time, however, actors may see reasons to pose limits to the 'natural' character of such trends and may wish to counteract their adverse consequences. In order to try to manage these developments, nation states can make treaties and other arrangements. In these cases issues about judicial competence will arise. It may be political will that is critical in the first place, in which case we are in the realm of the normative. The description–prescription oppositions at stake here are set out in Table 8.1.

Although implementation researchers may be committed to changing reality, the nature of their trade makes them engaged primarily in the quest for truth, rather than in the quest for appropriate action. Contrastingly, practitioners in public administration may also practise intellectual cogitation, but first and

Table 8.1   Description/prescription oppositions

	Empirical	Normative
General	Social and economic trends Reform ideologies	Principles
Specific	Institutional environments	Context-bound application

foremost they are working under an imperative to act. Unlike social scientists, government actors always have to act. In the practice of governance, the general and the specific, the normative and the empirical are linked together in concrete answers to the questions about what to do, here and now. What they see as appropriate action is in an important way related to the composite nature of the specific context of that action. As argued, reform ideologies and social and economic trends may be less manipulable than, in a causal way, influential in the context involved. More or less the same applies for the institutional environment; for an individual actor this is not only to a large extent given, but also has a character that varies in time and space. In normative terms there may be reasons to uphold certain general principles.

Two sets of general normative principles are guiding the deeds of government actors: those of the rule of law or *Rechtsstaat*, and those of democracy (see also Chapter 2). The *Rechtsstaat* implies the fact that government behaviour is subject to law; therefore there are institutional arrangements to maintain the rule of law in a legitimate way. In those institutions values like justice, equity and fairness are expressed. Equal treatment of equal cases is a highly valued principle here. Democracy involves the freedom of speech, the right of self-organization and other rights as laid down in the Universal Declaration of Human Rights. Specific institutions, particularly representative organs and general elections that are regularly held, are needed to provide for the guaranteed consummation of these rights. There is a third set of principles that has been more controversial: the principles embodied in what is called the Welfare State. Rather than an intended and well-designed 'project', the welfare state can be seen as a set of desired but unintended by-products of collective action. When there is steady economic growth, in combination with the rule of law and some form of democracy, the possibility arises for social exchanges and the realization of a proper level of prosperity for the average citizen. A variety of types of welfare state can be observed, within which different values are expressed, like equality and solidarity, or social control and minimum benefits. These varying principles may be related to political and institutional contexts (see Esping-Andersen, 1990).

It is implementation that keeps all these institutions performing their functions in society. Therefore, implementation always matters. In the last instance, the implementation of public policy entails the maintenance of values collectively seen as important (Vickers, 1965). Finally, the *res publica* and the wellbeing of the *polis* itself are at stake. So it is important to ask what kind of advice to practitioners implementation studies have to offer.

Advice from implementation studies

The conventional view of the policy process is that it entails a 'sequential pattern of action involving a number of functional categories of activity that can be analytically distinguished'. As we indicated in Chapter 1, the essence of that image is that the policy process can be decomposed into a number of successive phases or stages. It was then noted in Chapter 6 that this has been the subject of criticism but it was argued that it is undesirable to write off the 'stages model' of the policy process completely. There may be theoretical reasons (see DeLeon, 1999b), but, just as important, empirical ones for not doing so. Although the stages model of the policy process may not provide researchers with a tool 'to grasp how the entire system works *in verifiable* ... theory' (ibid.: 28), it, indeed, fulfils heuristic functions in both the study and practice of public administration. In the latter world the perceived phased character of the policy process supplies actors with insight into their own positions in that process, and, related to that, provides clues about how to act. Additional to, but distinguished from, this cognitive function of the stages heuristic is the normative function that gives sense, direction and legitimacy to the things actors at various positions in the policy process are expected to do.

Illustrating the way this perspective offers a point of departure to relate knowledge and action, the top-down theorists examined in Chapter 3 formulate conditions of effective implementation and argue that what happens at the so-called 'implementation stage' will influence the actual policy outcome. Hence they argue that the probability of a successful outcome will be increased if, at the stage of policy design, thought is given to potential problems of implementation. It is acknowledged that these preconditions are at the same time the reasons why in practice the phenomenon of 'perfect implementation' does not occur.

We have also noted that this sort of approach with its explicit or implicit focus on the explanation of a specific 'implementation gap' can often be connected to a 'reform' orientation. It is this orientation towards improvement that makes analysts formulate the kinds of checklists presented in Chapter 3 on pp. 48–5. They want to formulate recommendations for policy-makers, whom they see as both competent and legitimized to pursue measures by which the formation and implementation of policies can be improved. Because these policy-makers are seen as in command of the vertical chain implied by the stage model, the successive stages as distinguished in that model are used as 'coat hangers' for the respective elements of advice to them. The analytical rationality of presentational logic (aiming at z means starting with a and then going to b, and so on) and the normative wish to formulate advice for policy-makers in a system of representative democracy strengthen each other here. This orientation of 'reform' can be observed in many of the implementation studies aiming at description and/or explanation that have been published since the beginning of the 1970s. These pursue the kind of research agenda established by theorists like Pressman and Wildavsky, Van Meter and Van Horn, and Sabatier and Mazmanian (see Chapter 3).

Recommendations in detail

The next question is then what kind of concrete advice to policy-makers can be found in those studies. In a survey of 300 of such publications, O'Toole (1986) searched for policy recommendations for implementation. He shows, first, that most of the scanned publications, in fact, contain few detailed recommendations. He suggests that 'prescription is rarely a central focus of work in the implementation literature' (ibid.: 191). Second, O'Toole observes that the advice offered often seems largely unsupported by the empirical research base. Third, much of the advice offered in the literature on multi-actor implementation is contradictory. O'Toole speaks of situations in which social scientific findings are sometimes used for the 'buttressing of established perspectives, as symbolic and pseudo-authoritative support for positions already staked out' (ibid.: 196). O'Toole explains his findings in terms of the normative disagreement in the field, particularly on what constitutes 'success', and the fact that the empirical theory is not well advanced. The state of the field's development imposes 'a real constraint on the quality of advice available for those in the policy process' (ibid.: 198). There is a 'lack of focus and cumulation'. The recommendations that can be found often take on a proverbial character. (He echoes here Simon's famous analysis of the contradictory 'proverbs' of administration [1945].) Referring to a set of principles apparently so sensible that they can serve to guide action from the centre, aiming at maximizing the probability of implementation success, O'Toole speaks of the 'top-down perspective's conventional wisdom'. This 'conventional wisdom' implies a policy design in which the degree of required behavioural change is kept low; a structure of implementation as simple as possible in which the number of actors is minimized; the taking into consideration of the problems of implementation during the initial stages of policy formation; and attributing the responsibilities for the implementation of a specific policy to units sympathetic to that policy (O'Toole, 1986: 200).

Clearly the lists of conditions favourable for policy implementation, cited above, are part of this conventional wisdom.[1] From a 'bottom-up' perspective, O'Toole adds a criticism of the elements mentioned here. He states that the kind of efforts at central control as presented direct attention to variables that, in general, are difficult or impossible to manipulate. The productive effects and necessity of conflict, negotiation and politics during implementation are ignored. Potentially important participants in the implementation process are neglected. The fact that many policy problems can only be addressed through widespread discretion, local presence and an adaptive implementation mode is overlooked. Actually, in O'Toole's view, the 'conventional wisdom' concerns an attempt to perform the impossible: '[D]ecide all the important questions at the outset (thus ignoring the learning that must perforce take place as policy problems are actually tackled)' (ibid.: 201).

Since O'Toole's (1986) scan of the implementation literature, many more implementation studies have been performed. So many that it becomes even more difficult to be fully comprehensive. The result of that multitude of implementation studies has been the adding of a few new variables to the list so long already. Looking at this problem in the abstract it may be believed that if only we could work with more complex models, a way of weighting the influence of different variables might be discovered. Modern computational techniques seem to support this contention. Yet, in practice the problem then becomes one of finding the data to be fitted into such a model. 'Heroic assumptions' and the imposition of elaborate *'ceteris paribus'* clauses become essential, but then undermine the empirical use of the model.

Rothstein (1998) points out that it is not clear what to make of lists of variables and checklists like those presented above. They say

> [nothing] about which factors are more important than others, and under what conditions, or which types of programmes are harder to implement than others, and not much about which organizational forms are suitable for which tasks. Many of the factors seem so obvious as to be trivial'. (ibid.: 69)

Besides, in many implementation studies that aim at description of the implementation of a particular policy or at the explanation of a specific implementation gap, there has been an orientation toward failure. Hence Elmore argues: 'Analysis of social policy has come to consist of explaining why things never work as intended; a high level of knowledge about social policy has come to be equated with a fluent cynicism' (1983: 213).

Pressman and Wildavsky's emphasis on the problems of multiple clearance points, engendered a similar pessimism. For Goggin et al. (1990), this message provided a reason to plead for research designs meant to avoid any preoccupation with what could be seen as 'exceptional failure'. Unless adequate attention to the relationship between causal and manipulable variables is guaranteed, descriptive implementation studies cannot provide any specific advice for practitioners about how to handle concrete circumstances.

More knowledge-based advice

Sometimes, however, real new insights are gained that may have constructive consequences for the actions practitioners can take. The chance that this will happen is enhanced by the degree to which the research design has a systematic and explicitly accumulative character. Brown et al. (1998), for instance, investigated the function of local partnerships in the implementation of a geographical information system (GIS) in the USA. They found, first, that

> [P]artnerships are neither more nor less successful than single-organizational arrangements; multi-actor outcomes themselves are contingent on more nuanced features of the case. Second, structurally more complex arrangements do not lead to higher spending, although such institutional settings do seem to be associated with reduced outcomes as measured in certain ways. Finally, while the number of units involved in decision making is significant and somewhat negative in relation to outcomes, the use

of formal procedures and leadership that inspires motivated contributions by participants can offer distinct advantages in multi-unit arrangements. (Brown et al., 1998: 522–3)

On the basis of these findings Brown et al. formulate some clear recommendations: '(M)anagers interested in gaining the benefits of GIS [the concerned information system – MH/PH] should institute formal procedures, develop strong leadership and cap growth in the number of actors involved and the number of resources shared' (ibid.: 522).

Keiser and Meier (1996) investigated child-support enforcement in the USA. A federal law requires the American states to locate absent parents, establish paternity, determine child-support obligations, enforce support obligations and collect support payments. In each state a central office establishes the rules and regulations governing child support in that state and monitors the activities of local officials. The authors remark that, because the child-support enforcement bureaucracy exists in a macro-structural arrangement with states at the apex, it is appropriate to study that bureaucracy's enforcement by examining and comparing state-level outputs. As categories within which the authors formulate central variables, the authors distinguish policy design variables (policy context, policy coherence, target population characteristics, tractability), bureaucratic variables, political forces, task requirements and economic capacity. The first broad hypothesis is that policy design plays a role in determining enforcement level. The second one argues that local implementation forces determine enforcement level. The research findings show support for the broad assumption that policy design matters. The results are consistent with the hypothesis that the policy context and tractability of the policy problem have an impact on enforcement success. In contrast, the authors observe that policy coherence and target population characteristics do not seem to play a strong role in affecting enforcement; they may be sufficient conditions but they are not necessary. Keiser and Meier point out that the findings show that:

policy context can communicate priorities to a bureaucracy if these changes fit with bureaucratic values, even if the statute does not state explicitly a change in priorities. Claims that priority specification in statutes are necessary conditions to enforcement success may be erroneous. Public managers and policy makers do not, therefore, need to be overly concerned with controlling the bureaucracy with coherent legislation. (ibid.: 359)

It may be noticed that Keiser and Meier, aiming at testing a few hypotheses while examining state-level outputs, formulate some recommendations about policy design as practised by state and federal policy-makers, while Brown et al., looking at the local level, direct their advice to public managers working at that level. An example that similarly mixes top-down and bottom-up perspectives in an interesting way is Fiorino's description of a reform strategy pursued in American environmental regulation. He shows the 'backward mapping' character of that strategy and concludes that such a strategy may be appropriate if there is a lack of political consensus on the *need for* and the *form of* change or 'when mechanisms for implementing change are unreliable' (1997: 261). Having started his investigation 'at the bottom', Fiorino ends up with some suggestions for 'the top', while Brown et al. formulate recommendations for managers at that 'bottom'.

Hogwood and Gunn (1984), acknowledging that many so-called 'implementation failures' can be traced to inadequate policies, criticize 'bottom-uppers' for taking an oppositional stance to elected officials and for refraining from giving any advice to them. They do not see why the view from the top is necessarily less valid than that from other positions, and argue that the implications of a bottom-up view become less attractive when specific examples are examined. For instance, 'if a Home Secretary is committed to better relations between policemen and black youths, should we view with equanimity the persistence of "street-level" police attitudes and action which are openly racist?' Or, 'if Parliament decided to move from left-hand to right-hand drive on our roads, would we be happy to leave to "negotiation" between road-users, local authorities, and the central government such questions as when, how, and whether the change-over should take effect?' (Hogwood and Gunn, 1984: 208). Analyzing the differences between the top-down and bottom-up perspectives further as far as the relationship between theory and practice issues is concerned, O'Toole (2001) notes an important underlying normative difference. Top-down analysts often express themselves in support of a representative regime and the consistent execution of choices made by political leaders. On the other hand, bottom-uppers endorse the emergence of the policy contributions of actors far from the oversight of political principals. From this major difference stem another two. Top-downers see implementation primarily as a matter of 'assembling action in support of the intentions and orders of political leaders', while bottom-uppers look at it as 'mobilizing the energies of disparate stakeholders to make sensible choices in congealing problem solving around a complex, context-specific, and dynamic policy issue'. In the former view the primary focus is on issues of compliance and monitoring; in the latter on innovation, collaboration and creativity (ibid.: 10).

Linder and Peters (1987) suggest that the general message of bottom-up studies, although mostly implicit, seems to be that practitioners in implementation should do what they think they should do to implement a policy. The proposition that the outcome of policy-making is determined at the 'street-level', is converted into a normative stance. Descriptive and prescriptive statements are thus blurred, and the empirical and the normative are not separated. Against that view, Linder and Peters argue that implementation is only one reason why policies do not succeed. Besides, they argue, 'governance is not about negotiation, it is about the use of legitimate authority' (ibid.: 464). Rather than 'admitting defeat and turning the potential domination of implementation by lower echelons of the public bureaucracy and the environment into a virtue', it is important to design effective policies and effective implementation systems (ibid.: 474). DeLeon (1999a), on the other hand emphasizes the need for greater clarity about the normative perspectives in both top-down and bottom-up work. DeLeon describes the top-down view as 'more democratic' in that a policy is chosen by elected representatives while with the bottom-up perspective it is crafted by local bureaucrats. Nevertheless he opposes Matland (1995), who states that street-level bureaucrats are not particularly responsible to their constituents, calling this a peculiar contention. DeLeon pleads for a greater emphasis on a participatory-democratic orientation to implementation, 'buttressed by more of a post-positivist orientation and methodology' (1999a: 330). We see here the shadow of debates about the respective merits of representative and more participatory forms of democracy (cf. Chapter 5, pp. 103–4).

O'Toole argues that there is a need to improve implementation theory while at the same time giving attention to the needs of practical decision-makers. However, he remains cautious: 'There have not been striking successes evident thus far in finding ways of linking theoretical efforts with practical advice' (2001: 32). This remark draws attention to the specific relation between the world of analysis and the world of practice. There sometimes is, but more often is not, a one-to-one relationship at stake in which the analyst gives direct advice to the practitioner about what to do. Scholarly attention to the relationship between knowledge and policy suggests that in general there is an 'enlightenment function' rather than an instrumental use of academic knowledge in the practice of public policy (Weiss, 1977; Cohen and Lindblom, 1979; Scott and Shore, 1979).

The logic of political-administrative practice is different from the one expressed in academic knowledge. The former practice is often driven by 'position' or 'situational logic' rather than 'knowledge'. As noted above, for the practitioner the question that constantly needs to be answered is: How to act? Moreover, that question has to be answered in a wide range of different institutional arrangements and power configurations, varying not only between practitioners but also from case to case for the same practitioner as well. If, as suggested here, propositions of the kind embodied in top-down advice to practitioners seldom amount to very much, this means that, if implementation scholars want to take the relationship between theory and practice seriously, they need to specify contexts from the beginning to the end. Therefore, it is the identification of these contexts that will be central to the second half of this chapter.

Policy settings

Some implementation researchers have acknowledged the need to specify different ways of organizing public administration, relating types of government measures to 'operative conditions'. In the epilogue of an interesting volume on the empirical study of governance, Ellwood (2000) pleads for a specification of jurisdictions, policy types and government problems.

In Chapter 4, efforts to use policy typologies to help to distinguish different kinds of implementation situations were discussed. It was suggested that traditional approaches based upon the studies of Lowi do not work. Matland (1995), however, approaches this subject without such a taxonomy. He suggests possibilities by emphasizing a more general approach to the recognition of the way the

Table 8.2   Matland's analysis of the impact of conflict and ambiguity upon implementation

	Low conflict	High conflict
Low ambiguity	*Administrative implementation* Resources	*Political implementation* Power
	Example: smallpox eradication	Example: bussing
	An activity where there is a generally shared straightforward objective	A straightforward but strongly contested activity
High ambiguity	*Experimental implementation* Contextual conditions	*Symbolic implementation* Coalition strength
	Example: Headstart	Example: community action agencies
	A complex policy where cause/effect mechanisms are little understood	Response to a demand for policy where there is neither a strong coalition nor clarity about what can be achieved

Source: simplified version of the table in Matland (1995: 160). Clarifications have been added in the table because Matland uses old examples from the United States that may mean little to some readers.

different characteristics of policies have implications for the way these policies are implemented. He uses his distinction between issues about the extent of policy ambiguity on the one hand and issues about conflict on the other, to develop the matrix set out in Table 8.2.

In Table 8.2, 'administrative implementation' needs little explanation. Matland describes this as where there are the 'prerequisite conditions for a rational decision process' the ideal situation for the application of a top-down approach. With 'political implementation' he says 'implementation outcomes are decided by power' (1995: 163). His example, 'bussing', refers to the contested issue of the reduction of educational segregation by the bussing of children to schools outside their immediate neighbourhoods. In the case of 'political implementation' Matland argues that theories that emphasize interactions and policy/implementation feedback are particularly applicable, while those that stress decision-making at the micro-level are less so. In the case of 'experimental implementation', 'contextual conditions', meaning environmental influences on outcomes, are likely to be important: 'Program mutations arise as different organizations implement different policies in different environments' (1995: 166). There are complex feedback and learning issues to consider in this case, and bottom-up approaches to analysis are particularly likely to be applicable. 'Symbolic implementation' involves high conflict despite the vagueness of policy. The strength of coalitions, particularly at the local level, tends to determine outcomes. Professional values and allegiances may be important for these. Matland's example of 'community action' is very much an area where

	Certainty: Large	Certainty: Little
Agreement: Large	Technical problems	Untamed technical problems
Agreement: Little	Political problems	Wicked problems

Figure 8.1   Policy problems classified according to the impact of levels of certainty and agreement

Source: Hoppe (1989)

programmes have not satisfied the aspirations of participants either at the top or bottom. Much more significant examples may occur in areas where ambitious but ambiguous aspirations to effect health improvements or crime reductions offer significant opportunities for policy development through the implementation process by professional coalitions.

Matland's article appears to offer some important suggestions about the need to think about implementation as differing in relation to the varying character of the policies to be implemented. His concern to distinguish issues in terms of the complexity of implementation is also found with writers who have stressed that their particular concern is to address the implementation of 'wicked problems' (see Chapter 4, p. 69). In this context, Koppenjan and Klijn (2004: 29) present a model originally developed by Hoppe (1989) using two dimensions:

• certainty on (scientific) knowledge;
• (societal) agreement on problem formulation.

Hence the four quadrants set out in Figure 8.1. But Koppenjan and Klijn elaborate this with a particular emphasis on institutional complexity as a source of problem complexity. Here we go on to examine the extent to which further context may be provided by institutional settings, affecting how the policy issues concerned are handled.

Institutional environments

There is an increasing volume of comparative work exploring differences between characteristics of national, political and policy systems. Above we made the distinction between the rule of law, democracy and the welfare state. Documenting the ways in which authors have studied institutional variety, we more or less follow that distinction while specifying it into a number of explanatory concerns getting attention in diverse parts of social science. These concerns regard:

• differences between constitutional arrangements and their implications for political decision-making (constitutional systems);
• differences in policy styles, in general, with particular reference to the overall organization of administration (public-administrative styles);

- differences between ways in which governments manage social policy and the economy (social-economic regimes); and
- differences in approaches to regulatory policy (implementation regimes).

The state of knowledge accumulated in social science has not reached a stage where it is feasible to put these related approaches to comparison between nation states together in one coherent theory on institutional environment. Indeed, given competition between academics, competing typologies are perhaps inevitable. We will not here try to make a new contribution to the comparative typologies. Instead we want to highlight a number of themes. The sorts of concerns mentioned here can be addressed as regarding, successively, constitutional systems, public-administrative styles, social-economic regimes, and implementation regimes.

Constitutional systems

At the constitutional end there are two dimensions that have been highlighted in Lijphart's more recent work (1999):

- Majoritarian versus consensus systems.
- Unitary versus federal systems.

On both dimensions England (but not the UK where a new federalism is emerging) stands out, with its most dramatic manifestation being the systematic squeezing out of local government autonomy. Conversely Switzerland may be seen as the extreme case in the opposite 'box'.

It seems reasonable to expect that the first of the distinctions will be reflected, not merely at the level of political agenda-setting but also through the whole system, including at the implementation 'stage'. Then the second has the same implication: that federalism requires accommodations to be reached in a context within which the constitutional division of powers leaves matters for negotiation. A great deal here hinges upon the policy formation/policy implementation distinction explored earlier in the book. In that context and elsewhere the complications federalism contributes to implementation theory have been explored. The possibility was identified that accommodations associated with the earlier 'stages' have been made before a policy reaches the implementation 'stage'. In relation to that, it is compatible with the conceptualization of the policy process outlined in this book to suggest that 'high level' constitutional differences will have some effect, so that some systems are much more likely than others to involve the delegation of some crucial decision processes.

Public-administrative styles

The second body of comparative work to which we want to refer is the policy styles literature. This has taken its cue from a distinction drawn by Dyson (1980) between strong and weak states, a notion particularly influenced by his interest in German administration. Later writers have seen that distinction as too simplistic. Richardson has advanced (1982) (and Bovens, 't Hart and Peters, 2001 have worked with) a model embodying two dimensions:

- an anticipatory style as opposed to a reactive one;
- a consensus-seeking style as opposed to one that tends to impose decisions on society.

Of course, there may be ways of connecting these two dimensions to those used by Lijphart. Since we are not here trying to formulate some comprehensive comparative theory, all we can note is that the authors who have worked with this distinction have not done so. On the contrary, for example, Bovens, 't Hart and Peters put the UK and The Netherlands together as countries where the anticipatory style is evident. Richardson moreover uses the dimensions to identify four quadrants:

- anticipatory and consensus-seeking;
- anticipatory and imposing decisions;
- reactive and consensus-seeking;
- reactive and imposing decisions.

Following the same logic as before, as far as this is concerned, we merely want to suggest that inasmuch as there are different detectable styles, they can be expected to have implications for differences in implementation. Certainly if somewhat broadly conceived as 'political-administrative styles', they may be connected with, for example, Matland's categories. The issues in his low ambiguity/high conflict box will be tackled rather differently in a country with a reactive and consensus-seeking style than in one with an anticipatory and decision-imposing style.

Social-economic regimes

The third body of comparative work we want to consider is that which concerns differences in ways in which governments manage to combine social and economic desiderata. The leading insights here are addressed under the heading of 'regime theory', originally developed by Esping-Andersen (1990). In the academic field of comparative social policy, differences in regimes now are the subject of a vast literature (see Arts and Gelissen, 2002 and Hill, 2006, Chapter 2 for surveys). Much of this is about policy content rather than the policy process and does not concern us here. However, the theory is underpinned by a contrast between political systems. This contrast particularly concerns that between liberal market societies (with the United States as the strongest example, and other Anglophone nations following in its wake) and what Esping-Andersen calls 'conservative regimes' where state-led development was important for the development of welfare systems. There is a third type of regime, the social-democratic regime of Scandinavia, but it is the contrast between the 'liberal' and the 'conservative' that is important for the analysis here. That contrast has an echo in theoretical work on the management of the economy, where economic activity has been seen as more co-ordinated, with government playing a key role in the conservative rather than in the liberal systems (Hall and Soskice, 2001).

In relation to social policy Esping-Andersen draws out a contrast between the extensive use of social assistance benefits in the liberal regimes as opposed to social insurance in the conservative ones. As far as implementation is concerned, that may be simply a policy difference, but the question that this kind of theory raises is about the extent to which differences in responses to policy problems have implications for differences in implementation. Social insurance embeds a structure of rights, leading to unitary implementation, in a way that policy based on social assistance does not. The contrast in respect of the management of the economy, however, may be the more dramatic one. The co-ordination of economic activity calls for fine tuning of implementation, while a system that leaves much to the market may imply a clear-cut regulatory structure within which economic enterprise gets on with the job. Van Waarden (1999a) here sees the United States as a country with a legalistic market oriented system in contrast to The Netherlands. However, he draws a contrast between the United States and the other market society he looks at, the UK, seeing regulation as pragmatic (as in The Netherlands) there. Then, however, he is putting together the Hall and Soskice dimension with the anticipatory/reactive dimension in Richardson's approach.

Implementation regimes

Van Waarden (1999a) made a comparative investigation of differences between nations in their style of regulation, in the use of preferred certain policy instruments in modes of network formation and in enforcement routines. At the end he asks: Does nation matter here? Van Waarden argues that the national differences in handling political and administrative issues discussed in the successive chapters of the edited volume are related to the institutional environment, particularly the political, juridical and public service institutions specific to each respective country. He suggests looking together at policy styles and regulatory styles, using those terms as equivalents. Part of the regulatory style is the enforcement style: the style in the stage of implementation, enforcement and sanctioning. Parallel to the term we used in the previous paragraph we would propose 'implementation regime' as the overarching concept here.

In a further chapter, Van Waarden (1999b) goes on to explain civil servants' behaviour from the national differences as presented above. His assumption is that this behaviour is, to a large extent, pre-structured by the macro-institutional framework within which they are working. As clusters of factors Van Waarden mentions the political, juridical and administrative institutions of the state. Also important are the separation of public and private law; the degree and nature of constitutional checks and balances on the political and administrative exercise of power; the recruitment, selection and training of civil servants; and their professional identity. In addition, civil servants' styles are related to the structure of the civil society (position of societal organizations, and so on); the general political culture; and basic norms and values (for example, levels of trust in government). One of Van Waarden's findings is that the stronger the checks on the implementation activities of civil servants in a country, the greater their inclination to execute rules 'according to the book', in order to protect themselves from possible liability claims or public accountability.

Institutional variation and implementation

In the range presented above it is only the last type of differences that seems, *prima facie*, to relate directly to implementation. However, all types mentioned here are relevant inasmuch as – following the stance taken throughout this book on the importance of seeing inter-connections within the policy process – the conditions under which policy is generated influence those under which it is implemented. Furthermore, implicit within these approaches to comparison is an institutionalist perspective acknowledging that 'the organization of political life makes a difference' (March and Olsen, 1984: 747). Embedded within that is a view that attention needs to be paid not merely to the most obvious manifestations of that organization, in constitutional forms, but also to its ideological and cultural forms. Attention to what can be summarized as 'the institutional dimension' is evident in much policy analysis. An extensive literature exists on the extent to which policy change is constrained or channelled into pathways (Bridges, 2000; Mahoney, 2000; Pierson, 2000).

Also in implementation studies themselves, apart from policy settings the institutional dimension sometimes gets more than implicit attention. In seeking to explain implementation in Hungary, O'Toole (1994), for instance, stresses the necessity to include the multi-level character of institutional contexts in the research design of implementation studies. In a later paper, O'Toole (2001) makes a distinction between 'core circumstances' and 'external circumstances'. With the former, O'Toole refers to the objectives, information and power of those involved in the implementation process. External circumstances he conceives as working through, and thus perhaps modifying, the core circumstances. 'An implementation manager, equipped with the basic logic, can consider a particular circumstance and identify which, if any, external circumstances might potentially alter the value of one of the central variables' (ibid.: 32). In addition, O'Toole also indicates the need to specify the identity of the 'practitioners' who are dealing with implementation. Elsewhere, O'Toole (1993) warned against a too mechanistic view on ways to link 'problems' and 'structures', as is argued for in the so-called 'contingency approach' (Scharpf, 1986).

As noted at the beginning of this section, we have drawn upon a number of different, unco-ordinated, comparative theoretical approaches. Our concern is not to say that these approaches solve the problems posed by the diversity of implementation arrangements. However, although they do not lead us to some neat categorization of ideas, they do suggest ways in which institutional contexts need to be taken into account in implementation theory and research. As far as recommendations to practitioners are concerned, it is pertinent to note that while international policy learning or policy borrowing is widespread, many policies transferred in this way either run into difficulties or are radically transformed in a new institutional context (see Dolowicz et al., 2000; Rose, 2004).

It seems obvious that since empirical reality is characterized by a multi-dimensional variety, action in the practice of that reality takes many forms. Also before and beyond implementation studies, scholars in social science made attempts to get, conceptually, a grip on that variety of context-bound forms of action.

Operational governance in context

Modes of governance

On several dimensions contextual variety can be observed; above we did so concerning policy settings and institutional environments. Within the latter category we distinguished between constitutional systems, public-administrative styles, social-economic regimes and implementation regimes, as sub-categories of dimensions specifying the nature of these institutional environments. In several parts of social science there have been attempts to develop taxonomies to typify, more in general, settings of social interaction. Varying along lines of academic discipline, such contributions often have a conceptual nature. Etzioni (1961), for instance, looks at the reasons why people in organizations comply with rules. Calling power 'an actor's ability to induce or influence another actor to carry out his directives or any norms he supports' (ibid.: 4), Etzioni states that power differs according to the means employed to make the subjects comply. These means may be physical, material or symbolic. He distinguishes coercive, remunerative and normative power (Figure 8.2). Next, Etzioni defines involvement as the 'eval-uative orientation of an actor to an object, characterized in terms of intensity and direction' (ibid.: 9). Etzioni distinguishes between alienative, calculative and moral involvement. The first type refers to an involvement with a negative ori-entation, such as the one experienced by conscripted men and women in basic training. Calculative involvement designates either a negative or a positive ori-entation with low intensity (compare the relationships of merchants with con-tinuous business contacts). Moral involvement concerns a positive orientation of high intensity, like that of a devoted member of a political party.

Etzioni combines the two groups of concepts – kinds of power and kinds of involvement – as dimensions of a typology of compliance relations. He then argues that three combinations are more likely than others; these are marked X in Figure 8.2. These 'congruent' combinations are alienative involvement and coercive power, calculative involvement and remunerative power and moral

KINDS OF POWER	KINDS OF INVOLVEMENT		
	Alienative	Calculative	Moral
Coercive	X		
Remunerative		X	
Normative			X

Figure 8.2   A typology of compliance relations
Source: based on Etzioni (1961: 12).

involvement and normative power. Next, Etzioni wants to examine the relationship between compliance and goals. He therefore distinguishes between three types of organizational goals: order, economic and cultural goals. In the first type, prohibiting deviant behaviour is important. The production of commodities and services is central in organizations with economic goals, while organizations with culture goals 'institutionalize conditions needed for the creation and preservation of symbolic objects, their application, and the creation or reinforcement of commitments to such objects' (ibid.: 73). Etzioni expects that organizations serving order goals will tend to have a coercive compliance structure; those serving economic goals will tend to have a utilitarian compliance structure; and organizations serving culture goals will tend to have a normative compliance structure. His general argument is that effective organizations show a balanced mix: the levels of coercion and alienation are low, while those of remuneration and calculation are high, as well as those of normative and moral involvement.

An analysis with some similarities to Etzioni's is found in Lindblom's *Politics and Markets* (1977). The latter depicts some elementary mechanisms of 'social control': authority, exchange and persuasion (ibid.: 12). He defines authority as existing 'whenever one, several or many people explicitly or tacitly permit someone else to make decisions for them for some category of acts' (ibid.: 17–8). Following the legitimate exercise of authority is the basis of the membership of formal organizations like churches, clubs, corporations and unions. A government is a formal organization *par excellence*: '[C]onsequently, the authority relationship is the bedrock on which government is erected. Authority is as fundamental to government as exchange is to the market system' (ibid.: 13). Persuasion is a 'ubiquitous form of social control' appearing in three variants: propaganda, commercial advertising and 'mutual persuasion'. With the latter variant Lindblom refers to the "free competition of ideas" [as] fundamental to liberal democracy' (ibid.: 13).

Since Etzioni and Lindblom developed their typologies, similar threefold conceptualizations have been used frequently and with wider applications. Boulding (1990), an economist, for instance, speaks of 'three faces of power'. He distinguishes the following dimensions along which variants of power can be identified: the nature of its consequences, characteristic behaviour and the sort of institutions by which power is exercised. On the first dimension, Boulding distinguishes destructive power, productive power, and integrative power.

Corresponding to these three categories are three kinds of characteristic behaviour: threat, exchange and love. As related institutions, Boulding mentions those of, respectively, political and military power (such as tax, the army); economic power (firms, households); and social power (family, churches, non-profit organizations). He acknowledges that all of these categories are 'fuzzy sets' (ibid.: 24), which means, for example, that integrative power also has a destructive and productive aspect. Nevertheless, Boulding sees these classifications as a necessary way of dealing with complex reality.

Thompson et al. (1991) talk about hierarchies, markets and networks as three general models of social coordination. Ouchi (1991) distinguishes between bureaucracies, markets and clans. Bradach and Eccles (1991) refer to authority, price and trust. Colebatch and Larmour (1993) focus on the process of organizing. Following certain 'patterns of action' people draw on existing models. They may organize by 'following rules defined by hierarchic authority' (bureaucracy); through 'individual exchanges which serve their interests' (market); or by 'acting in ways which are appropriate for some group of which they are a part' (community) (ibid.: 104). In the 'bureaucratic' model of organization, authority and rules are organizing principles; in the 'market' model, incentives and prices are central; while in the 'community' model, norms, values and networks are key factors (ibid.: 17).

Referring to Colebatch and Larmour, Parsons observes that in the real world of public service delivery there are almost always mixes (1995: 492). As Colebatch and Larmour state: 'The task is to identify the nature of the mix, not to place the organization into one box or another' (1993: 80). Parsons distinguishes four sorts of such mixes: a governmental mix, regarding layers of government; a sectoral mix, concerning public–private relationships; an enforcement mix, regarding modes of enforcement; and a value mix, referring to underlying values (1995: 492). For the enforcement or compliance mix, particularly relevant here, Parsons makes a distinction between two dimensions. The organizational settings of the enforcement mix obviously will vary, and because of that, so will the modes of enforcement. Parsons states that when the mode of organization is hierarchy, enforcement requires 'effective methods of command and the use of coercion or threat to ensure compliance with authoritative rules'. In the market mode of organization the problem of gaining compliance will be perceived as one 'rooted in self-interested behaviour'. Network or 'community' organizational forms 'will rely on the operation of custom, tradition, common moral codes, values and beliefs, love, a sense of belonging to a "clan" (see Ouchi, 1991), reciprocity, solidarity and trust' (Parsons, 1995: 518–19).

The two dimensions referred to are used by Parsons to position the classifications made by some authors. In Table 8.3 we give an adaptation of Parsons' scheme.

The range of variants following on the conceptualizations developed by Etzioni and Lindblom suggest their general validity. Their function is that they include both 'conditions for ordered rules' and 'governing mechanisms'. In Table 8.3 these are referred to, respectively, as modes of organization and modes of compliance. The terms quoted stem from Milward and Provan's definition of governance

Table 8.3   Modes of organization and modes of compliance

	Modes of organization		
Modes of compliance	Hierarchy/ Bureaucracy	Market	Network/ Community
Etzioni (1961)	Coercive	Remunerative	Moral
Lindblom (1977)	Authority	Exchange	Persuasion
Rigby (1964, 1990)	Command	Contract	Custom
Boulding (1990)	Threat	Exchange	Love
Bradach and Eccles (1991)	Authority	Price	Trust

Source: extension and adaptation of Parsons (1995: 518).

(1999: 3). Indeed, the two dimensions enable the description and analysis of any related empirical phenomenon on the scale of separate organizations as well as on system scale. In fact, all the mode of organization/mode of compliance combinations included here in the columns under the labels of hierarchy, market and networks refer to what can be called *modes of governance*.

In Chapter 1, we gave definitions of the concept of governance, while in Chapter 5 we positioned the study of public policy implementation in its socio-historic context. What we addressed as *the governance paradigm* we related to the current age of neo-interventionism. There we made clear that in this book we are treating 'governance' as an analytical concept that can be used as a general label for studying action in the public domain. In Chapter 6, we elaborated the concept into an analytical framework that with its multiple dimensions may serve as an alternative to the stages heuristic. On a meta-level, asking the questions who, what, where, on which scale, and how, the framework can be helpful to give focus to governance research. Being in line with the treatment of the term governance we gave in these previous chapters, the conceptualization 'modes of governance' specifies the forms governance in practice can take. As such, it needs some elaboration.

Pierre and Peters (2000) describe contemporary governance as having a 'multi-level' character. International, national and sub-national processes of governance are interlinked in a negotiated fashion. They see an emerging role of international organizations, taking over specific tasks of nation states. Seen from the level of the latter, Pierre and Peters speak of tasks 'moving up'; where greater importance is achieved by regions, localities and communities, they describe tasks as 'moving down'; while an increasing relevance of phenomena like privatization is called the 'moving out' of government tasks. Under the heading of 'models of governance' Pierre and Peters sketch three 'scenarios': towards 'reasserting control'; 'letting other regimes rule'; and towards 'communitarism, deliberation, and direct democracy'. In doing so, they use the concept of governance and its distinctive modes in an effort to generalize about historical trends. In Chapter 5 of this book, in fact, something similar was done in describing the successive paradigms. Given the broad definition of the concept as adopted from O'Toole (2000a), the contemporary governance paradigm entails not a singular but several 'modes of governance', each with equal analytical relevance. Given the action imperative implied by the principles of the rule of law and democracy, and to a certain extent by those of the welfare state, the answer to the question 'How to act?' for practitioners in public administration differs from context to context. Therefore, it seems relevant to give a further conceptual elaboration of what since Etzioni and Lindblom have been identified as three fundamental modes of governance. In particular, it may be possible to reflect on the consequences of governance by *authority*, *transaction*, or *persuasion* for implementation. Doing so we make the link both with Lindblom's terminology and the conceptualization of governance we gave in Chapters 1, 5 and 6.

Three governance roles

In the *authority* mode of governance the central subject of government action is regulation and imposition. The delivery of products and services is seen as having an exclusive ('public good') character, like flood control or assistance benefits. There are both a constitutional basis and a democratic mandate that justify the government's monopoly position here. The term 'government' refers to an array of political-administrative actors acting under a legitimate mandate. Making directive decisions and seeing that they are managed accordingly are the core focus of the political and administrative functionaries involved. In a metaphorical way this role of government can be labelled as that of a *Chief Executive Officer* (CEO) (for an elaboration see Hupe and Klaassen, 2000).

The second mode of governance, governance by *transaction*, implies a stress on the creation of frameworks in which other actors can perform, while at the same time there is a task to evaluate and ensure that these frameworks keep functioning well. These tasks are founded in a corresponding constitutional basis and democratic mandate. Legislation is important, as well as institutional design, especially the institutionalization of oversight. The role of government is one of a regulator and *inspector*.

In the third mode, governance by *persuasion*, inviting to participate is central. The constitutional basis and democratic mandate regard end-situations as what are to be aimed at. Objectives are strived for in joint efforts between government and other actors in society. Vision and the development of a basis of consensus are essential. Government has a role as *chairperson* or *régisseur* here. The latter metaphor refers to a stage play, in which the actors do the work. The play director or *régisseur* is important for the interpretation of the play and of the actors' roles, but remains invisible during the performance itself. As with chairing a meeting, the essence of practising governance as *régie* is inviting actors to contribute to a collectively produced result. The chairperson as well as the *régisseur* may have high ambitions, they are highly dependent on others, as well.

Although choices between these modes of governance may be influenced by many considerations, including political ideology, they are given equivalent status here as alternatives with different implications for control over implementation. The appropriateness of each of the three modes of governance depends on the character of the circumstances involved. Just as the contexts adequate for application vary, so do the action consequences of each separate mode of governance. How to manage implementation in context, case by case, depends to a large extent on the specific configuration of factors, including political will. This is why simple rules for implementation, generalizable across all contexts, are inapplicable. What is possible, however, is specifying the characteristics of corresponding *modes of operational governance* (Table 8.4). We are echoing Matland's general point about seeing implementation in its policy context here, but specify the issues about the identification of that context in a way that also connects it to institutional configurations.

Modes of operational governance

In Chapter 6, we conceived the implementation part of governance as *operational* governance. Realizing the decisions made and getting things done: these sorts of activities take different forms, according to the specific place (locus) in the political-societal relations concerned. Thus managing implementation may take the form of, respectively, managing policy processes (on the system scale), managing inter-organizational relations (on the scale of organizations) and managing external and internal contacts (by individual persons).[2] Given these three forms of managing implementation, what kind of action consequences on a conceptual level for each one can be identified as corresponding with the modes of governance pictured above?

For the governance-by-authority mode, the congruent action perspective is the *enforcement perspective* on managing implementation. In this perspective, management via inputs is central. Managing policy processes implies the assignment of an explicit responsibility to fulfil such a task when and where the specific policy is applied. At the same time this requires adequate attention, in the formulation of policy and in decision-making on laws and policy programmes, to the clear assignment of responsibilities. For the management of inter-organizational relations, clarity about tasks and spheres of competence is essential. For individual street-level bureaucrats or their chiefs, for instance, managing external and internal contacts means taking care of standard operating procedures and ensuring compliance with them, demonstrating leadership, enhancing motivation and internalization, and providing training on the job.

The perspective on managing implementation congruent with governance by transaction can be called the *performance perspective*. Here management on outputs takes place. In the managing of policy processes, creating 'interfaces' is important. At the directional level – next to the operational level of action – appropriate policy frameworks need to be provided. Enhancing contract compliance is a key activity in the daily process of managing inter-organizational relations. Managing interaction is all about enhancing and maintaining a service orientation. Compliance with output targets is important.

Table 8.4 Modes of operational governance

	Label of mode		
Operational activities	'Enforcement' (Management via inputs)	'Performance' (Management via outputs)	'Co-Production' (Management via outcomes as shared results)
Managing policy processes	Making mandates explicit	Creating 'interfaces'	Appealing for responsibility
Managing inter-organizational relations	Creating clarity on tasks and competences Taking care of sufficient resources	Enhancing contract compliance	Realizing partnerships
Managing (external and internal) inter-personal contacts	Enhancing motivation and internalization. Realizing compliance to standard operating procedures Leadership Training on the job	Enhancing and maintaining service orientation Rewarding target compliance	Enhancing professionalization Organizing response
Central management mechanism	*'Rules'*	*'Contract'*	*'Trust'*

For governance via persuasion, the compatible perspective is the *co-production perspective* on managing implementation. The focus is managing outcomes as shared results (Whitaker, 1980; Parks et al., 1981). Managing of policy processes here means leaving discretion to other actors and inviting them to participate. For the managing of inter-organizational relations, this implies, for instance, realizing 'implementation partnerships' (Hupe, 1993a). Micro-management involves enhancing professionalization and institutionalizing client participation. Peer assessment is important, as well as establishing complaint procedures.

Coherent implementation demands appropriate vertical connections. In the ideal-typical congruence of governance by *authority* with an *enforcement* perspective on managing implementation, there is a vertical chain-like link between what can be called the 'implementation setting', that is the situation at the street-level, the policy setting and the broader institutional environment. In the alternative ideal-typical situation of governance by *transaction*, connected with a *performance* perspective on managing implementation, the couplings are looser (contracts), although still vertical. As opposed to the chain metaphor it is appropriate to speak of a vertical rope. With the loose couplings and a more co-ordinated character of the relationships among actors, in the case of governance by *persuasion* with a *co-production* perspective on implementation, the metaphor (if any) of a woven thread may be used.

Illustrations

The argument developed here may be illustrated with the use of some examples. For the first mode of governance/mode of operational governance combination the protection against fire supplies an illustration. Representative organs will provide the Executive with a clear mandate to design an effective fire-protection policy. In such a policy the outcomes are specified: fires must be prevented and, when they occur, must immediately be extinguished. Although there always will be normal bureaucratic politics, during the formulation of and decision-making on this policy, no major conflicts are to be expected. Depending on the specific macro-institutional environment, fire protection may be seen as a legitimate government monopoly. Then there will hardly be any alternative power sources, while the required technical competence will be 'in-house'. Because the consequences of fires can be fatal, the stake of the responsible political functionaries is high. In a policy setting that shows such a combination of high ambitions and a large degree of independence, such a mix of political will and material competence, ideal-typically the *governance-by-authority* mode of governance can be seen as appropriate.

If the implementation of the fire-protection policy takes place in a unitary system of inter-governmental relations, then the character of the authority of the political-administrative layer most proximate to the operational fire brigades clearly is an executive one. Consistently, the vertical relation will be one of subordination. There may be a local or regional network in which the fire brigade is one public utility department among others, but competence and responsibilities are unambiguously formulated and exclusively assigned. At the street-level, the variety of regimes is relatively low: as far as extinguishing fires is concerned, the fire brigade is the dominant organization. It is a task-oriented organization with a specific *esprit de corps*. While the firefighters are highly trained, they work within a strict system of rules. The implementation style in their organization may be not 'administrative' in the desk-bound sense, but it certainly is far from commercial. In general, people affected by a fire comply with the orders given to them by the members of the fire brigade.

Alternatively, in many societies, refuse collection is organized through contracts, using a mode of control through contracts that are able to specify standards of performance for regularly undertaken routine tasks. Contract enforcement then involves checking processes to ensure compliance. Contracts are regularly reviewed and the availability of other potential implementing agents helps to secure this. The third mode is particularly found where complex services requiring high levels of creativity are involved, in medicine and teaching, for example. Here neither the strict rule system within which firefighters exercise their discretion nor the contractual framework used to govern refuse collection may be appropriate. Rather, the model suggests there is a need for a more creative relationship between those who seek to control these activities and the people who perform them, in which communications flow both ways.

Ambiguous reality

The degree of 'steering' ambitions and the perception on self-competence can, in their combination, be seen as preconditions for governance; although perhaps not the only ones. Apart from other relevant factors, in a democratic *Rechtsstaat* the answers to questions on steering ambitions (*What do we want?*) and self-perceived government competence (*What are we able to do ourselves?*) given on the directional level seem of guiding importance for implementing action.[3] Implementation studies have shown, however, how problematic such actions can be. Against that background the analytical constructions presented here may fulfil heuristic functions. At the same time it is obvious that reality is often different. First, it may show a greater variety of phenomena than captured in these constructions. For instance, within the implementation of one policy different implementation strategies may be used. In an analysis of multi-organization partnerships that uses a model very like that outlined here, Lowndes and Skelcher (1998) speak of a 'partnership life cycle'. Within this, 'pre-partnership collaboration is characterized by a network mode of governance'. 'Partnership creation and collaboration' involves the use of hierarchy to establish formalized procedures; 'partnership programme delivery' is by market 'mechanisms of tendering and contract'; and in 'partnership termination' there is 'a re-assertion of a network governance mode' (ibid.: 320). While we may be dubious about this attempt to generalize on the basis of studies of urban regeneration partnerships in England, the important point here is the idea of variation of practices over what may be seen as a single implementation process.

Second, some phenomena can be perceived as problematic. Looking at the 'street-level', Terpstra and Havinga (1999) give an inventory of the intrinsic problems that can be expected there. Problematic aspects of rule-led bureaucracies are – also thought of in an analytical construction – red tape; legalism and formalism; insufficient tailor-made case treatment; and lack of an orientation to effectiveness. For corporate or market-oriented implementation organizations the authors mention as negative aspects the fact that moral, political and professional values are subordinate to cost control and efficiency; and these may enhance the chance of arbitrariness. Problematic aspects of professional implementation organizations concern their uncontrollability (in terms of costs, deviation from formal rules). Democratic 'steering' of these organizations is difficult (Terpstra and Havinga, 1999: 51).

Besides, new policies may be introduced at system scale that require an adaptation of the given institutional arrangements, for instance, in relation to the character of authority given to a specific public-administrative layer (competence and allocation of resources). One can imagine, however, that such an adaptation does not take place. It is also possible that the trajectory of an existing policy, the vertical connections, has become obsolete and needs attention. These deficiencies concerning the structural dimensions of institutional settings may have consequences for the management of inter-organizational relations. In the macro-locus of the political-administrative system, for example, conflicts may have become visible in the legitimate policy-formation, that work through in the implementation of that policy. It may even be the case that the constitutional basis for a policy is controversial. Authors like Wittrock and DeLeon (1986) and Ferman (1990) observe that implementers of such a policy may function then as an extra check in the system of government.

An especially problematic situation is apparent when, in the vertical connections, structural discrepancies have grown between what is actually happening at the street-level and what relevant stake-holders assess as appropriate at the directional level in the locus of the political-administrative system as a whole. In particular, this may be the case when at the street-level, in a relative autonomy, a specific *implementation culture* has developed. Especially in such circumstances, more or less different from the situations and connections as ideal-typically supposed, the actors involved may evaluate both the configuration of factors concerning the two major preconditions of governance mentioned above and the feasibility of changing that given configuration. According to the character of the system of inter-governmental relations concerned, the locus of the guidance from the directional level may vary. Generally, in the last resort, what is legitimately wanted in the locus of the political-administrative system as a whole will provide the leading clues here.

Non-congruent mixes

The general action imperative implies that implementation action is required whatever the nature of the mix of settings: in congruent as well as non-congruent ones. Non-congruent here refers to a 'multi-mode of governance' mix of the settings. Such a mix is present when for a certain policy, for example, at the street-level a service orientation is being asked for (*transaction* mode of governance), while the inter-organizational relations (still) have a 'command' character (*authority* mode). Non-congruency may also imply the connection between the practised implementation perspective and the character of the given mix of settings. Stressing at random the specific and binding character of central governmental authority and responsibilities in managing a certain policy process (*enforcement* perspective), for instance, may create tensions in a network-like institutional setting (*persuasion* mode of governance).

These kinds of non-congruent configurations of contextual factors form the reality practitioners are used to deal with, and often have to accept. As far as they provide more room to manoeuvre, non-congruent mixes, both of settings and of mode of governance/managing implementation perspective combinations, can even be functional for the tasks at hand. However, the more seriously certain situations of implementation are being judged as structurally dysfunctional, or the more frequently this happens, the greater the likelihood that relevant actors – irrespective of layer, but acting on the constitutive and directional levels of governance – will see the need to enhance congruence between the composite elements of those mixes. Negotiation, for instance, can be functional in a process of co-production between residents, associations and local government in a network configuration aiming at consensus about the exact location of a youth centre in a neighbourhood. Similarly, however, negotiation between the same actors in that neighbourhood would be seen as entirely dysfunctional if practised in the process of policy formation and implementation concerning the infrastructure for the local supply of drinking water.

The constructions made above are designed to be helpful in a cognitive and analytical way. The extent to which they provide a heuristic assisting with the diagnosis of the specific context practitioners have to deal with, remains open. It is certain, however, that the presented constructions will rarely be observed in their pure forms; unless in political-administrative rhetoric. Instead, in many cases, mixed ('hybrid') forms will occur. Knowing when to accept non-congruent or incongruent configurations of contextual factors and make the best of them; or, instead, when to change them, cannot be prescribed by any checklist. It is clear that determining the relevance and relative weight of the dimensions mentioned here, in concrete action situations, is a matter of judgement, and, finally, a 'political' matter. In all these cases statements about the appropriate mode of control depend upon judgements which involve other considerations as well as those relating to implementation control.

In particular, the use of the 'performance' mode of operational governance is the subject of controversy, inasmuch as privatized modes of policy delivery are seen to have merits separate from concerns about effective implementation – the facilitation of citizen choice and the achievement of additional contributions from the private sector. A particular paradox here, however, is that one of the arguments used in favour of a loosening of public control over services (implying at least partial privatization) is that services can be more innovative if released from the 'dead hand' of government. This is an argument used in the UK, for example, for quasi-independent schools and hospitals. The approach to implementation advocated there can be seen as a hybrid form between the performance and the co-production modes of operational governance. There is then, in fact, a lively debate between those who see this as a feasible form and those who argue that it is difficult to secure co-production in the context of a contract. The conceptualization offered here can, we suggest, assist with the examination of this.

Conclusion

Now, at the end of this chapter, we can reposition implementation in terms of the need to relate it to the concept of governance, which we have stressed. Given the three levels of governance we distinguished in Chapter 6, what we called *directional governance* is at the heart of all the activities mentioned. This level of governance action entails the guiding formulation plus decision-making on public tasks. Roughly speaking, we are dealing here with what we defined in Chapter 1 as policy formation. Kiser and Ostrom (1982) pointed to the importance of another level, that of constitutional design. In our view, the level of *constitutive governance* is relevant in other loci of political–societal relations than that of the centre, as well. At sub-layers such as the street-level, too, the creation of settings is an important task. For individuals, this means the internalization of specific values and norms, from which action is influenced. Implementation, then, refers to that part of governance that involves activities in relation to public tasks implied by the directional decisions on those tasks. In the beginning of the third millennium 'implementation of public policy' takes various forms, but they all can be approached as concerned with the operational part of governance. In short, implementation can be seen as *operational governance*.

Identifying and specifying dimensions of contextual variety, in this chapter we structured the multiplicity of environments and circumstances practitioners have to deal with as contexts of action. The central theme of this chapter has been that in order to relate the insights derived from the academic study of implementation to the 'action imperative' practitioners are facing, there is a need to analyze the contexts within which implementation acts occur. Matland's insight involves highlighting two of these:

- what is to be implemented, cannot be explored through any neat policy typology, but rather in terms of the level of ambiguity embodied in policy goals;
- the power context.

Then, we contended, there is a need to consider the institutional context (including within that notion the cultural context). This is something to which various efforts to develop comparative analyses of government and of policy make a contribution, albeit in more or less tentative ways. Our position is that all the attempts by political scientists or analysts of public administration to compare nations in these terms must have a bearing upon implementation analysis, given the way in which the latter is integrated into the policy process as a whole.

From there we went on to some considerations about modes of governance, elaborating the kind of conceptualizations provided by authors like Etizoni and Lindblom further towards analyzing the practice of managing implementation. When approaching them from an analytical point of view, in this chapter we treated the three ideal-typical modes of governance and corresponding modes of operational governance as each offering models for the management of implementation, with their respective strengths and weaknesses for this task depending upon the policy delivery activity at stake. In the multiple contexts in which practitioners of public administration are acting, the application of these modes will vary from situation to situation. Likewise, the judgements on the appropriateness of the application of the distinguished congruent combinations will differ with the assessment of the specific configuration of factors in the circumstances at hand. Within that configuration we identified the level of steering ambition ('willing') and the level of competence ('being able') as among the possibly most relevant factors. Instead of, for instance, equating governance only with network management, the plea for contextualization made here essentially implies recognizing alternative modes of governance. If governance is multiple, so is managing implementation as concerning the *operational* part of it.

Notes

1 In a summary of the 'top-down perspective's conventional wisdom', O'Toole (1986) refers to Mazmanian and Sabatier (1981) and Pressman and Wildavsky (1984). At the same time he mentions O'Toole and Montjoy (1984) as well.

2 Berman (1978) makes a distinction between 'macro-implementation' and 'micro-implementation'. For the distinction between locus and focus, see Chapter 1 of the present book.

3 Pierre and Peters (2000) speak of a 'state-centered' conception of governance. They give both empirical and normative reasons for such a stance. It is interesting that they do not hesitate to use the term 'steering' in this context. We share the considerations given by these authors in the following sense. Given the context at hand, in the practice of public administration it may be deemed appropriate that certain tasks in the public domain are fulfilled by so-called 'private' actors. 'Private' then may refer to business corporations or non-profit organizations. Normatively, in our view the decision to have such tasks fulfilled this way needs an explicit legitimation. After all, such a decision concerns a 'value choice' (Rothstein, 1998) with a *public* character. The decision on the 'appropriateness' can be seen as a result of an analytically supported political assessment 'on the spot'. In that assessment the specific combination of available ambition and perceived self-competence may be important.

9

THE FUTURE OF IMPLEMENTATION STUDIES

Contents

Introduction

As the final chapter in this book, we need to provide our key conclusions. We do this by addressing the question: what future for implementation studies from our observed state of the art can be justified? Has, indeed, the subject become 'yesterday's issue'?, as one of us rhetorically asked a number of years ago (Hill, 1997). The answer given in the introductory chapter of this book remains the answer in this last chapter: 'No'. We think the study of implementation has a future – although perhaps a different one than it seemed to have back in the 1970s.

In this chapter we return to the objectives of studying implementation (second section). What was it all about? Next, by way of a substantive rather than a systematic summary of the argument of the book, we highlight some of our findings from the preceding chapters (third section). We continue by sketching some developments that can be judged as enhancing the study of implementation of public policies – under whatever contemporary heading (fourth section). The chapter ends with a concluding fifth section.

The objective of studying implementation

In an academic discipline several questions may lead the quest for truth. After all, in the division of labour between 'science' and 'society' both parties have legitimate expectations from each other. Programmatic and methodological considerations may embody the lines of distinction between science and other trades in society. Fundamentally, this is not different for *social* science ('or the social sciences'). In the study of politics and public administration, too, it ultimately is the combination of an orientation towards the accumulation of knowledge, on the one hand, and the ways in which this knowledge is being gained, on the other, that make practising that study not the same as writing a novel or giving a yoga workshop.

Of course, from there the debate starts about the implications of the nature of the object of those disciplines in social science for the ways in which that object should be approached. In this book we have addressed implementation theory and research as a sub-discipline of political science and public administration. As we have suggested throughout this book, much theorizing about implementation since the late 1990s has been within a variant of the study of public administration described as public management.

In our view, this means that all of the preceding statements made in this section go for implementation studies as well. As a consequence, we see the following sorts of concerns in this sub-discipline: descriptive concerns (the most realistic way to describe implementation processes); theoretical and methodological concerns (how to research implementation); and normative concerns (raising issues about whose will should prevail in the implementation of policy). Through the history of the sub-discipline – let us say since the publication of Pressman and Wildavsky's book in 1973 – these concerns have remained important. It means that when we identify the objectives of studying implementation, we should differentiate between teaching, research and consultancy.

It is clear that scholars, engaged as they are in exercises in scientific enquiry, in principle are driven by the same search for the truth, despite the question of whether these exercises take the form of teaching, doing research or giving advice. Yet the fact, for example, that policy analysis is a mixture of 'analysis of' policy and 'analysis for' policy (Gordon et al., 1977) indicates that the core preoccupations of those offering theoretical propositions will differ. Our assumption is that the stances taken by authors on implementation may, to a certain extent, be influenced by the kind of concern they are led by. What we described as descriptive; theoretical and methodological; and normative concerns may imply, quite pragmatically, different objectives associated with, respectively, teaching, research; and consultancy. In fact, on a meta-level, different kinds of questions are leading. In teaching, the objective is transferring knowledge: What knowledge and insights are available? Theory and research aim to contribute to the accumulation of that knowledge and insights: Given what we know, what can we explain? In consultancy, the objective is to give advice to practitioners: How can knowledge be used to act?

Teaching about implementation

As far as teaching is concerned, there is a need to be as comprehensive as possible, identifying the multitude of factors that influence implementation and the range of interpretations of their impact. Therefore there will tend to be a bias away from simplification. Analysis will be essentially 'of policy', and there is likely to be some attention to the difficulties of explaining action. Obviously, therefore, within accounts of implementation offered by some teachers there will be interpretative perspectives influenced by postmodern challenges to generalization and the accumulation of hypotheses (see pp. 38–40). The word 'some' is important in that last sentence; we certainly do not generalize here about all teachers. The important point is that while, in our view, such perspectives place serious constraints upon research activities they do not necessarily inhibit teaching about implementation. Hence we find Fox (in Palumbo and Calista, 1990) supporting arguments for a wide view of the policy arena and a broad time span, and also arguing for the consideration of 'multiple standpoints'. Fox rejects a total shift away from positivism, but argues: 'to the positive benefits of modern social science must be added respect for the disciplined employment of sound intuition itself born of experience not reducible to models, hypotheses, quantification, "hard" data, or little pieces of incorrigible fixity' (ibid.: 211).

Yanow develops a related argument for an 'interpretive' approach, with an emphasis on 'interpretations of policy language, legislative intent or implementing actions' (Yanow, 1993) to the study of implementation, questioning the quest for one best way of studying the subject.

Researching implementation

As the teaching perspective is likely to embrace all philosophical and methodological standpoints, and to be able to tolerate complex and possibly conflicting explanations, we have started with that. By contrast, the research perspective tends to involve efforts to restrict the span of attention, recognize the specificity of policy and operational contexts and confine the number of variables to be examined to a relatively small number. The formulation of hypotheses will generally be required in which identification of dependent and independent variables will be attempted, and *ceteris paribus* clauses are likely to be used. Quantification and comparison will be seen as important. While we do not want to suggest that all who engage in implementation research are positivists in any strict sense, those concerns of traditional positivist research are likely to be in evidence. Hence it is from the particularly research-orientated implementation theorists like May and Winter, and public management researchers like Meier and O'Toole, that we see strong attempts to limit the span of theoretical attention, at least in respect of any particular research project.

There is also inevitably an issue in respect of the research concern about funding and other support for work on implementation. It is not surprising to find a top-down orientation, or at least a search for 'what works', in the writings of those whose approach to implementation analysis is particularly linked to research concerns. For many of the people who fund research work want to see efforts to answer specific questions about differences in implementation, and often about the reasons for what is called implementation 'success' and 'failure'.

Advising about Implementation

These practical concerns also apply to the consultancy orientation in implementation theory, with the difference that there will often not be the same pressure for the systematic testing of hypotheses in this case. We find thus the impact of consultancy in the domination, particularly in the early implementation work, of the search for a series of concrete propositions ('rules for successful implementation'). It would be unfair, however, to suggest that the consultancy approach is always orientated towards simplification. There is an interesting tradition of stressing complexity, in which the consultant role is to help clients to cope with this. We see this most saliently in the long career of Eugene Bardach (1977, 1998) with his emphasis upon 'fixing games' and identifying key roles in those games. Similarities exist in work in the UK in which inter-organizational complexity is stressed, with early but influential publication on the roles of 'reticulists' (Friend et al., 1974) The latter term refers to actors working across organizational boundaries and contemporary work on how best successful partnerships can be formed (see particularly Hudson and Hardy, 2002). A related development in The Netherlands is the elaboration of propositions about network management (Koppenjan and Klijn, 2004).

While consultants in the strict sense need clients who pay for their advice, there is nevertheless in implementation studies work in which normative concerns are central. In many cases these concerns include challenges to the normative simplicity of the top-down perspective, which takes it for granted that successful implementation means compliance with the wishes of dominant actors. We speak here of what is implicitly consultancy, but without specific clients, although perhaps 'advocacy' is a better word. In this sense we see authors, such as Rothstein, whose particular concerns are with highlighting the normative questions embedded in implementation studies. Also studies can be observed from authors who specifically identify themselves with concerns other than of those 'at the top'. A grass-roots view of democracy is explicitly embodied in some of Hjern and Hull's work (1982). Contrary to many of the simplifications of his view which stress the power to 'subvert' policy, Michael Lipsky's original analysis of street-level bureaucracy is concerned to recognize the validity of the perspectives of low-level officials *and* of the public to whom they relate. More explicitly Yanow's concern about policy meaning (1993) applies to implementation an aspiration to inform people outside the usually identified 'stakeholders'. This view parallels Fox and Miller's defence of the postmodernist approach to the exploration of discourse as contributing to the empowerment of the powerless (1995).

As indicated above, we do not suggest that those who have theorized about implementation belong explicitly and strictly to one of the three categories of teachers, researchers or consultants (in a narrow or wider sense). After all, many individual implementation scholars fulfil two or all these three roles – although perhaps not always at the same time. We do suggest, however, that participation in one or more of these activities may have had some influence on approaches to theory, in terms of stances on the divergences identified in the subsequent chapters of this book. These divergences particularly regard:

- approaches to the top-down/bottom-up synthesis, and especially the normative issues that are embedded in it;
- treatment of the policy formation/implementation boundaries;
- the attention given to complexity, and particularly to networks;
- simplification and the specification of policy- and contextual differences.

In the following section we highlight some of our findings from the previous chapters, by way of summarizing the argument unfolded in this book.

The study of governance in operation

We started from the position, set out in Chapter 1, that within political science and public administration a sub-discipline concerned with policy implementation seems to have been established. The introductory remarks included explanations about the terminology we accordingly have used in the book. In Chapter 2, we gave attention to the subject of implementation in general, looking at its societal embedding and at theoretical elements that are relevant to the subject, although coming from a different background. Next we reviewed the literature about implementation, in Chapters 3 and 4. There we observed that it was a development from a long-standing concern to explain, and probably try to reduce, the 'gap' between the initial formulation of the goals of a public policy and the actual results of that policy. In fact, attention for the relation between intentions and achievements dates far back; otherwise the pyramids in Egypt could not have been built.

The history of 'public policy' as the nominator for the strivings connecting intentions and achievements of government actors, however, is relatively young. It is seen little before the rise of the modern state. Furthermore, the period in which public policy implementation as a modern phenomenon under corresponding labels has been studied is even shorter. It seems defendable to mark the beginning of that period with the publication of Pressman and Wildavsky's influential book *Implementation* in 1973. We showed that the 'mainstream' implementation literature, broadly speaking originating from that book, to some extent supplemented, and to some extent bypassed, other relevant literature on politics, public law and public organizations. Within the specific implementation literature a lively debate developed, dominated by arguments about whether 'top-down' or 'bottom-up' views of implementation were more appropriate. While that argument was partly about methodology, it was perhaps primarily driven by concerns about accountability. The top-down preoccupation with the elimination of the 'gap' between formulation and output contrasted with the bottom-up view that this phenomenon was a product of the inevitable, and perhaps desirable, participation of other actors in 'later stages' of the policy process.

Then, as is the way with debates of this kind, gradually the literature moved away from a simple confrontation between the top-down and bottom-up perspectives on studying implementation. Authors became critical of the 'misery' kind of approach that led top-downers to be preoccupied with a process of policy modification. From a methodological point of view it was recognized that it is much more fruitful to seek to understand and explain the implementation (sub-) process as such, than to be preoccupied by a need to explain an inevitable 'gap'. From a normative point of view it was recognized: (1) that there are alternative views about the accountability of public policy that cannot be resolved by an academic literature; and (2) that in many situations the exploration of the way alternative 'accountabilities' can fuse together is a more fruitful way forward for those anxious to control implementation than a preoccupation with domination by any single party.

Chapter 5 then added to that review the perspective that the evolution of the debate needs to be seen not simply in terms of a developing academic argument, but also in its relationship to a changing perspective on the role of government in society. The latter has involved what we, alongside many other contemporary writers, see as an evolution from *government* to *governance*. As the essence of that phrase we see the de-coupling of actor and activities; of locus and focus. Governance, of course, remains practised by government, but this may take various forms. The need to specify actor/activities combinations may lead to distinctions between sorts of governance, like corporate governance, government governance or public governance. In fact, however, paraphrasing Bozeman's (1987) motto one could state: *All* governance is public.

We then asked what the implications would be of what we labelled as *the governance paradigm* for the old issues about implementing public policy. It was noted that there are authors who see in these new developments the 'death' of the study of implementation. We agree that governance makes the top-down/bottom-up debate seem rather dated, and the top-down control emphasis in the work of some of the top-down writers particularly irrelevant. Implementation theory has developed and moved away from that debate to take on board complexity in respect both of the process and of the related issues of control. Nevertheless it seems wrong to see the implementation perspective as no longer appropriate. On the contrary, in our view it is the very complexity of the issues facing modern governance that makes it important to continue giving attention to implementation: in practice as well as in studying it. One of the virtues of the work of the early top-down theorists was that they emphasized issues of purposive action and control over policy processes. Those issues remain important regardless of the stance one takes on who should be in control. While we recognize that there has been a tendency in some postmodernist writing on public administration to see the policy process as having a shapeless, 'garbage can', character, we share the more widespread concern about the need to raise questions about how policy processes may be influenced.

Having identified the prevalence of what we described as a governance paradigm, in Chapter 6 we explored the theoretical consequences of looking at implementation from a governance perspective. We reviewed the functionality of the stages model and explored the pros and cons of alternative general frameworks. It was in that chapter, too, that we gave an elaboration of the Multiple Governance Framework developed as a way to reframe the policy process.

We have elaborated through Chapters 6 to 8 what it means to do research on implementation and to try to make recommendations based on that, given the prevalence of the governance paradigm, on the one hand, and the state of knowledge about implementation, on the other. For that purpose we addressed the agenda of issues that we identified in Chapter 4 as characteristic of the present state of implementation theory. The search for a synthesis, noted in that chapter, invites implementation researchers to explain explicitly and as specified as possible what it is that needs explanation. If 'implementation' is an object of research at all, the question where in a policy process policy formation ends and implementation begins has to be handled methodologically. Next to that it is important to consider how to deal theoretically and methodologically with the fact that many policy processes involve a multiplicity of administrative layers. While network analysis has broadened the horizontal dimension in implementation research, specifying inter-organizational relationships is needed. As far as the vertical dimension is concerned, the fact should be acknowledged that differences in managerial action refer to an important, but only one set of factors causing varying agency responses. On the borders of those agencies citizens as clients, and other actors affected by the policy involved, function as stakeholders whose actions may influence the implementation of that policy as well. And then there are macro-environmental factors that may be hard to control, but nevertheless may have a pertinent influence, too. Measuring the impact of all these factors may be difficult, certainly in their relationships. This is why we think it is important not to champion either quantitative or qualitative research methods exclusively.

While researching in this field is one thing, practitioners, working under an action imperative, may welcome advice how to implement public policies. The search for truth in academia is paralleled by the quest for appropriate action in the practice of public administration. In Chapter 8, we explored the various dimensions of the situations in which governance is being practised. There we also tried to elaborate conceptually the kind of general insights about the ways actors can 'steer' the behaviour of other actors as developed by authors like Etzioni and Lindblom. Although reality almost always is ambiguous – or rather, because of that – it remains relevant to specify contexts for action. After all, it is in implementation as the operational part of governance that 'good intentions' materialize.

Promising developments

As indicated, we do not see studying implementation as an obsolete matter; that study will continue, under whatever heading. Preferring to give this book 'an open end', rather than to aim at closing an ongoing discussion, it seems relevant to identify some lines that may gain momentum in the future. Overviewing the field, we see three sorts of such developments.

First, there are the implementation studies, called simply that. It can be stated as a fact that the multi-disciplinary attention to the subject of implementation continues as before. Just as there was practice and study of implementation before it became something that could be called a paradigm, this will be the case after that paradigm has been succeeded by newer ones. As Saetren (2005) has evidenced on the basis of a comprehensive bibliometrical study, many implementation studies are still being done. They may often be single case studies and policy field-related – which may make them less visible – but there still is a critical mass of *mainstream implementation studies*, in the literal sense.

As a second development renewed attention to issues of implementation can be observed in the literature on what is called 'multi-level governance'. Looking at governing across more than one administrative layer – as we would formulate the subject matter – researchers, for instance, are interested in the 'implementation' of directives of the European Union by the various member states. In that context the traditional questions about the relationship between policy implementation and policy formation are posed anew. Elsewhere, we have pointed out some methodological traps associated with such research (Hupe and Hill, 2003). In particular, there is the possibility that 'implementation' is presupposed where, in fact, legitimate policy co-formation is at stake. Because of the contemporary preoccupation with traditional issues, perhaps the label *neo-implementation studies* is appropriate here.

Third, there are studies of 'implementation' performed under different headings. The kind of research recognized by Kettl (2000) and O'Toole (2000a) as promising and, actually, advancing 'implementation studies' can be valued as broadening perspectives and enhancing chances for the development of new insights and the use of new sources of knowledge. The systematic research that some scholars do, particularly American ones, makes a substantial theoretical-empirical contribution to the accumulation of knowledge. If this knowledge concerns what still can be called the sub-discipline of public policy implementation studies, or something else, in our view is of secondary importance. One of the characteristics of these studies is that, instead of theorizing about what should be the elements of a comprehensive, overarching *grand theory* (constantly adding new variables), they focus on confronting existing knowledge about a relatively narrowly defined subject, in a systematic way, with relevant sets of data. Next to this kind of study, it can be expected that, if certain requirements are met (see Chapter 7), the linking of large quantities of data with parsimoniously formulated formal models (Meier and O'Toole, 2001; see also Torenvlied, 2000) may advance the field – either in the narrow or in a broader sense.

In the context of this third category, two contemporary trends in the study of public administration seem worthy of note. One is that one can observe a rise of studies in which explicitly performance is being analyzed. Since the 1980s the measuring of the results of government action, in all kinds of variants, has attracted attention (Pollitt and Bouckaert, 2004; Bouckaert and Halligan, 2007;

see also Ferlie et al., 2005). This is both in the practice and in the study of public administration, then usually addressed as public management. It is this trend, an ideological movement with real consequences, which made us talk in Chapter 5 about the New Public Management paradigm. Recently, in a limited number of empirical studies making connections between various sorts, 'public service performance' as dependent variables and specific other variables on the explanatory side gets particularly explicit attention (Boyne et al., 2006).

The other trend is in policy studies; that the degree of rigour seems to be increasing. Although the volume *Theories of the Policy Process* hardly contains 'theories' in the meaning given by Ostrom and adopted by us in Chapter 6, it does give an informative overview of what Sabatier (2007), the editor, calls 'more promising' theoretical approaches. If one takes a closer look at the eight approaches, one can identify a variety of ways to conceptualize what, in fact, can be called 'performance'. All of the approaches aim at explaining variation; although the social constructivist one, as presented by Ingram et al. (2007), perhaps not exactly at causal explanation. Some of the approaches want to explain policy change or policy adoption, but the Advocacy Coalition Framework (Sabatier and Weible, 2007) and the Multiple Streams Framework (Zahariadis, 2007) explicitly focus on explaining policy outputs and outcomes. What is relevant here is not the question whether these approaches justifiably are labelled 'frameworks'. Rather, the fact is remarkable that certainly the latter two are interested in explaining variation in what can be, but is not, called *performance*: not from a public management but *from a policy studies perspective*.

And then, in a way, we seem to be back with what implementation studies were all about. After all, the subject matter of these studies, as formulated by O'Toole (2003a: 273), still concerns 'what happens between the establishment of policy and its impact in the world of action'.

Conclusion

In Chapter 4, we reported on the state of the art of implementation studies at the beginning of the twenty-first century. We started accumulating the material for that chapter in the first edition of this book while believing that we could assemble a comprehensive database of implementation studies carried out during the 1990s. This belief proved to be mistaken; given the diversity of the subject we soon discovered that it was an impossible task. Studies claiming to be about implementation had been carried out without reference to the mainstream theoretical literature, while excellent insights relevant to the theoretical debate had been provided by studies apparently indifferent to that mainstream.[1]

Actually this is the situation right now, as well. On the one hand, the days of the policy-implementation paradigm are over, as we argued in Chapter 5. At the same time, however, the implementation, as legitimately as possible, of decisions agreed upon in the face of collective ambitions goes on, while still deemed necessary – to say the least. The labels and concepts may change, that fact fundamentally does not. As long as collective ambitions are strived at, governance (or whatever it may be called in the future) will be practised. And as long as that is the case, it will be considered worthwhile to study the operational part of that governance.

This situation justifies sustained academic attention to what in this book has been addressed as implementing public policy. Such attention may keep the threefold form we distinguished in the second section of this chapter. One may see a certain analogy here with the *trias gubernandi* presented in Chapter 6. In theory and research the leading meta-question directs the quest for truth (cf. the directional level). In consultancy, the leading meta-question is about putting knowledge into practice (cf. the operational level). The meta-question leading in teaching and the objective of documenting and transferring knowledge relate to maintaining the state of the (sub-) discipline as institution. Then we are talking about the constitutive level (cf. the title of the present chapter).

Thus specifying academic attention implies – here as well – distinguishing between actor and activities. As indicated, many scholars are engaged both in research and teaching, and often also in consultancy. When writing this book, however, it was particularly concerns related to teaching that we had in mind. Eventually, presenting once in a while what knowledge and insights are available may contribute to establishing the conditions necessary for the academic work of the future. In this book, therefore, we have brought together many insights relevant for all who teach about implementation. We did so, recognizing throughout that a scholarly activity in an applied discipline should make positive contributions both to the accumulation of new evidence from research and to the passing on of ideas for action.

Note

1 For the past three months one of us has been receiving a service provided for the journals published by Sage (only therefore a fraction of the total journals published) in which he is notified of articles with some reference to 'policy implementation'. Such notifications come in at a rate of about 30 articles a week, from journals of many kinds (education, environmental studies, health studies, sociology, psychology etc. – with political science featuring only rarely).

REFERENCES

Following standard Dutch practice names containing the forms 'van', 'in't', "t,' 'ter', do not appear here in the alphabetical order indicated by the prefix. Thus, for example, H.R. van Gunsteren comes in the place appropriate to Gunsteren. The exception to this rule is two American authors – Van Meter and Van Horn – who are normally indexed under the letter 'v' in English publications.

Aalders, M.V.C. (1987) *Regeltoepassing in de ambtelijke praktijk van Hinderwet en Bouwtoezichtafdeling*. Groningen: Wolters-Noordhoff.
Aberbach, J.D., Putnam, R.D. and Rockman, B.A. (1981) *Bureaucrats and Politicians in Western Democracies*. Cambridge, MA: Harvard University Press.
Abma, T. (1999) 'Introduction: narrative perspectives on program evaluation', in T. Abma (ed.) *Telling Tales: On Evaluation and Narrative. Advances in Program Evaluation*, Vol. 6. Greenwich, CT: JAI Press, pp. 1–27.
Aldrich, H.E. (1976) 'Resource dependence and inter-organizational relations: local employment service offices and social services sector organizations', *Administration and Society*, 7(4): 419–54.
Alford, R.R. (1975) *Health Care Politics: Ideological and Interest Group Barriers to Reform*. Chicago: University of Chicago Press.
Algemene Rekenkamer (1987) *Privatisering Staatsvissershavenbedrijf*. The Hague: Staatsuitgeverij.
Algemene Rekenkamer (1998) *Privatisering van het ABP*. The Hague: Sdu Uitgevers.
Allison, G.T. (1971) *Essence of Decision: Explaining the Cuban Missile Crisis*. Boston: Little, Brown and Company.
Anderson, J.E. (1975) *Public Policy-Making*. New York: Praeger.
Argyris, C. (1964) *Integrating the Individual and the Organization*. New York: Wiley.
Arts, W. and Gelissen, J. (2002) 'Three worlds of welfare capitalism or more?' *Journal of European Social Policy*, 12(2): 137–58.
Atkinson, P. (1985) *Language, Structure and Reproduction: An Introduction to the Sociology of Basil Bernstein*. London: Methuen.
Bailey, S.K. and Mosher, E.K. (1968) *ESEA: The Office of Education Administers a Law*. Syracuse, NY: Syracuse University Press.
Baldwin, R. (1995) *Rules and Government*. Oxford: Clarendon Press.
Banks, L., Haynes, P., Hill, M. and Balloch, S. (2006) *Changes in Communal Provision for Adult Social Care, 1991–2001*. York: Joseph Rowntree Foundation.
Bardach, E. (1977) *The Implementation Game: What Happens after a Bill Becomes a Law*. Cambridge, MA: MIT Press.
Bardach, E. (1998) *Getting Agencies to Work Together: The Practice and Theory of Managerial Craftsmanship*. Washington, DC: Brookings Institution Press.
Bardach, E. and Lesser, C. (1996) 'Accountability in human services collaboratives – For what? And to whom?', *Journal of Public Administration Research and Theory*, 6(2): 197–224.
Barrett, S. (2004) 'Implementation studies: time for a revival? Personal reflections on 20 years of implementation studies', *Public Administration* 82(2): 249–62.

Barrett, S.M. and Fudge, C. (1981a) 'Examining the policy–action relationship', in S.M. Barrett and C. Fudge (eds), *Policy and Action: Essays on the Implementation of Public Policy*. London: Methuen, pp. 3–34.

Barrett, S.M. and Fudge, C. (1981b) 'Reconstructing the field of analysis', in S.M. Barrett and C. Fudge (eds), *Policy and Action: Essays on the Implementation of Public Policy*. London: Methuen, pp. 249–78.

Barrett, S.M. and Fudge, C. (eds) (1981c) *Policy and Action: Essays on the Implementation of Public Policy*. London: Methuen.

Barrett, S.M. and Hill, M.J. (1981) 'Report to the SSRC Central–Local Government Relations Panel on the "core" or theoretical component of the research on implementation', unpublished.

Baudrillard, J. (1973) *Le miroir de la production ou l'illusion critique du matérialisme historique*. Tournai: Casterman.

Baudrillard, J. (1981) *Simulacres et simulation*. Paris: Galilée.

Beck, U. (1992) *Risk Society: Towards a New Modernity*. London: Sage.

Bellamy, C. and Taylor, J. (1992) 'Informatisation and new public management: an alternative agenda for public administration', *Public Policy and Administration*, 7(3): 29–41.

Benson, J.K. (1975) 'The inter-organizational network as a political economy', *Administrative Science Quarterly*, 20(2): 229–49.

Benson, J.K. (1977) 'Organizations: a dialectical view', *Administrative Science Quarterly*, 22(1): 1–21.

Benson, J.K. (1982) 'A framework for policy analysis', in D.L. Rogers and D.A. Whetten (eds), *Interorganizational Coordination: Theory, Research and Implementation*. Ames: Iowa State University Press, pp. 137–76.

Bentley, A.F. (1967) *The Process of Government*. Cambridge, MA: The Belknap Press.

Berke, J.S., Kirst, M.W., Bailey, S.K. and Britell, J.K. (1972) *Federal Aid to Education: Who Benefits? Who Governs?* Lexington, KY: Heath.

Berman, P. (1978) 'The study of macro- and micro-implementation', *Public Policy*, 26(2): 157–84.

Bevir, M. and Rhodes, R.A.W. (2000) 'Analysing networks: from typologies of institutions to narratives of beliefs', paper presented by Rod Rhodes on 24 January at a staff seminar of the Department of Public Administration, Erasmus University, Rotterdam.

Blau, P.M. (1955) *The Dynamics of Bureaucracy: A Study of Interpersonal Relations in Two Government Agencies*. Chicago: University of Chicago Press.

Boaden, N. (1971) *Urban Policy-Making: Influences on County Boroughs in England and Wales*. Cambridge: Cambridge University Press.

Bouckaert, G. and Halligan, J. (2007) *Managing Performance: International Comparisons*. London/New York: Routledge.

Boulding, K.E. (1990) *Three Faces of Power*. Newbury Park, CA: Sage.

Bovens, M.A.P., Derksen, W., Witteveen, W.J., Kalma, P. and Becker, F. (1995) *De verplaatsing van de politiek*. Amsterdam: Wiardi Beckman Stichting.

Bovens, M.A.P. and 't Hart, P. (1996) *Understanding Policy Fiascoes*. New Brunswick, NJ: Transaction Publishers.

Bovens, M., 't Hart, P. and Peters, B.G. (eds) (2001) *Success and Failure in Public Governance*. Cheltenham: Edward Elgar.

Bowe, R., Ball, S.J. and Gold, A. (1992) *Reforming Education and Changing Schools: Case Studies in Policy Sociology*. London: Routledge.

Bowen, E.R. (1982) 'The Pressman–Wildavsky paradox', *Journal of Public Policy*, 2(1): 1–21.

Boyne, G.A., Meier, K.J., O'Toole, Jr., and Walker, R.M. (eds) (2006) *Public Service Performance: Perspectives on Measurement and Management*. Cambridge: Cambridge University Press.

Bozeman, B. (1987) *All Organizations are Public: Bridging Public and Private Organizational Theories*. San Francisco: Jossey-Bass.

Braak, M. ter (1931) *Afscheid van domineesland*. Brussel: Stols.

Bradach, J.L. and Eccles, R.G. (1991) 'Price, authority and trust: from ideal types to plural forms', in G. Thompson, J. Frances, R. Levacic and J. Mitchell (eds), *Markets, Hierarchies and Networks: The Coordination of Social Life*. London: Sage, pp. 277–92.

Braybrooke, D. and Lindblom, C.E. (1963) *A Strategy of Decision: Policy Evaluation as a Social Process*. New York: Free Press of Glencoe.

Bressers, J.T.A. and Ringeling, A.B. (1989) 'Beleidsinstrumenten in drie arena's: Beleidsvorming, uitvoering en doorwerking', *Beleidswetenschap*, 3(1): 3–24.

Bridges, A. (2000) 'Path dependency, sequence, history, theory', *Studies in American Political Development*, 14: 109–12.

Brooks, D. (2000) *Bobos in Paradise: The New Upper Class and How They Got There*. New York: Simon & Schuster.

Brown, M.M., O'Toole, L.J., Jr, and Brudney, J.L. (1998) 'Implementing information technology in government: an empirical assessment of the role of local partnerships', *Journal of Public Administration Research and Theory*, 8(4): 499–525.

Burns, T.R. and Stalker, G.M. (1961) *The Management of Innovation*. London: Tavistock Publications.

Campbell, E. (2001) 'Prosecution and diversion: implementing a policy initiative'. PhD thesis, University of Newcastle upon Tyne.

Castells, M. (1996) *The Rise of the Network Society*. Cambridge, MA: Blackwell.

Cater, D. (1964) *Power in Washington: A Critical Look at Today's Struggle to Govern in the Nation's Capital*. New York: Random House.

Challis, L., Fuller, S., Henwood, M., Klein, R., Plowden, W., Webb, A., Whittingham, P. and Wistow, G. (1988) *Joint Approaches to Social Policy: Rationality and Practice*. Cambridge: Cambridge University Press.

Chan, H.S., Wong, K.-K., Cheung, K.C. and Lo, J.M.-K. (1995) 'The implementation gap in environmental management in China: the case of Guangzhou, Zhengzhou, and Nanjing', *Public Administration Review*, 55(4): 333–40.

Chaney, C.K. and Saltzstein, G.H. (1998) 'Democratic control and bureaucratic responsiveness: the police and domestic violence', *American Journal of Political Science*, 42(3): 745–68.

Chapman, R.A. (1970) *The Higher Civil Service in Britain*. London: Constable.

Cho, C-L., Kelleher, C.A., Wright, D.S and Yackee, S.W. (2005) 'Translating national policy objectives into local achievements across planes of governance and among multiple actors: second-order devolution and welfare reform implementation', *Journal of Public Admnistration, Research and Theory*, 15(1): 31–54.

Choi, Y.-C. (1999) *The Dynamics of Public Service Contracting: the British Experience*. Bristol: Policy Press.

Cimitile, C.J., Kennedy, V.S., Lambright, W.H., O'Leary, R. and Weiland, P. (1997) 'Balancing risk and finance: the challenge of implementing unfunded environmental mandates', *Public Administration Review*, 57(1): 63–74.

Clark, M.J. (1997) 'Implementation of aged care policy in the Australian federal system', *Australian Journal of Public Administration*, 56(3): 53–64.

Clarke, J. and Newman, J. (1997) *The Managerial State: Power, Politics and Ideology in the Remaking of Social Welfare*. London: Sage.

Clegg, S.R. (1990) *Modern Organizations: Organization Studies in the Postmodern World*. London: Sage.

Cline, K.D. (2000) 'Defining the implementation problem: organizational management versus cooperation', *Journal of Public Administration Research and Theory*, 10(3): 551–71.

Coase, R.H. (1937) 'The nature of the firm', *Economica*, 4: 386–405.

Cohen, D.K. and Lindblom, C. (1979) 'Solving problems of bureaucracy: a limit on social science', *American Behavioral Scientist*, 22 (5): 54–60

Cohen, M.D., March, J.G. and Olsen, J.P. (1972) 'A garbage can model of organizational choice', *Administrative Science Quarterly*, 17(1): 1–25.

Colebatch, H.K. and Larmour, P. (1993) *Market, Bureaucracy and Community: A Student's Guide to Organisation*. London: Pluto Press.

Cox, R.H. (1989) *Corporation and social policy: the Development of the modern Dutch welfare state'*, PhD dissertation, Indiana University, Bloomington.

Creveld, M. van (1996) 'The fate of the state', *Parameters*, 26(1): 4–19.

Cronin, T.E. (1980) *The State of the Presidency*. 2nd edn. Boston: Little, Brown and Company.

Crozier, M. (1964) *The Bureaucratic Phenomenon*. Chicago: University of Chicago Press.

Crozier, M. and Friedberg, E. (1980) *Actors and Systems: The Politics of Collective Action*. Chicago: University of Chicago Press.

Daalder, H. (1966) 'The Netherlands: opposition in a segmented society', in R.A. Dahl (ed.), *Political Opposition in Western Democracies*. New Haven, CT: Yale University Press, pp. 188–236.

Daemen, H. and Schaap, L. (eds) (2000) *Citizen and City: Developments in Fifteen Local Democracies in Europe*. Delft: Eburon.

Dahl, R. (1961) *Who Governs? Democracy and Power in an American City*. New Haven, CT: Yale University Press.

Danziger, J.N. (1978) *Making Budgets: Public Resource Allocation*. Beverly Hills, CA: Sage.

Davies, H.T.O., Nutley, S.M. and Smith, P.C. (eds) (2000) *What Works?*, Bristol: Policy Press.

Davis, G., Wikeley, N.J. and Young, R. (1998) *Child Support in Action*. Oxford: Hart.

Davis, K.C. (1969) *Discretionary Justice: A Preliminary Inquiry*. Baton Rouge, LA: Louisiana State University Press.

Dekker, P. (1998) 'Nonprofit sector, civil society and volunteering: some evidence and questions from the Netherlands and the rest of Western Europe', *Third Sector Review*, 4(2): 125–43.

DeLeon, P. (1999a) 'The missing link revisited: contemporary implementation research', *Policy Studies Review*, 16(3/4): 311–38.

DeLeon, P. (1999b) 'The stages approach to the policy process: What has it done? Where is it going?', in P.A. Sabatier (ed.), *Theories of the Policy Process*. Boulder, CO: Westview Press, pp. 19–32.

Derrida, J. (1993) *Spectres de Marx: L'état de la dette, le travail du deuil et la nouvelle Internationale*. Paris: Galilée.

Derthick, M. (1970) *The Impact of Federal Grants: Public Assistance in Massachusetts*. Cambridge, MA: Harvard University Press.

Derthick, M. (1972) *New Towns In-Town: Why a Federal Program Failed*. Washington, DC: Urban Institute.

Dewey, J. (1927) *The Public and its Problems*. New York: Holt.

Dewey, J. (1935) *Liberalism and Social Action*. New York: Capricorn Books.

Dicey, A.V. (1905) *Lectures on the Relations between Law and Public Opinion in England during the Nineteenth Century*. London: Macmillan.

DiMaggio, P.J. and Powell, W.W. (1983) 'The iron cage revisited: institutional isomorphism and collective rationality in organizational fields', *American Sociological Review*, 48(1): 147–60.

Dolbeare, K.M. and Hammond, P.E. (1971) *The School Prayer Decisions: From Court Police to Local Practice*. Chicago: University of Chicago Press.

Dolowitz, D.P., Hulme, R., Nellis, M. and O'Neill, F. (2000) *Policy Transfer and British Social Policy: Learning from the USA?* Buckingham: Open University Press.

Douglas, M.T. (1982) *In the Active Voice*. London: Routledge and Kegan Paul.

Dowding, K. (1995) 'Model or metaphor? A critical review of the policy network approach', *Political Studies*, 43: 451–63.

Dror, Y. (1986) *Policymaking Under Adversity*. New Brunswick, NJ: Transaction Publishers.

Dror, Y. (1989) *Public Policymaking Reexamined*. 2nd edn. New Brunswick, NJ: Transaction Publishers.

Drucker, P.F. (1995) 'The network society', *The Wall Street Journal Europe*, 30 March.

Dryzek, J.S. (1990) *Discursive Democracy: Politics, Policy, and Political Science*. Cambridge: Cambridge University Press.

Dunleavy, P. (1991) *Democracy, Bureaucracy and Public Choice: Economic Explanations in Political Science*. New York: Prentice Hall.

Dunn, W.N. (1981) *Public Policy Analysis: An Introduction*. Englewood Cliffs, NJ: Prentice Hall.

Dunsire, A. (1978a) *The Execution Process*, Vol. 1: *Implementation in a Bureaucracy*. Oxford: Martin Robertson.

Dunsire, A. (1978b) *The Execution Process*, Vol. 2: *Control in a Bureaucracy*. Oxford: Martin Robertson.

Dunsire, A. (1995) 'Administrative theory in the 1980s: a viewpoint', *Public Administration*, 73(1): 17–40.

Durant, R.F. (1984) 'EPA, TVA and pollution control: implications for a theory of regulatory policy implementation', *Public Administration Review*, 44(4): 305–15.

Durant, R.F. (1985) *When Government Regulates Itself: EPA, TVA, and Pollution Control in the 1970s*. Knoxville, TN: University of Tennessee Press.

Durant, R.F. (1993) 'Hazardous waste, regulatory reform, and the Reagan revolution: the ironies of an activist approach to deactivating bureaucracy', *Public Administration Review*, 53(6): 550–60.

Durant, R.F. and Legge, J.S., Jr (1993) 'Policy design, social regulation, and theory building: lessons from the traffic safety policy arena', *Political Research Quarterly*, 46(3): 641–56.

Dworkin, R.M. (1977) *Taking Rights Seriously*. London: Duckworth.

Dyson, K. (1980) *The State Tradition in Western Europe*. Oxford: Martin Robertson.

Easton, D. (1953) *The Political System*. New York: Alfred A. Knopf.

Easton, D. (1965) *A Framework for Political Analysis*, Englewood Cliffs, NJ: Prentice Hall.

Edelenbos, J. (2000) *Proces in vorm: Procesbegeleiding van interactieve beleidsvorming over lokale ruimtelijke projecten*. Utrecht: Lemma.

Edelenbos, J. and Monnikhof, R.A.H. (eds) (2001) *Lokale interactieve beleidsvorming: Een vergelijkend onderzoek naar de consequenties van interactieve beleidsvorming voor het functioneren van de lokale democratie*. Utrecht: Lemma.

Edelman, M.J. (1971) *Politics as Symbolic Action: Mass Arousal and Quiescence*. New York: Academic Press.

Eisinger, P.K. (1988) *The Rise of the Entrepreneurial State: State and Local Economic Development Policy in the United States*. Madison, WI: University of Wisconsin Press.

Ellwood, J.W. (2000) 'Prospects for the study of the governance of public organizations and policies', in C.J. Heinrich and L.E. Lynn, Jr (eds), *Governance and Performance: New Perspectives*. Washington, DC: Georgetown University Press, pp. 319–35.

Elmore, R.F. (1978) 'Organizational models of social program implementation', *Public Policy*, 26(2): 185–228.

Elmore, R.F. (1980) 'Backward mapping: implementation research and policy decisions', *Political Science Quarterly*, 94(4): 601–16.

Elmore R.F. (1983) 'Social policy-making as strategic intervention', in E. Scidman, ed. *HandBook of Social Intervention*. Beverly Hills: Sage, pp. 212–36

Elster, J. (1998) *Deliberative Democracy*. Cambridge: Cambridge University Press.

Esping-Andersen, G. (1990) *The Three Worlds of Welfare Capitalism*. Cambridge: Polity.

Ester, P., Halman, G.C.J.M. and Mooz, R.G. de, eds (1983) *The Individualizing Society: Value Change in Europe and North America*. Tilburg: Tilburg University Press.

Ethridge, M.E. and Percy, S.L. (1993) 'A new kind of public policy encounters disappointing results: implementing learnfare in Wisconsin', *Public Administration Review*, 53(4): 340–7.

Etzioni, A. (1961) *A Comparative Analysis of Complex Organizations: On Power, Involvement, and Their Correlates*. New York: Free Press.

Ewalt, J.A.G. and Jennings, E.T. (2004) 'Administration, governance, and policy tools in welfare policy administration' *Public Administration Review*, 64(4); 449–62.

Exworthy, M., Berney, L. and Powell, M. (2002) 'How great expectations in Westminster may be dashed locally: the implementation of national policy on health inequalities', *Policy and Politics*, 30(1): 79–96.

Exworthy, M. and Powell, M. (2004) 'Big windows and little windows: implementation in the "congested state"', *Public Administration*, 82(2): 263–81.

Falkner, G., Hartlapp, M. and Treib, O. (2007) 'Worlds of compliance: why leading approaches to European Union implementation are only "sometimes-true" theories', *European Journal of Political Research*, 46: 395–416.

Ferlie, E., Lynn, L.E. and Pollitt, C. (2005) *The Oxford Handbook of Public Management*. Oxford: Oxford University Press.

Ferman, B. (1990) 'When failure is success: implementation and Madisonian government', in D.J. Palumbo and D.J. Calista (eds), *Implementation and the Policy Process: Opening Up the Black Box*. New York: Greenwood Press, pp. 39–50.

Fernández, J-L., Kendall, J., Davey, V. and Knapp, M. (2007) 'Direct payments in England: factors linked to variations in local provision', *Journal of Social Policy*, 36(1): 97–122.

Fielding, N. and Fielding, J. (1991) 'Police attitudes to crime and punishment', *British Journal of Criminology*, 31(1): 568–90.

Fiozino, D.Y. (1997) 'Strategies for regulatory reform: Forward compared to backward mapping', *Policy Studies Journal*, 25(2): 249–65.

Fischer, F. (1980) *Politics, Volumes and Public Policy. The Problem of Methodology*. Boulder, Colorado: Westview Press.

Fischer, F. (1995) *Evaluating Public Policy*. Chicago: Nelson-Hall.

Fix, M. and Kenyon, D. (eds) (1990) *Coping with Mandates*. Washington, DC: Urban Institute Press.

Flynn, N. (1993) *Public Sector Management*, 2nd edn. New York: Harvester Wheatsheaf.

Flynn, R., Williams, G. and Pickard, S. (1996) *Markets and Networks: Contracting in Community Health Services*. Buckingham: Open University Press.

Fox, C.J. (1990) 'Implementation research: why and how to transcend positivist methodologies', in D.J. Palumbo and D.J. Calista (eds), *Implementation and the Policy Process: Opening Up the Black Box*. New York: Greenwood Press, pp. 199–212.

Fox, C.J. and Miller, H.T. (1995) *Postmodern Public Administration: Toward Discourse*. Thousand Oaks, CA: Sage.

Frederickson, G. (1999) 'The repositioning of American public administration', John Gaus Lecture at the annual meeting of the American Political Science Association, Atlanta, CA.

Freidson, E. (1970) *Professional Dominance: The Social Structure of Medical Care*. New York: Atherton Press.

Friend, J.K., Power, J.M. and Yewlett, C.J.L. (1974) *Public Planning: The Inter-Corporate Dimension*. London: Tavistock Publications.

Frissen, P.H.A. (1999) *Politics, Governance and Technology: A Postmodern Narrative on the Virtual State*. Cheltenham: Edward Elgar.

Fry, G.K. (1984) 'The development of the Thatcher government's "Grand Strategy" for the civil service: a public policy perspective', *Public Administration*, 62(3): 322–36.

Fukuyama, F. (1992) *The End of History and the Last Man*. New York: Free Press.

Fulton Committee (1968) *Report of the Committee on the Civil Service*, Cmnd 3638. London: HMSO.

Gains, F. (1999) 'Implementing privatization policies in "Next Steps" agencies', *Public Administration*, 77(4): 713–30.

Galligan, D.J. (1986) *Discretionary Powers: A Legal Study of Official Discretion*. Oxford: Clarendon Press.

Gerth, H.H. and Mills, C.W. (eds) (1947) *From Max Weber: Essays in Sociology*. London: Kegan Paul, Trench, Trubner.

Giddens, A. (1984) *The Constitution of Society: Outline of the Theory of Structuration*. Berkeley, CA: University of California Press.

Giddens, A. (1998) *The Third Way: The Renewal of Social Democracy*. Cambridge: Polity.

Gill, J. and Meier, K.J. (2000) 'Public administration research and practice: A methodological manifesto', *Journal of Public Administration Research and Theory*, 10(1): 157–99.

Glennerster, H., Matsaganis, M., Owens, P. with Hancock, S. (1994) *Implementing GP Fundholding: Wild Card or Winning Hand?* Buckingham: Open University Press.

Goggin, M.L., Bowman, A.O'M., Lester, J.P. and O'Toole, L.J., Jr (1990) *Implementation Theory and Practice: Toward a Third Generation*. Glenview, IL: Scott Foresman/Little, Brown and Company.

Gordon, I., Lewis J. and Young. K. (1977) 'Perspectives on policy analysis', *Public Administration Bulletin*, 25: 26–30.

Gormley, W.T., Jr (1996) 'Regulatory privatization: a case study', *Journal of Public Administration Research and Theory*, 6(2): 243–60.

Gouldner, A.W. (1954) *Patterns of Industrial Bureaucracy*. New York: Free Press of Glencoe.

Graaf, H. van de and Hoppe, R. (1989) *Beleid en politiek*. Bussum: Coutinho.

Gray, A. and Jenkins, B. (1995) 'From public administration to public management: reassessing a revolution?', *Public Administration*, 73(Spring): 75–99.

Gray, J. (2007) *Black Mass: Apocalyptic Religion and the Death of Utopia*. London: Allen Lane.

Greca, R. (2000) 'Institutional co-governance as a mode of co-operation between various social service carriers and providers', *Public Management*, 2(3): 379–95.

Greenwood, R., Hinings, C.R. and Ranson, S. (1975) 'Contingency theory and the organization of local authorities; Part I: Differentiation and integration', *Public Administration*, 53(1): 1–23.

Grimshaw, R. and Jefferson, T. (1987) *Interpreting Policework: Policy and Practice in Forms of Beat Policing*. London: Allen & Unwin.

Guba, E.G. and Lincoln, Y.S. (1987) 'The countenances of fourth-generation evaluation: description, judgment and negotiation', in D.J. Palumbo (ed.), *The Politics of Program Evaluation*. Newbury Park, CA: Sage, pp. 202–34.

Guéhenno, J-M. (1993) *La fin de la démocratie*. Paris: Flammarion.

Gunn, L. (1978) 'Why is implementation so difficult?', *Management Services in Government*, 33(4): 169–76.

Gunsteren, H.R. van (1976) *The Quest for Control*. London: John Wiley and Sons.

Gunsteren, H.R. van (1998) *A Theory of Citizenship: Organizing Plurality in Contemporary Democracies*. Boulder, CO: Westview Press.

Halberstam, D. (1972) *The Best and the Brightest*. London: Barrie & Jenkins.

Hall, P.A. (1986) *Governing the Economy: The Politics of State Intervention in Britain and France*. Cambridge: Polity.

Hall, P.A. and Soskice, D. (2001) *Varieties of Capitalism: The Institutional Foundations of Comparative Advantage*. Oxford: Oxford University Press.

Ham, C. (1992) *Health Policy in Britain: The Politics and Organisation of the National Health Service*, 3rd edn. London: Macmillan.

Ham, C. and Hill, M.J. (1984) *The Policy Process in the Modern Capitalist State*. New York: St. Martins Press.

Hammond, K.R. and Adelman, L. (1978) 'Science, values and human judgment', in K.R. Hammond (ed.), *Judgment and Decision in Public Policy Formation*. Boulder, CO: Westview Press. pp. 119–41.

Hanf, K.I. (1993) 'Enforcing environmental laws: the social regulation of co-production', in M. Hill (ed.), *New Agendas in the Study of the Policy Process*. Hemel Hempstead: Harvester Wheatsheaf, pp. 88–109.

Hanf, K.I. and Scharpf, F.W. (eds) (1978) *Interorganizational Policy Making: Limits to Coordination and Central Control*. London: Sage.

Harbin, G., Gallagher, J.J., Lillie, T. and Eckland, J. (1992) 'Factors influencing state progress in the implementation of Public Law 99–457, Part H', *Policy Sciences*, 25(2): 103–15.

Harden, I. (1992) *The Contracting State*. Buckingham: Open University Press.

Hardy, B., Turrell, A. and Wistow, G. (1992) *Innovations in Community Care Management*. Aldershot: Avebury.

Hargrove, E.C. (1975) *The Missing Link: The Study of the Implementation of Social Policy*. Washington, DC: Urban Institute.

Hargrove, E.C. (1983) 'The search for implementation theory', in R.J. Zeckhauser and D. Leebaert (eds), *What Role for Government? Lessons from Policy Research*. Durham, NC: Duke University Press, pp. 280–94.

Heclo, H.H. (1972) 'Review article: policy analysis', *British Journal of Political Science*, 2(1): 83–108.

Heinemann, R.A., Bluhm, W.T., Peterson, S.A. and Kearny, E.N. (1990) *The World of the Policy Analyst: Rationality, Values and Politics*. Chatham, NJ: Chatham House Publishers.

Heinrich, C.J. and Lynn, Jr., L.E. (eds) (2000) *Governance and Performance: New Perspectives*, Washington, DC: Georgetown University Press.

Hendriks, F. and Toonen, T. (eds) (1998) *Schikken en plooien: De stroperige staat bij nader inzien*. Assen: Van Gorcum.

Hennessy, P. (1989) *Whitehall*. London: Secker and Warburg.

Herzberg, F. (1966) *Work and the Nature of Man*. New York: World Publishing Times Mirror.

Hickson, D.J., Hinings, C.R., Lee, C.A., Schneck, R.E. and Pennings, J.M. (1971) 'A strategic contingencies theory of intraorganizational power', *Administrative Science Quarterly*, 16(2): 216–29.

Hill, M. (1972) *The Sociology of Public Administration*. London: Weidenfeld and Nicolson.

Hill, M. (1997) 'Implementation theory: yesterday's issue?', *Policy and Politics*, 25(4): 375–85.

Hill, M. (2005) *The Public Policy Process*. Harlow: Pearson.

Hill, M. (2006) *Social Policy in the Modern World*. Oxford: Blackwell.

Hill, M. and Bramley, G. (1986) *Analysing Social Policy*. Oxford: Blackwell.

Hill, M. and Hupe, P. (2006) 'Analysing policy processes as multiple governance: accountability in social policy', *Policy and Politics*, 34(3): 557–73.

Hirsch, W.Z. (1995) 'Factors important in local governments' privatization decisions', *Urban Affairs Review*, 31(2): 226–43.

Hjern, B. (1982) 'Implementation research: the link gone missing', *Journal of Public Policy*, 2(3): 301–8.

Hjern, B. and Hull, C. (1982) 'Implementation research as empirical constitutionalism', in B. Hjern and C. Hull (eds), *Implementation Beyond Hierarchy*. Amsterdam: Elsevier (special issue of *European Journal of Political Research*), pp. 105–15.

Hjern, B. and Porter, D.O. (1981) 'Implementation structures: a new unit of administrative analysis', *Organization Studies*, 2(3): 211–27.

HMSO (1991) *Raising the Standard: The Citizen's Charter*. Cm 1599. London: HMSO.

HM Treasury (2004) *Risk Management Assessment Framework: A Tool for Departments*. London: HM Treasury.

HM Treasury (2005) *Managing Risks to the Public: Appraisal Guidance*. London: HM Treasury.

Hofland, H.J.A. (2005) 'Totale democratisering', *NRC Handelsblad*, 6 May.

Hogwood, B.W. (1995) 'Public policy', *Public Administration*, 73(Spring): 59–73.

Hogwood, B.W. and Gunn, L. (1984) *Policy Analysis for the Real World*. Oxford: Oxford University Press.

Holdaway, S. (1983) *Inside the British Police: A Force at Work*. Oxford: Blackwell.

Hollifield, J.F. (1990) 'Immigration and the French state: problems of policy implementation', *Comparative Political Studies*, 23(1): 56–79.

Hood, C.C. (1976) *The Limits of Administration*. London: John Wiley.

Hood, C.C. (1991) 'A public managament for all seasons?', *Public Administation*, 69 (spring): 3–190

Hood, C.C. (1998) *The Art of the State: Culture, Rhetoric, and Public Management*. Oxford: Clarendon Press.

Hood, C.C. and Jackson, M. (1991) *Administrative Argument*. Aldershot: Dartmouth.

Hoogerwerf, A. (ed.) (1978) *Overheidsbeleid: Een inleiding in de beleidswetenschap*. Alphen aan den Rijn: Samsom.

Hoppe, R. (1989) *Het Beleidsprobleem geproblematiseerd*. Muiderberg: Cotinho.

Hoppe, R., Graaf, H. van de and Dijk, A. van (1987) 'Implementation research and policy design', *International Review of Administrative Sciences*, 53(4): 581–604.

Howlett, M. (1991) 'Policy instruments, policy styles and policy implementation: national approaches to theories of instrument choice', *Policy Studies Journal* 19(2): 1–21.

Howlett, M. and Ramesh, M. (2003) *Studying Public Policy*. Don Mills, ONT: Oxford University Press.

Huber, J.D. and Shipan, C.R. (2002) *Deliberate Discretion? The Institutional Foundations of Bureaucratic Autonomy*. Cambridge: Cambridge University Press.

Huby, M. and Dix, G. (1992) *Evaluating the Social Fund*. London: HMSO.

Hudson, B. (1987) 'Collaboration in social welfare: a framework for analysis', *Policy and Politics*, 15(3): 175–82.

Hudson, B. and Hardy, B. (2002) 'What is a successful partnership and how can it be measured?' in C. Glendinning, M. Powell and K. Rumney (eds), *Partnerships, New Labour and the Governance of Welfare*. Bristol: Policy Press.

Hudson, B., Hardy, B., Henwood, M. and Wistow, G. (1997) *Inter-Agency Collaboration*. Leeds: Nuffield Institute of Health.

Hudson, B., Hardy, B., Henwood, M. and Wistow, G. (1999) 'In pursuit of inter-agency collaboration in the public sector: what is the contribution of theory and research?', *Public Management*, 1(2): 235–60.

Hufen, J.A.M. and Ringeling, A.B. (eds) (1990) *Beleidsnetwerken: Overheids–semi-overheids-en particuliere organisaties in wisselwerking*. The Hague: VUGA.

Hupe, P.L. (1990) 'Implementing a meta-policy: the case of decentralisation in The Netherlands', *Policy and Politics*, 18(3): 181–91.

Hupe, P.L. (1993a) 'The politics of implementation: individual, organisational and political co-production in social services delivery', in M. Hill (ed.), *New Agendas in the Study of the Policy Process*. Hemel Hempstead: Harvester Wheatsheaf, pp. 130–51.

Hupe, P.L. (1993b) 'Beyond pillarization: the (post-)welfare state in The Netherlands', *European Journal of Political Research*, 23(4): 359–86.

Hupe, P.L. (1994) 'Het betwiste primaat van de politiek', in P. de Jong, A.F.A. Korsten, A.J. Modderkolk and I.M.A.M. Pröpper (eds), *Verantwoordelijkheid en ver antwoording in het openbaar bestuur: Congrespublikatie 1994*. The Hague: VUGA, pp. 61–70.

Hupe, P.L. (1996) 'Uitvoering als partnership', in Divosa (ed.) *Kantelende werelden: Veranderingen in de beleids- en uitvoeringspraktijk van sociale diensten*, Utrecht congres publicatie Divosa.

Hupe, P.L. (2000) 'De paradox van interactief bestuur', in P.B. Lehning (ed.), *De beleidsagenda 2000: Strijdpunten op het breukvlak van twee eeuwen*. Bussum: Coutinho, pp. 129–45.

Hupe, P.L. (2007) *Overheidsbeleid als politiek: Over de grondslagen van beleid*. Assen: Koninklijke Van Gorcum.

Hupe, P.L. and Hill, M. (2006) 'The three action levels of governance: re-framing the policy process beyond the stages model', in B.G. Peters and J.Pierre (eds), *Handbook of Public Policy*, London: Sage.

Hupe, P.L. and Hill, M. (2007) 'Street-level bureaucracy and public accountability', *Public Administration*, 85(2): 279–300.

Hupe, P.L. and Klaassen, H.L. (2000) 'De zichtbare staat: over sturingsconcepties en onderhandelen', in P.L. Hupe, M.A. Beukenholdt-ter Mors and H.L. Klaassen (eds), *Publiek onderhandelen: Een vorm van eigentijds besturen*. Alphen aan den Rijn: Samsom, pp. 257–85.

Hupe, P.L. and Klaassen, H.L. (2001) 'De zichtbare staat: modellen van overheids beleidsvoering', *Openbaar Bestuur*, 11(6/7): 2–6.

Hupe, P.L. and Meijs, L.C.P.M. (2000) *Hybrid Governance: The Impact of the Nonprofit Sector in The Netherlands*. The Hague/Rotterdam/Baltimore: Social and Cultural Planning Office/Erasmus University/Johns Hopkins University.

Huxham, C. (2000) 'The challenge of collaborative governance', *Public Management*, 2(3): 337–57.

Immergut, E.M. (1992) 'The rules of the game: the logic of health policy-making in France, Switzerland and Sweden', in S. Steinmo, K. Thelen and F. Longstreth (eds), *Structuring Politics: Historical Institutionalism in Comparative Analysis*. Cambridge: Cambridge University Press, pp. 57–89.

Ingraham, P.W. (1987) 'Toward more systematic consideration of policy design', *Policy Studies Journal*, 15(Winter): 611–28.

Ingram, H. and Schneider, A. (1990) 'Improving implementation through framing smarter statutes', *Journal of Public Policy*, 10(1): 67–88.

Ingram, H., Schneider, A.L. and DeLeon, P. (2007) 'Social construction and policy design', in P.A. Sabatier (ed.), *Theories of the Policy Process*. Boulder, CO: Westview Press, pp. 3–17.

Israel, J.I. (1995) *The Dutch Republic: Its Rise, Greatness, and Fall, 1477–1806*. Oxford: Clarendon Press.

Jachtenfuchs, M. (1995) 'Theoretical perspectives on European governance', *European Law Journal*, 1(2): 115–33.

Jacob, H. and Lipsky, M. (1968) 'Outputs, structures, and power: an assessment of changes in the study of state and local politics', *The Journal of Politics*, 30(2): 510–38.

Jenkins, W.I. (1978) *Policy Analysis: A Political and Organisational Perspective*. London: Martin Robertson.

Jenkins-Smith, H. (1991) 'Alternative theories of the policy process: reflections on research strategy for the study of nuclear waste policy', *Political Science and Politics*, June: 157–66.

Jewell, C.J. (2007) *Agents of the Welfare State*. New York and Basingstoke: Palgrave Macmillan.

Jewell, C.J. and Glaser, B.E. (2006) 'Towards a general analytic framework, organizational settings, policy goals and street-level behaviour', *Administration and Society*, 38(3): 335–64.

John, P. (1998) *Analysing Public Policy*. London: Pinter.

John, P. (2001) *Local Government in Western Europe*. London: Sage.

Jordan, A.G. and Richardson, J.J. (1987) *British Politics and the Policy Process: An Arena Approach*. London: Allen & Unwin.

Jowell, J. (1973) 'The legal control of administrative discretion', *Public Law*, 18: 178–220.

Kagan, R.A. (1978) *Regulatory Justice: Implementing a Wage–Price Freeze*. New York: Russell Sage Foundation.

Kaufman, H. (1960) *The Forest Ranger: A Study in Administrative Behavior*. Baltimore, MD: Johns Hopkins University Press.

Keiser, L.R. and Meier, K.J. (1996) 'Policy design, bureaucratic incentives, and public management: the case of child support enforcement', *Journal of Public Administration Research and Theory*, 6(3): 337–64.

Keiser, L.R., Mueser, P.R. and Choi, S-W. (2004) 'Race, bureaucratic discretion and the implementation of welfare reform', *American Journal of Political Science*, 48(2): 314–27.

Keiser, L.R. and Soss, J. (1998) 'With good cause: bureaucratic discretion and the politics of child support enforcement', *American Journal of Political Science*, 42(4): 1133–56.

Kelly, M. (1994) 'Theories of justice and street-level discretion', *Journal of Public Administation Research and Theory*, 4(2): 119–40.

Kettl, D.F. (2000) 'Public administration at the millennium: the state of the field', *Journal of Public Administration Research and Theory*, 10(1): 7–34.

Kickert, W.J.M. (1996) 'Bestuurskunde in de Verenigde Staten: ontwikkelingen in historisch-maatschappelijke context', *Bestuurskunde*, 5(3): 122–33.

Kickert, W.J.M. (1997) 'Public governance in The Netherlands: an alternative to Anglo-American "managerialism"', *Public Administration*, 75(4): 731–52.

Kickert, W.J.M. (1998) *Aansturing van verzelfstandigde overheidsdiensten: Over publiek management van hybride organisaties*. Alphen aan den Rijn: Samsom.

Kickert, W.J.M., Klijn, E.H. and Koppenjan, J.F.M. (eds) (1997) *Managing Complex Networks: Strategies for the Public Sector*. London: Sage.

Kickert, W.J.M. and van Vught, F.A. (eds) (1995) *Public Policy and Administration Sciences in The Netherlands*. Hemel Hempstead: Prentice Hall/Harvester Wheatsheaf.

Kingdon, J.D. ([1984] 1995) *Agendas, Alternatives and Public Policies*. Boston: Little, Brown and Company.

Kingsley, J.D. (1944) *Representative Bureaucracy: An Interpretation of the British Civil Service*. Yellow Springs, OH: Antioch Press.

Kiser, L.L. (1984) 'Towards an institutional theory of citizen co-production', *Urban Affairs Quarterly*, 19(4): 485–510.

Kiser, L.L. and Ostrom, E. (1982) 'The three worlds of action: a metatheoretical synthesis of institutional approaches', in E. Ostrom (ed.), *Strategies of Political Inquiry*. Beverley Hills, CA: Sage, pp. 179–222.

Klijn, E.H. (1996) 'Analysing and managing policy processes in complex networks: a theoretical examination of the concept policy network and its problems', *Administration and Society*, 28(1): 90–119.

Klijn, E.H. (1997) 'Policy networks: an overview', in W.J.M. Kickert, E.H. Klijn and J.F.M. Koppenjan (eds), *Managing Complex Networks: Strategies for the Public Sector*. London: Sage, pp. 14–34.

Klijn, E.H. and Koppenjan, J.F.M. (2000) 'Public management and policy networks: foundations of a network approach to governance', *Public Management*, 2(2): 135–58.

Knegt, R. (1986) *Regels en redelijkheid in de bijstandsverlening: Participerende observatie bij een Sociale Dienst*. Groningen: Wolters-Noordhoff.

Knill, C. and Lenschow, A. (1998) 'Coping with Europe: the impact of British and German administrations on the implementation of EU environmental policy', *Journal of European Public Policy*, 5(4): 595–614.

Knoepfel, P. (1986) 'Distributional issues in regulatory policy implementation: the case of Air Quality Control Policies', in A. Schnaiberg, N. Watts and K. Zimmermann (eds), *Distributional Conflicts in Environmental Policy*. Aldershot: Gower, pp. 363–79.

Knoepfel, P. (1997) *Conditions pour une mise en œuvre efficace des politiques environnementales*, Cahier de l'IDHEAP no 167. Chavannes-près-Renens: IDHEAP.

Knoepfel, P. and Weidner, H. (1982) 'Formulation and implementation of air quality control programmes: patterns of interest consideration', *Policy and Politics*, 10(1): 85–109.

Knoepfel, P., Larrue, C., Varone, F. and Hill, M. (2007). *Public Policy Analysis*, Bristol: Policy Press.

Knoke, D. (1990) *Policy Networks: The Structural Perspective*. Cambridge: Cambridge University Press.

Kooiman, J. (ed.) (1993) *Modern Governance: New Government–Society Interactions*. London: Sage.

Kooiman, J. (1999) 'Social-political governance: overview, reflections and design', *Public Management*, 1(1): 67–92.

Kooiman, J. (2003) *Governing as Governance*. London: Sage.

Kooiman, J. and van Vliet, M. (2000) 'Self-governance as a mode of societal governance', *Public Management*, 2(3): 359–77.

Koppenjan, J.F.M. (1991) 'Falen en leren rond de paspoortaffaire: De hardleersheid van een ministerie geanalyseerd', *Beleid & Maatschappij*, 18(1): 20–30.

Koppenjan, J.F.M. and Klijn, E-H. (2004) *Managing Uncertainties in Networks*. London: Routledge.

Krause, G.A. (1996) 'The institutional dynamics of policy administration: bureaucratic influence over securities regulation', *American Journal of Political Science*, 40(4): 1083–121.

Kuhn, T.S. (1970) *The Structure of Scientific Revolutions*, 2nd edn. Chicago: University of Chicago Press.

Kuypers, G. (1973) *Grondbegrippen van politiek*. Utrecht: Het Spectrum.

Kuypers, G. (1980) *Beginselen van beleidsontwikkeling* (2 vols). Muiderberg: Coutinho.

Lampinen, R. and Uusikylä, P. (1998) 'Implementation deficit: why do member states not comply with EU directives?', *Scandinavian Political Studies*, 21(3): 231–51.

Lane, J.-E. (1987) 'Implementation, accountability and trust', *European Journal of Political Research*, 15(5): 527–46.

Lane, J.-E. and Ersson, S.O. (2000) *The New Institutional Politics: Performance and Outcomes*. London: Routledge.

Lash, S. (1988) 'Postmodernism as a regime of signification', *Theory, Culture & Society*, 5(2/3): 311–36.

Lasswell, H.D. (1935/1938) *Politics: Who Gets What, When, How*. Cleveland OH: Meridian Books.

Lasswell, H.D. (1951) 'The policy orientation', in D. Lerner and H.D. Lasswell (eds), *The Policy Sciences*. Stanford, CA: Stanford University Press.

Lasswell, H.D. (1956) *The Decision Process: Seven Categories of Functional Analysis*. College Park, MD: University of Maryland.

Lasswell, H.D. (1970) 'The emerging conception of the policy sciences', *Policy Sciences*, 1(1): 3–14.

Laumann, E.O. and Knoke, D. (1987) *The Organizational State: Social Choice in National Policy Domains*. Madison, WI: University of Wisconsin Press.

Lawson, T.R. (2000) 'A structural model of socio-political governance with an example of application in the United States', *Public Management*, 2(3): 417–34.

Lerner, D. and Lasswell, H.D. (eds) (1951) *The Policy Sciences*. Stanford, CA: Stanford University Press.

Lester, J.P., Bowman, A.O'M., Goggin, M.L. and O'Toole, L.J., Jr (1987) 'Public policy implementation: evolution of the field and agenda for future research', *Policy Studies Review*, 7(1): 200–16.

Lester, J.P. and Goggin, M.L. (1998) 'Back to the future: the rediscovery of implementation studies', *Policy Currents*, 8(3): 1–9.

Leuchtenburg, W.E. (1963) *Franklin D. Roosevelt and the New Deal*, 1932–1940. New York: Harper & Row.

Lijphart, A. (1975) *The Politics of Accommodation: Pluralism and Democracy in the Netherlands*. Berkeley, CA: University of California Press.

Lijphart, A. (1999) Patterns of Democracy. New Haven, CT: Yale University Press.

Lindblom, C.E. (1959) 'The science of muddling through', *Public Administration Review*, 19(2): 79–88.

Lindblom, C.E. (1965) *The Intelligence of Democracy: Decision Making through Mutual Adjustment*. New York: Free Press.

Lindblom, C.E. (1977) *Politics and Markets: The World's Political-Economic Systems*. New York: Basic Books.

Lindblom, C.E. and Woodhouse, E.J. (1993) *The Policy-Making Process*, 3rd edn. Englewood Cliffs, NJ: Prentice Hall.

Linder, S.H. and Peters, B.G. (1987) 'A design perspective on policy implementation: the fallacies of misplaced prescription', *Policy Studies Review*, 6(3): 459–75.

Lipsky, M. (1971) 'Street-level bureaucracy and the analysis of urban reform', *Urban Affairs Quarterly*, 6: 391–409.

Lipsky, M. (1980) *Street-Level Bureaucracy: Dilemmas of the Individual in Public Services*. New York: Russell Sage Foundation.

Lowi, T.J. (1972) 'Four systems of policy, politics, and choice', *Public Administration Review*, 32(4): 298–310.

Lowndes, V. and Skelcher, C. (1998) 'The dynamics of multi-organizational partnerships: an analysis of changing modes of governance', *Public Administration*, 76(Summer): 313–33.

Lukes, S. (1974) *Power: A Radical View*. London: Macmillan.

Lynn, L.E. Jr (1981) *Managing the Public's Business: The Job of the Government Executive*. New York: Basic Books.

Lynn, L.E. Jr (1987) *Managing Public Policy*. Boston, Mass: Little Brown.

Lynn L.E. Jr (1996a) *Public Management as Arts, Science, and Profession*. Chatham, NJ: Chatham House.

Lynn, L.E. Jr (1996b) 'Assume a network: Reforming mental health services in Illinois', *Journal of Public Administration Research and Theory*, 6(2): 297–314.

Lynn, L.E. Jr (2003) 'Public management', in B.G. Peters and J. Pierre (eds) *Handbook of Public Administration*, London: Sage.

Lynn, L.E., Jr (2006) *Public Management: Old and New*. New York and London: Routledge.

Lynn, L.E. Jr, Heinrich, C.J. and Hill, C.J. (1999) 'The empirical study of governance: theories, models, methods', paper presented at the Workshop on Models and Methods for the Empirical Study of Governance, University of Arizona, Tucson.

Lynn, L.E. Jr, Heinrich, C.J. and Hill. C.J. (2000a) 'Studying governance and public management: challenges and prospects', *Journal of Public Administration Research and Theory*, 10(2): 233–61.

Lynn, L.E. Jr Heinrich, C.J. and Hill, C.J. (2000b) 'Studying Governance and Public Management: Why? How? In Heinrich and Lynn (eds) *Governance and Performance: New Perspectives*, Washington, DC: Georgetown University Press.

Lynn, L.E. Jr, Heinrich, C.J. and Hill C.J. (2001) *Improving Governance: A New Logic for Empirical Research*. Washington, DC: Georgetown University Press.

Lyotard, J.-F. (1979) *La condition postmoderne: Rapport sur le savoir*. Paris: Les Editions de Minuit.

Mack, R. (1971) *Planning and Uncertainty*. New York: John Wiley.

Mahoney, J. (2000) 'Path dependency in historical sociology', *Theory and Society*, 29(4): 507–48.

March, J.G. and Olsen, J.P. (1984) 'The new institutionalism: organizational factors in political life', *The American Political Science Review*, 78(3): 734–49.

March, J.G. and Olsen, J.P. (1989) *Rediscovering Institutions: The Organizational Basis of Politics*. New York: Free Press.

March, J.G. and Olsen, J.P. (1996) 'Institutional perspectives on political institutions', *Governance*, 9(3): 248–64.

Marsh, D. and Rhodes, R.A.W. (eds) (1992) *Implementing Thatcherite Policies: Audit of an Era*. Buckingham: Open University Press.

Mashaw, J.L. (1983) *Bureaucratic Justice: Managing Social Security Disability Claims*. New Haven, CT: Yale University Press.

Matland, R.E. (1995) 'Synthesizing the implementation literature: the ambiguity–conflict model of policy implementation', *Journal of Public Administration Research and Theory*, 5(2): 145–74.

Mattesich, P. and Monsey, B. (1992) *Collaboration: What Makes it Work?* St Paul, MN: Amherst H. Wilder Foundation.

Maupin, J.R. (1993) 'Control, efficiency, and the street-level bureaucrat', *Journal of Public Administration Research and Theory*, 3(3): 335–57.

May, P.J. (1993) 'Mandate design and implementation: enhancing implementation efforts and shaping regulatory styles', *Journal of Policy Analysis and Management*, 12(4): 634–63.

May, P.J. (1994) 'Analyzing mandate design: state mandates governing hazard-prone areas', *Publius*, 24(2): 1–16.

May, P.J. (1995) 'Can cooperation be mandated? Implementing intergovernmental environmental management in New South Wales and New Zealand', *Publius*, 25(1): 89–113.

May, P.J. and Burby, R.J. (1996) 'Coercive versus cooperative policies: comparing intergovernmental mandate performance', *Journal of Policy Analysis and Management*, 15(2): 171–201.

May, P.J and Winter, S.C. (2008) 'Politicians, managers, and street-level bureaucrats: influences on policy implementation', to be published in *Journal of Public Administration Research and Theory*.

Maynard-Moody, S. and Musheno, M. (2000) 'State agent or citizen agent: two narratives of discretion', *Journal of Public Administration Research and Theory*, 10(2): 329–58.

Maynard-Moody, S., Musheno, M.C. and Palumbo, D.J. (1990) 'Street-wise social policy: resolving the dilemma of street-level influence and successful implementation', *The Western Political Quarterly*, 43(4): 833–48.

Mayo, E. (1933) *The Human Problems of an Industrial Civilisation*. Cambridge, MA: Harvard University Press.

Mazmanian, D.A. and Sabatier, P.A. (eds) (1981) *Effective Policy Implementation*. Lexington, KY: Lexington Books.

Mazmanian, D.A. and Sabatier, P.A. (1983) *Implementation and Public Policy*. Glenview, IL: Scott, Foresman.

McGregor, D. (1960) *The Human Side of Enterprise*. New York: McGraw-Hill.

McGregor, E.B. Jr. (1993) 'Toward a theory of public management success', in B. Bozeman (ed.), *Public Management: The State of the Art*. San Francisco: Jossey-Bass, pp. 173–85.

Meer, F.M. van der and Roborgh, L.J. (1993) *Ambtenaren in Nederland: Omvang, bureaucratisering en representativiteit van het ambtelijk apparaat*. Alphen aan den Rijn: Samsom Tjeenk Willink.

Meier, K.J. (1999) 'Are we sure Lasswell did it this way? Lester, Goggin and implementation research', *Policy Currents*, 9(1): 5–8.

Meier, K.J. and Gill, J. (2000) *What Works: A New Approach to Program and Policy Analysis*. Boulder, CO: Westview Press.

Meier, K.J. and McFarlane, D.R. (1995) 'Statutory coherence and policy implementation: the case of family planning', *Journal of Public Policy*, 15(3): 281–98.

Meier, K.J. and O'Toole, L.J., Jr (2001) 'Managerial strategies and behavior in networks: a model with evidence from U.S. public education', *Journal of Public Administration Research and Theory*, 11(3): 271–93.

Meier, K.J. and O'Toole, L.J. Jr (2003) 'Public management and educational performance: the impact of managerial networking', *Public Administration Review*, 63(6): 689–99.

Meier, K.J., Stewart, J., Jr and England, R.E. (1991) 'The politics of bureaucratic discretion: educational access as an urban service', *American Journal of Political Science*, 35(1): 155–77.

Merton, R.K. (1957) *Social Theory and Social Structure*. Glencoe, IL: Free Press.

Meyer, J.W. and Rowan, B. (1977) 'Institutionalized organizations: formal structure as myth and ceremony', *American Journal of Sociology*, 83(1): 340–63.

Meyers, M.K., Glaser, B. and MacDonald, K. (1998) 'On the front lines of welfare delivery: are workers implementing policy reforms?', *Journal of Policy Analysis and Management*, 17(1): 1–22.

Milward, H.B. (1996) 'Introduction to the symposium on the Hollow State: Capacity, control, and performance in interorganizational settings', *Journal of Public Administration Research and Theory*, 6(2): 193–5.

Milward, H.B. and Provan, K.G. (1999) 'How networks are governed', unpublished paper.

Milward, H.B., Provan, G. and Else, B.A. (1993) 'What does the "Hollow State" look like?', in B. Bozeman (ed.), *Public Management: The State of the Art*. San Francisco: Jossey-Bass, pp. 309–32.

Milward, H.B. and Snyder, L.O. (1996) 'Electronic government: linking citizens to public organizations through technology', *Journal of Public Administration Research and Theory*, 6(2): 261–75.

Mitchell, D. (1991) *Income Transfers in Ten Welfare States*. Aldershot: Avebury.

Moe, R.C. (1994) 'The "Reinventing Government" exercise: misinterpreting the problem, misjudging the consequences', *Public Administration Review*, 54(2): 111–22.

Moe, T.M. (1982) 'Regulatory performance and presidential administration', *American Journal of Political Science*, 26(2): 197–224.

Montfort, A.J.G.M. van (1991) *De regels van het huis: Ambtelijke regeltoepassing bij de gemeentelijke woonruimteverdeling*. Groningen: Wolters-Noordhoff.

Moran, M. and Wood, B. (1993) *States, Regulation and the Medical Profession*. Buckingham: Open University Press.

Morgan, G. (1986) *Images of Organization*. Beverly Hills, CA: Sage.

Morgan, G. (1993) *Imaginization: The Art of Creative Management*. Newbury Park, CA: Sage.

Murray, C. (2006) 'State intervention and vulnerable children: implementation revisited', *Journal of Social Policy*, 35(2): 211–28.

Nakamura, R.T. (1987) 'The textbook policy process and implementation research', *Policy Studies Review*, 7(1): 142–54.

Nathan, R.P. (1983) *The Administrative Presidency*. New York: John Wiley.

Newman, J. (2001) *Modernising Governance*. London: Sage.

Newton, K. and Sharpe, L.J. (1977) 'Local output research: some reflections and proposals', *Policy and Politics*, 5(1): 61–82.

Ohmae, K. (1995) *The End of the Nation State: The Rise of Regional Economies*. London: HarperCollins.

Osborne, D.E. and Gaebler, T.A. (1992) *Reinventing Government: How the Entrepreneurial Spirit is Transforming the Public Sector*. Reading, MA: Addison-Wesley.

Ostrom, E. (2007) 'Institutional rational choice: an assessment of the institutional analysis and development framework', in P.A. Sabatier (ed.), *Theories of the Policy Process*. Boulder, CO: Westview Press, pp. 3–17.

O'Toole, L.J., Jr (1986) 'Policy recommendations for multi-actor implementation: an assessment of the field', *Journal of Public Policy*, 6(2): 181–210.

O'Toole, L.J., Jr (1988) 'Strategies for intergovernmental management: implementing programs in interorganisational networks', *Journal of Public Administration*, 25(1): 43–57.

O'Toole, L.J., Jr (1989a) 'Alternative mechanisms for multiorganizational implementation: the case of wastewater management', *Administration and Society*, 21(3): 313–39.

O'Toole, L.J., Jr (1989b) 'Goal multiplicity in the implementation setting: subtle impacts and the case of wastewater treatment privatization', *Policy Studies Journal*, 18(1): 1–20.

O'Toole, L.J., Jr (1993) 'Interorganizational policy studies: lessons drawn from implementation research', *Journal of Public Administration Research and Theory*, 3(2): 232–51.

O'Toole, L.J., Jr (1994) 'Economic transition, constitutional choice, and public administration: implementing privatization in Hungary', *Journal of Public Administration Research and Theory*, 4(4): 493–519.

O'Toole, L.J., Jr (1995) 'Rational choice and policy implementation', *American Review of Public Administration*, 25(1): 43–57.

O'Toole, L.J., Jr (1996) 'Hollowing the infrastructure: revolving loan programs and network dynamics in the American states', *Journal of Public Administration Research and Theory*, 6(2): 225–42.

O'Toole, L.J., Jr (1997) 'Networking requirements, institutional capacity, and implementation gaps in transitional regimes: the case of acidification policy in Hungary', *Journal of European Public Policy*, 4(1): 1–17.

O'Toole, L.J., Jr (2000a) 'Research on policy implementation: assessment and prospects', *Journal of Public Administration Research and Theory*, 10(2): 263–88.

O'Toole, L.J., Jr (2000b) 'Different public managements? Implications of structural context in hierarchies and networks', in J.L. Brudney, L.J. O'Toole, Jr, and H.G. Rainey (eds), *Advancing Public Management: New Developments in Theory, Methods, and Practice*. Washington, DC: Georgetown University Press, pp. 19–32.

O'Toole, L.J., Jr (2001) 'The theory–practice issue in policy implementation research', *paper presented at the Economic and Social Research Council Seminar Series*, seminar three, University of Cambridge.

O'Toole, L.J., Jr and Meier, K.J. (1999) 'Modeling the impact of public management: implications of structural context', *Journal of Public Administration Research and Theory*, 9(4): 505–26.

O'Toole, L.J., Jr and Montjoy, R.S. (1984) 'Interorganizational policy implementation: a theoretical perspective', *Public Administration Review*, 44(6): 491–503.

Ouchi, W.G. (1991) 'Markets, bureaucracies and clans', in G. Thompson, J. Frances, R. Levacic and J. Mitchell (eds) *Markets, Hierarchies and Networks: The Coordination of Social Life*. London: Sage, pp. 246–55.

Page, E.C. (1985) *Political Authority and Bureaucratic Power: A Comparative Analysis*. Brighton: Wheatsheaf Books.

Palumbo, D.J. (ed.) (1987) *The Politics of Program Evaluation*. Newbury Park, CA: Sage.

Palumbo, D.J. and Calista, D. (eds) (1990) *Implementation and the Policy Process*. New York: Greenwood Press.

Parks, R.B., Baker, P.C., Kiser, L., Oakerson, R., Ostrom, E., Ostrom, V., Percy, S.L., Vandivort, M.B., Whitaker, G.P. and Wilson, R. (1981) 'Consumers as coproducers of public services: some economic and institutional considerations', *Policy Studies Journal*, 9(Summer): 1001–11.

Parsons, W. (1995) *Public Policy*. Aldershot: Edward Elgar.

Patton, M.Q. (1978) *Utilization-Focused Evaluation*. Newbury Park, CA: Sage.

Peck, E. and 6, P. (2006) *Beyond Delivery: Policy Implementation and Sense-making and Settlement*. Basingstoke: Palgrave Macmillan.

Peters, B.G. and Pierre, J. (2001) 'Developments in intergovernmental relations: towards multi-level governance', *Policy and Politics*, 29(2): 131–5.

Peters, B.G. and Pierre, J. (eds) (2003) *Handbook of Public Administration*. London: Sage.

Peters, B.G. and Pierre, J. (eds) (2006) *Handbook of Public Policy*. London: Sage.

Peters, T.J. (1990) 'Part one: Get innovative or get dead', *California Management Review*, 33(1): 9–26.

Pettigrew, A., Ferlie, E. and McKee, L. (1992) *Shaping Strategic Change: Making Change in Large Organizations: The Case of the National Health Service*. London: Sage.

Pierre, J. and Peters, B.G. (2000) *Governance, Politics and the State*. New York: St Martin's Press.

Pierson, P. (2000) 'Increasing returns, path dependence and the study of politics', *American Political Science Review*, 92(4): 251–67.

Pitts, D. (2005) 'Diversity, representation and performance: evidence about race and ethnicity in public organizations', *Journal of Public Administration Research and Theory*, 15(4): 615–31.

Pollitt, C. (1990) *Managerialism and the Public Services: The Anglo-American Experience*. Oxford: Blackwell.

Pollitt, C. and Bouckaert, G. (2004) *Public Management Reform: A Comparative Analysis*. Oxford: Oxford University Press.

Popper, K.R. (1959) *The Logic of Scientific Discovery*. London: Hutchinson.

Powell, M., Exworthy, M. and Berney, L. (2001) 'Playing the game of partnership', in R. Sykes, C. Bochel and N. Ellison (eds), *Social Policy Review 13: Developments and Debates: 2000–2001*. Bristol: Policy Press, pp. 39–62.

Pressman, J.L. and Wildavsky, A. (1984) *Implementation*, 3rd edn. Berkeley, CA: University of California Press (1st edn, 1973; 2nd edn, 1979).

Pröpper, I.M.A.M. and Steenbeek, D.A. (1999) *De aanpak van interactief beleid: Elke situatie is anders*. Bussum: Coutinho.

Provan, K.G. and Milward, H.B. (1991) 'Institutional-level norms and organizational involvement in a service-implementation network', *Journal of Public Administration Research and Theory*, 1(4): 391–417.

Pusey, M. (1991) *Economic Rationalism in Canberra: A Nation-Building State Changes its Mind*. Cambridge: Cambridge University Press.

Rae, D. and Taylor, M. (1971) 'Decision rules and policy outcomes', *British Journal of Political Science*, 1(1): 71–90.

Reichard, G.W. (1988) *Politics as Usual: The Age of Truman and Eisenhower*. Arlington Heights, IL: Harlan Davidson.

Reiner, R. (1992) *The Politics of the Police*, 2nd edn. New York: Harvester Wheatsheaf.

Rhodes, R.A.W. (1981) *Control and Power in Central–Local Government Relations*. Farnborough: Gower.

Rhodes, R.A.W. (1988) *Beyond Westminster and Whitehall: The Sub-Central Governments of Britain*. London: Unwin Hyman.

Rhodes, R.A.W. (1992) 'Beyond Whitehall: researching local governance', *Social Sciences*, 13: 2.

Rhodes, R.A.W. (1996a) 'The new governance: governing without government', *Political Studies*, 44(4): 652–67.

Rhodes, R.A.W. (1996b) 'From institutions to dogma: tradition, eclecticism, and ideology in the study of British public administration', *Public Administration Review*, 56(6): 507–16.

Rhodes, R.A.W. (1997) *Understanding Governance: Policy Networks, Governance, Reflexivity and Accountability*. Buckingham: Open University Press.

Riccucci, N.M. (2005) *How Management Matters: Street-Level Bureaucrats and Welfare Reform*. Washington, DC: Georgetown University Press.

Riccucci, N.M and Meyers, M.K. (2004) 'Linking passive and active representation: the case of frontline workers in welfare agencies', *Journal of Public Administration, Research and Theory*, 14(4): 585–97.

Richards, D. and Smith, M.J. (2002) *Governance and Public Policy in the UK*. Oxford: Oxford University Press.

Richards, S. (1992) 'Changing patterns of legitimation in public management', *Public Policy and Administration*, 7(3): 15–28.

Richardson, J. (ed.) (1982) *Policy Styles in Western Europe*. London: Allen and Unwin.

Rigby, T.H. (1964) 'Tradition, market and organizational societies and the USSR', *World Politics*, 16(4): 539–47.

Rigby, T.H. (1990) *The Changing Soviet System: Mono-organizational Socialism from its Origins to Gorbachev's Restructuring*, Aldershot, Hants: Edward Elgan.

Ringeling, A.B. (1978) *Beleidsvrijheid van ambtenaren: Het spijtoptantenprobleem als illustratie van de activiteiten van ambtenaren bij de uitvoering van beleid*. Alphen aan den Rijn: Samsom.

Ringeling, A.B. (1993) *Het imago van de overheid: De beoordeling van prestaties van de publieke sector*. The Hague: VUGA.

Ripley, R.B. and Franklin, G.A. (1982) *Bureaucracy and Policy Implementation*. Homewood, IL: Dorsey Press.

Rist, R.C. (ed.) (1995) *Policy Evaluation: Linking Theory to Practice*. Aldershot: Edward Elgar.

Roe, E.M. (1994) *Narrative Policy Analysis: Theory and Practice*. Durham, NC: Duke University Press.

Rose, R. (1973) 'Comparing public policy: an overview', *European Journal of Political Research*, 1(1): 67–94.

Rose, R. (2004) *Learning from Comparative Public Policy: A Practical Guide*. London: Routledge.

Rosecrance, R.N. (1999) *The Rise of the Virtual State: Wealth and Power in the Coming Century*. New York: Basic Books.

Rossi, P.H. and Freeman, H. (1979) *Evaluation: A Systematic Approach*. Newbury Park, CA: Sage.

Rothstein, B. (1992) 'Labour-market institutions and working-class strength', in S. Steinmo, K. Thelen and F. Longstreth (eds), *Structuring Politics: Historical Institutionalism in Comparative Analysis*. Cambridge: Cambridge University Press, pp. 33–56.

Rothstein, B. (1998) *Just Institutions Matter: The Moral and Political Logic of the Universal Welfare State*. Cambridge: Cambridge University Press.

Ryan, N. (1995) 'Unravelling conceptual developments in implementation analysis', *Australian Journal of Public Administration*, 54(1): 65–80.

Ryan, N. (1996) 'Some advantages of an integrated approach to implementation analysis: a study of Australian industry policy', *Public Administration*, 74(4): 737–53.

Sabatier, P.A. (1986) 'Top-down and bottom-up approaches to implementation research: a critical analysis and suggested synthesis', *Journal of Public Policy*, 6(1): 21–48.

Sabatier, P.A. (1991) 'Toward better theories of the policy process', *Political Science and Politics*, 24 (June) 147–56.

Sabatier, P.A. ([1999]2007) 'The need for better theories', in P.A. Sabatier (ed.), *Theories of the Policy Process*. Boulder, CO: Westview Press, pp. 3–17.

Sabatier, P.A. (ed.) ([1999]2007) *Theories of the Policy Process*. Boulder, CO: Westview Press.

Sabatier, P.A. and Jenkins-Smith, H. (1993) *Policy Change and Learning: An Advocacy Coalition Approach*. Boulder, CO: Westview Press.

Sabatier, P.A. and Mazmanian, D.A. (1979) 'The conditions of effective implementation: a guide to accomplishing policy objectives', *Policy Analysis*, 5(4): 481–504.

Sabatier, P.A. and Mazmanian, D.A. (1980) 'The implementation of public policy: A framework of analysis', *Policy Studies Journal*, 8 (special issue): 538–60.

Sabatier, P.A and Weible, C.M. (2007) 'The advocacy coalition framework: innovations and clarifications', in P.A. Sabatier (ed.), ([1999]2007) *Theories of the Policy Process*. Boulder, CO: Westview Press, pp. 189–220.

Saetren, H. (2005) 'Facts and myths about research on public policy implementation: out-of-fashion, allegedly dead, but still very much alive and relevant', *The Policy Studies Journal*, 33(4): 559–82.

Satyamurti, C. (1981) *Occupational Survival: The Case of the Local Authority Social Worker*. Oxford: Blackwell.

Saward, M. (1997) 'In search of the hollow crown', in P.M. Weller, H. Bakvis and R.A.W. Rhodes (eds), *The Hollow Crown: Countervailing Trends in Core Executives*. Basingstoke: Macmillan, pp. 16–36.

Schama, S. (1987) *The Embarrassment of Riches: An Interpretation of Dutch Culture in the Golden Age*. New York: Knopf.

Scharpf, F.W. (1978) 'Interorganizational policy studies: issues, concepts and perspectives', in K.I. Hanf and F.W. Scharpf (eds), *Interorganizational Policy Making: Limits to Coordination and Central Control*. London: Sage, pp. 345–70.

Scharpf, F.W. (1986) 'Policy failure and institutional reform: why should form follow function?', *International Social Science Journal*, 38(2): 179–91.

Scharpf, F.W. (1997) *Games Real Actors Play: Actor-Centered Institutionalism in Policy Research*. Boulder, Colorado: Westview Press.

Schlager, E. (2007) 'A comparison of frameworks, theories and models of the policy process', in P.A. Sabatier (ed.), *Theories of the Policy Process*. Boulder, CO: Westview Press, pp. 3–17.

Schlesinger, A.M., Jr (1960) *The Politics of Upheaval*. Boston: Houghton Mifflin.

Scholz, J.T., Twombly, J. and Headrick, B. (1991) 'Street-level political controls over federal bureaucracy', *American Political Science Review*, 85(3): 829–50.

Schultze, C.L. (1968) *The Politics and Economics of Public Spending*. Washington, DC: Brookings Institution.

Schuyt, K. and Taverne, E. (2000) *1950: Welvaart in zwart-wit*. The Hague: Sdu Uitgevers.

Schwarz, M. and Thompson, M. (1990) *Divided We Stand: Redefining Politics, Technology, and Social Choice*. New York: Harvester Wheatsheaf.

Scott, R.A. and Shore, A.R. (1979) *Why Sociology Does Not Apply: A Study of the Use of Sociology in Public Policy*. New York: Elsevier.

Scott, W.R. (1995) *Institutions and Organizations*. Thousand Oaks, CA: Sage.

Selden, S.C. (1997) 'Representative bureaucracy: examining the linkage between passive and active representation in the farmers' home administration', *American Review of Public Administration*, 27(1): 22–42.

Selznick, P. (1949) *TVA and the Grass Roots: A Study in the Sociology of Formal Organization*. Berkeley, CA: University of California Press.

Selznick, P. (1957) *Leadership in Administration: A Sociological Interpretation*. New York: Row, Peterson.

Simon, H.A. (1945) *Administrative Behavior*. New York: Free Press.

Skocpol, T. (1995) *Social Policy in the United States: Future Possibilities in Historical Perspective*. Princeton, NJ: Princeton University Press.

Skocpol, T. and Finegold, K. (1982) 'State capacity and economic intervention in the early New Deal', *Political Science Quarterly*, 97(2): 255–78.

Smith, M.J. (1993) *Pressure, Power and Policy: State Autonomy and Policy Networks in Britain and the United States*. New York: Harvester Wheatsheaf.

Smith, S.R. and Smyth, J. (1996) 'Contracting for services in a decentralized system', *Journal of Public Administration Research and Theory*, 6(2): 277–96.

Smith, T. (1994) 'Post-modern politics and the case for constitutional renewal', *The Political Quarterly*, 65(2): 128–37.

Spence, D.B. (1997) 'Agency policy making and political control: modeling away the delegation problem', *Journal of Public Administration Research and Theory*, 7(2): 199–219.

Spicker, P. (2006) *Policy Analysis for Practice*. Bristol: Policy Press.

Stivers, C. (1994) 'The listening bureaucrat: responsiveness in public administration', *Public Administration Review*, 54(4): 364–9.

Stoker, R.P. (1991) *Reluctant Partners: Implementing Federal Policy*. Pittsburgh, PA: University of Pittsburgh Press.

Stoker, R.P. and Wilson, L.A. (1998) 'Verifying compliance: social regulation and welfare reform', *Public Administration Review*, 58(5): 395–405.

Stone, C. (1989) *Regime Politics: Governing Atlanta 1946–1988*. Lawrence, KS: University Press of Kansas.

Stone, D.A. (1989) 'Causal stories and the formation of policy agendas', *Political Science Quarterly*, 104(2): 281–300.

Stone, D.A. (2002) *Policy Paradox: The Art of Political Decision-Making*. New York: W.W. Norton and Company.

Strauss, A.L. (1978) *Negotiations: Varieties, Contexts, Processes, and Social Order*. San Francisco: Jossey-Bass.

Taylor, F.W. (1911) The Principles of Scientific Management. New York: Harper.

Terpstra, J. and Havinga, T. (1999) 'Uitvoering tussen traditie en management: Structuratie en stijlen van beleidsuitvoering', in W. Bakker and F. van Waarden (eds), *Ruimte rond regels: Stijlen van regulering en beleidsuitvoering vergeleken*. Amsterdam: Boom, pp. 40–67.

Thomas, H. (ed.) (1968) *Crisis in the Civil Service*. London: Blond.

Thompson, F. (1997) 'Defining the new public management', in L.R. Jones, K. Schedler and S.W. Wade (eds), *Advances in International Comparative Management*. Greenwich, CT: JAI Press, pp. 1–14.

Thompson, G., Frances, J., Levack, R. and Mitchell, J. (eds) (1991) *Markets, Hierarchies and Networks: The Coordination of Social Life*. London: Sage.

Thompson, J.D. (1967) *Organizations in Action: Social Science Bases of Administrative Theory*. New York: McGraw-Hill.

Thompson, J.R. and Jones, V.D. (1995) 'Reinventing the federal government: the role of theory in reform implementation', *American Review of Public Administration*, 25(2): 183–99.

Thompson, M., Ellis, R.J. and Wildavsky, A.B. (1990) *Cultural Theory*. Boulder, CO: Westview Press.

Toonen, T.A.J. (1990) 'The unitary state as a system of co-governance: the case of the Netherlands', *Public Administration*, 68(Autumn): 281–96.

Tops, P.E.W.M. (1999) 'Co-productie als bestuursstijl: ervaringen en vuistregels', *Bestuurswetenschappen*, 53(3): 201–25.

Torenvlied, R. (1996a) Besluiten in uitvoering: Theorieén over beleidsuitvoering modelmarig getoetst op sociale van reguleriy in drie gemeenten. Amsterdam: Thesis Publishers.

Torenvlied, R. (1996b) 'Political control of implementation agencies', *Rationality and Society*, 5(1): 25–50.

Torenvlied, R. (2000) *Political Decisions and Agency Performance*. Dordrecht/Boston/London: Kluwer Academic Publishers.

Torenvlied, R. and Thomson R. (2003) 'Is implementation distinct from political bargaining?' *Rationality and Society*, 15(1): 64–84.

Torre, E.J. van der (1999) *Politiewerk: Politiestijlen, community policing, professionalisme*. Alphen aan den Rijn: Samsom.

Truman, D. (1958) *The Governmental Process: Political Interests and Public Opinion*. New York: Knopf.

Twist, M.J.W. van (1994) *Verbale vernieuwing: Aantekeningen over de kunst van bestuur skunde*. The Hague: VUGA.

Valente, C.F. and Manchester, L.D. (1984) *Rethinking Local Services: Examining Alternative Delivery Approaches*. Washington, DC: International City Management Association.

Van Meter, D. and Van Horn, C.E. (1975) 'The policy implementation process: a conceptual framework', *Administration and Society*, 6(4): 445–88.

Veen, R.J. van der (1990) *De sociale grenzen van beleid: Een onderzoek naar de uitvoering en effecten van het stelsel van sociale zekerheid*. Leiden: Stenfert Kroese.

Veld, R.J. in 't (1984) *De vlucht naar Isfahan? Over bestuur, planning en de toekomst van het hoger onderwijs*. The Hague: VUGA Uitgeverij.

Vick, N., Tobin, R., Swift, P., Spandler, H., Hill, M., Coldham, T., Towers, C. and Waldock, H. (2006) 'An evaluation of the impact of the social care modernisation programme on the implementation of direct payments', *unpublished report of the Health and Social Care Advisory Service to the Department of Health*.

Vickers, G. (1965) *The Art of Judgment: A Study of Policy Making*. London: Chapman & Hall.

Visser, J. and Hemerijck, A.C. (1997) *'A Dutch Miracle': Job Growth, Welfare Reform, and Corporatism in the Netherlands*. Amsterdam: Amsterdam University Press.

Vliet, M. van (1993) 'Environmental regulation of business: options and constraints for communicative governance', in J. Kooiman (ed.), *Modern Governance: New Government–Society Interactions*. London: Sage, pp. 105–18.

Waarden, F. van (1999a) 'Ieder land zijn eigen trant?', in W. Bakker and F. van Waarden (eds), *Ruimte rond regels: Stijlen van regulering en beleidsuitvoering vergeleken*. Amsterdam: Boom, pp. 303–39.

Waarden, F. van (1999b) 'De institutionele grondslag van ambtelijke gewoonten', in W. Bakker and F. van Waarden (eds), *Ruimte rond regels: Stijlen van regulering en beleidsuitvoering vergeleken*. Amsterdam: Boom, pp. 340–74.

Wade, H.W.R. (1982) *Administration·Law*, 5th edn. Oxford: Oxford University Press.

Waldo, C.D. (1948) *The Administrative State: A Study of the Political Theory of American Public Administration*. New York: The Ronald Press Company.

Walker, R. and Lawton, D. (1988) 'Social assistance and territorial justice: the example of single payments', *Journal of Social Policy*, 17(4): 437–76.

Wamsley, G.L. (1990a) 'Preface', in G.L. Wamsley, R.N. Bacher, C.T. Goodsell, P.S. Kronenberg, J.A. Rohr, C.M. Stivers, O.F. White and J.F. Wolf, *Refounding Public Administration*. Newbury Park, CA: Sage, pp. 19–29.

Wamsley, G.L. (1990b) 'The agency perspective: public administrators as agential leaders', in G.L. Wamsley, R.N. Bacher, C.T. Goodsell, P.S. Kronenberg, J.A. Rohr, C.M. Stivers, O.F. White and J.F. Wolf (eds), *Refounding Public Administration*. Newbury Park, CA: Sage, pp. 114–62.

Weber, M. (1947) *The Theory of Social and Economic Organization*. Glencoe, IL: Free Press.

Weimer, D.L. (1993) 'The current state of design craft: borrowing, tinkering, and problem solving', *Public Administration Review*, 53(2): 110–20.

Weiss, C.H. (ed.) (1977) *Using Social Research in Public Policy Making*. Lexington, KY: Heath.

Weissert, C.S. (1994) 'Beyond the organization: the influence of community and personal values on street-level bureaucrats' responsiveness', *Journal of Public Administration Research and Theory*, 4(2): 225–54.

Whitaker, G.P. (1980) 'Coproduction: citizen participation in service delivery', *Public Administration Review*, 40(3): 240–6.

Wildavsky, A.B. (1979) *Speaking Truth to Power: The Art and Craft of Policy Analysis*. Boston: Little, Brown and Company.

Williams, W. (1971) *Social Policy Research and Analysis: The Experience in American Federal Social Agencies*. New York: American Elsevier.

Williams, W. (1980) *The Implementation Perspective: A Guide for Managing Social Service Delivery Programs*. Berkeley, CA: University of California Press.

Williamson, O.E. (1975) *Markets and Hierarchies: Analysis and Antitrust Implications: A Study in the Economics of Internal Organization*. New York: Free Press.

Wilson, J.Q. (1968) *Varieties of Police Behavior: The Management of Law and Order in Eight Communities*. Cambridge, MA: Harvard University Press.

Wilson, W. (1887) 'The study of administration', *Political Science Quarterly*, 2: 197–222.

Winter, S. (1990) 'Integrating implementation research', in D.J. Palumbo, and D.J. Calista (eds), *Implementation and the Policy Process: Opening Up the Black Box*. New York: Greenwood Press, pp. 19–38.

Winter, S.C. (1999) 'New directions for implementation research', *Policy Currents*, 8(4): 1–5.

Winter, S.C. (2003) 'Implementation perspectives: status and reconsideration', in B.G. Peters and J. Pierre (eds) *Handbook of Public Administration*. London: Sage. pp. 212–23.

Winter, S.C. (2005) 'Effects of casework: the relation between implementation and social effects in Danish integration policy', paper given at the Research Conference for Public Policy and Management, Washington DC, 3–5 November.

Winter, S.C. (2006) 'Implementation', in B.G Peters, and J. Pierre (eds), *Handbook of Public Policy*. London: Sage. pp. 151–66.

Wistow, G., Knapp, M., Hardy, B. and Allen, C. (1994) *Social Care in a Mixed Economy*. Buckingham: Open University Press.

Wittfogel, K.A. (1963) *Oriental Despotism: A Comparative Study of Total Power*. New Haven, CT: Yale University Press.

Wittrock, B. (1983) 'Governance in crisis and withering of the Welfare State: the legacy of the policy sciences', *Policy Sciences*, 15(3): 195–203.

Wittrock, B. and DeLeon, P. (1986) 'Policy as a moving target: a call for conceptual realism', *Policy Studies Review*, 6(1): 44–60.

Woll, P. (ed.) (1966) *Public Administration and Policy: Selected Cases*. New York: Harper & Row.

Wood, B.D. and Waterman, R.W. (1991) 'The dynamics of political control of the bureaucracy', *American Political Science Review*, 85(3): 801–28.

Woodward, J. (1965) *Industrial Organization: Theory and Practice*. London: Oxford University Press.

World Bank (2007) *A Decade of Measuring the Quality of Governance: Governance Matters 2007. Worldwide Governance Indicators. 1996–2006*. Washington, DC: World Bank.

Yanow, D. (1990) 'Tackling the implementation problem: epistemological issues in implementation research', in D.J. Palumbo and D.J. Calista (eds), *Implementation and the Policy Process: Opening Up the Black Box*. New York: Greenwood Press, pp. 213–28.

Yanow, D. (1993) 'The communication of policy meanings: Implementation as interpretation and text', *Policy Sciences*, 26(1): 41–61.

Yanow, D. (1996) *How Does a Policy Mean? Interpreting Policy and Organizational Actions*. Washington, DC: Georgetown University Press.

Young, H. (1989) *One of Us: A Biography of Margaret Thatcher*. London: Macmillan.

Zahariadis, N. (2007) 'The multiple streams framework: structure, limitations, prospects', in P.A. Sabatier (ed.), *Theories of the Policy Process*. Boulder, CO: Westview Press, pp. 65–92.

Zarefsky, D. (1986) *President Johnson's War on Poverty: Rhetoric and History*. Alabama: University of Alabama Press.

Zuurmond, A. (1994) *De infocratie: Een theoretische en empirische heroriëntatie op Weber's ideaaltype in het informatietijdperk*. The Hague: Phaedrus.

AUTHOR INDEX

Allison, Graham 8, 59, 166

Bardach, Eugene 48, 111, 153, 199
Barrett, Susan 7, 50, 54–5, 61, 62, 64, 66, 85, 104, 146
Benson, Kenneth 35, 53, 70, 148
Bovens, Mark 10, 61, 108, 165, 180

DeLeon, Peter 2, 8, 9, 91, 117, 119, 120, 136, 171, 175, 176, 192
Dunsire, Andrew 7, 10, 20, 43, 51, 83, 85, 86, 87, 90, 91, 92, 93, 106

Elmore, Richard 52, 53, 59, 173
Etzioni, Amitai 35, 46, 183, 184, 185, 187, 202
Exworthy, Mark 69, 78, 110, 147

Fischer, Frank 11, 17, 117
Franklin, Grace 34, 76, 77, 82
Fudge, Colin 7, 50, 54–5, 61, 62, 64, 66, 85, 104, 146

Giddens, Anthony 70, 93
Goggin, Malcolm 2, 44, 64, 65, 67, 72, 96, 99, 103, 112, 136, 141, 144, 145, 173
Gray, Andrew 20, 33, 34, 83, 84, 86, 89, 95, 106
Gunn, Lewis 4, 5, 6, 48, 49–51, 85, 89, 140, 141, 175
Gunsteren, Herman von 6, 155

Hanf, Kenneth 15, 53, 104, 153, 154
Hargrove, Erwin 8, 18, 19, 42, 43
Hart, Paul 't 10, 61, 165, 180
Heinrich, Corolyn 14, 33, 109, 121, 122
Hjern, Benny 43, 53–4, 55, 59, 64, 67, 68, 78, 85, 112, 199
Hogwood, Brian 4, 5, 6, 48, 49–51, 85, 89, 99, 140, 141, 175
Hoppe, Rob 5, 8, 111, 116, 178
Hudson, Bob 148, 149, 199
Hull, Chris 53–4, 59, 199

Jenkins, Bill 6, 20, 33, 34, 62, 83, 84, 86, 89, 106, 114, 118
Jenkins-Smith, Hank 6, 62, 114, 118
John, Peter 7, 12, 14, 84, 87, 117, 119

Kettl, Donald 84, 89, 90, 96–8, 100
Klijn, Erik-Hans 67–70, 71, 147, 178, 199
Koppenjan, Joop 67–70, 71, 147, 149, 178, 199
Kooiman, Jan 13, 14, 114, 126

Lane, Jan-Erik 59, 60, 78
Lasswell, Herbert 5, 6, 107, 115, 124
Lester, James 64, 65, 96, 103, 136
Lijphart, Arend 82, 91, 179, 180
Lindblom, Charles 5, 6, 8, 28, 65, 115, 117, 153, 166, 176, 184, 185, 187, 194, 202
Lipsky, Michael 15, 17, 26, 27, 35, 51–3, 54, 66, 78, 104, 117, 134, 150, 151, 152, 165, 199
Lynn, Laurence 13, 14, 15, 32, 33, 91, 109, 111, 121, 122, 131, 204

March, James 36, 37, 70, 182
Matland, Richard 73, 74, 75, 112, 131, 138, 176, 177, 178, 180, 188, 194
May, Peter 101, 141, 153, 159, 162, 198
Mazmanian, Daniel 7, 9, 48, 49, 50, 51, 53, 62, 112, 171, 195
Meier, Kenneth 73, 130, 148, 159, 174
Milward, H. Brinton 88, 111, 148, 185

Nakamura, Robert 6, 117, 118

Olsen, Johan 36, 37, 70, 182
Ostrom, Elinor 37, 115, 118, 119, 121, 122, 123, 124, 125, 126, 127, 128, 131, 194, 204
O'Toole, Laurence 7, 8, 12, 14, 15, 16, 64, 65, 70, 72–3, 90, 91, 98, 100–1, 104, 111, 112, 114, 130, 148, 155, 172, 175, 176, 182, 186, 195, 198, 203, 204

SUBJECT INDEX